Capitalism and the Equity Fetish

Robert Herian

Capitalism and the Equity Fetish

Desire, Property, Justice

Robert Herian
Law School
The Open University
Milton Keynes, UK

ISBN 978-3-030-66522-7   ISBN 978-3-030-66523-4   (eBook)
https://doi.org/10.1007/978-3-030-66523-4

This Palgrave Macmillan imprint is published by the registered company Springer Nature Switzerland AG
The registered company address is: Gewerbestrasse 11, 6330 Cham, Switzerland

For Chloe and Billy

FOREWORD

A spectre is haunting the common law, the spectre of Equity. This eerie insight is the rigorously argued and distinctively historical materialist theme and thesis of Robert Herian's provocative book. *Equity Fetishism* propounds the elaborate history and oneiric trajectory of an absence that jurists propagate and shore up by means of the phantasmatic image of an equity that will in Christian argot fulfil the law and so provide Complete Justice. In defiance of its institutional and jurisdictional demise, a spectral fetish object, a hidden pannomion, an ethereal Lady Justice is the form that the vanishing sign of equity plays upon the positive unconscious of law. As one English court put it, not without an aura of necrophilia, death or the abolition of the Court of Chancery "does not mean that equity is past childbearing; simply that its progeny must be legitimate—by precedent out of principle". An eerie equity, meaning here an exterior and other worldly dogma propels the paradox of affect in a law *sine affectu*.

The triggering instance of the book is that of the abolition of the distinction between law and equity, "the blending of the Courts into one Court of universal jurisdiction" in the Judicature Acts. In the debates preceding enactment, Lord Chancellor Campbell famously remarks that this annexation of equity "will render each Court competent to administer complete justice" and at a slightly later point he references "entire justice". In an act of administrative arrogation law takes equity 'in house' and makes it part of the legal *oikonomia*. Finally, the system is deemed, at least potentially, whole and equity is there to provide its last instance, a "more perfect justice". The description fits Francis Bacon's definition of Idols of the Theatre, of dogmas which are "but so many stage plays, representing worlds of their own creation after an unreal and scenic fashion". An image is fabricated to mask an absence or in more direct terms to hide an error which in this instance is a monotheistic belief in a singular and universal truth. Equity is Christian dogma as incorporated into law in the image of *æquitas naturalis*, of Lady Justice, of a veiled virgin variously and ineptly depicted in modernity as fairness, impartiality, principle or most directly as "the genius of common law".

What of death? Has abolition immortalized equity? Is justice, which Forcadel defines in *Cupido iurisperitus* (*Cupid's Law*) as "a disposition of the soul", and as a "constant will", to give to each their due, now wholly subsumed, cannibalized by law, and so buried in the interstices of juridical rules and their practices of abstraction? Is equity, to borrow a Schreberian turn of phrase, what law excretes—and the sublimated excrement becomes lawyer's gold? Certainly, the principle of equity is not especially evident in the various treatises, handbooks, and other introductory guides to law. In Stychin and Mulcahy, *Legal Methods and Systems*, it appears only in an extract from a work on the law of contracts, and in an historical aside, references courts that have been abandoned, and concepts of "the conscience of the King", and of "natural law" which have "long since disappeared from the rules of equity." Despite appearing under the heading "Key Concepts and Terminology", we are informed after the briefest of discussions that "there is little significance left in the distinction". Other texts, McLeod, on *Legal Method*, or Gillespie and Weare on *The English Legal System*, three is enough, simply and briefly note in addition the existence of equitable maxims derived somewhat nationalistically from antiquated and now dissolved courts of Chancery, and then refer any further inquiry to the Module on Equity and Trusts, where the concept generally gains equally minimal discussion in favour of rapid entry into the substantive rules for the preservation of wealth. It is also symptomatic that the *Critical Lawyers' Handbook* of 1992 makes no reference to equity, perhaps because equity in the sense of equality cannot plausibly be deemed a part of law. Depicted as both key and insignificant, a part of the vast host of the dead, a spectre that haunts in the excitations of juridical phantasms and the judge's desire, in the Christian will to do justice, there is more to this shroud, to this dead weight of history, than first meets the eye or is divulged by the learned authors of introductory works, handbooks, prolegomena, enchiridions and other propaedeutics of law.

One interpretation of the demise of the jurisdiction as an independent corrective or autonomous power to do justice would be to read it as juridical melancholia, an inability to let go of equity, a species of fort/da in which equity appears and disappears like the child's ball on a string. One should not take away the patient's denial and by the same token law's attachment to the divinity seems hard to untangle. It is also, of course, the case that to make the law requires breaking the law. This is hard to sell to the populace. Consider in this respect a case from 1824 concerned with covenants in a deed of land and specifically with the meaning of the word son. In *Hoffman v Porter*, the indenture dated 1800 transferred property to "Peter Hoffman and Son" and the question arose as to which of several sons of said Peter Hoffman could take "as purchaser by this description". The relevant law relating to strict settlements, and acknowledged by the Court, was that a conveyance to "the son of A, he having several sons, would be void for uncertainty". The covenant in question gave the son a right to "quiet enjoyment" of the property while title passed to the defendants. As Joyce would doubtless have put it, who is the father of any son that any son should love him or he any son? The mystical estate and apostolic succession from only begetter to only begotten is ever an incertitude: "*Amor matris*, subjective and objective genitive, is the only true thing in life". Paternity is a legal fiction and so the Judge is forced to fictive elaborations and to the quill of equity. Peter Hoffman and his son were to have quiet enjoyment. When the said Peter departed this life, the son should have inherited "all his rights and covenants in the land". We are then told that neither Peter nor, since his death, had his son the plaintiff "enjoyed the same quietly". The son had been "molested, & c. in the enjoyment thereof." This leads Judge Marshall to the conclusion that while the issue is not free from doubt, "Peter Hoffman and Son" was the title of a firm and the Son named was most likely the Son referenced by the name of the partnership: "the justice of the case is clearly with the plaintiff, is clearly in favour of giving validity to the conveyance, and, I do not think that law ought to be separated from justice, where it is at most doubtful."

A deed void in law, an indenture and covenant that failed to name the beneficiary, is reformed in equity so as to serve complete justice. The parchment fiction of a scriptural reality of title and deed is transformed, rewritten in equity, to read not "& Son" but "John Hoffman", *the* son of the father. The religious connotations of covenant in the background, the Judge is marshalling an exception to the rule despite there being nothing doubtful about its terms of application in these circumstances, only concern about its effects. The Judge's doubt concerns the certitude and not the incertitude of the rule. In the particular instance the application of the rule would threaten the apostolic passage from father to son. It would impact the mysterium of inheritance and the covenant of property remaining in the family. The disturbance of the quiet enjoyment of the deed by the dead had to be estopped in honour of the Christian order of succession, the sanctity of covenant and the reification of property. The law could not give up its invocation of a more complete justice, a *plus ultra*, a something more that is beyond the rule, that breaks the law and takes the name of Equity or Justice as the completion of the circle, the more perfect web and seamless whole. In Joycean argot the law sought the figure of maternity, a power hidden *in membris* genitive as the figure that defies both death and the letter of the law.

What then is it to grasp for what you don't have, to lunge towards a lost object and so strive to keep alive the spectre of the dead and the order of succession? The idols of the theatre, the dogma of tradition, gain a very specific focus and analysis in the concept of the fetish object. The vanishing sign of equity, and most specifically the fetish figure of Equity as Complete Justice (ECJ), are Herian's contribution to detailing exactly what the protection of private property—the interests of stakeholders—and the chimera of ECJ actually achieve in social outcomes. What law gives up without giving up is detailed in the subtle transformation of the meaning of equity from its primary juridical sense as fair and impartial justice, the originally Roman *æquitas naturalis*, to bearing an economic sense of equity as stock and capital value. Legal *oikonomia* is, to borrow from Selden, œconomy, the administration of things secreted behind the grand gestural sign of equity producing justice *in statu quo res erant ante bellum*, here meaning in apparent conformity to the state of things as they were before class war, sex war, race war, trans and culture wars. The religion of capitalism rests upon the opium of legality and most specifically here lodges its legitimacy upon the equity of its casuistry, the justice of the exception, the law beyond law that moved the Court in *Hoffman v Porter* to disinter the dead, and later allowed Lord Hoffman to assert correctively in a more recent decision, that "[t]he principles of equity have always had a strong ethical content and nothing which I say is intended to diminish the influence of moral values in their application."

After stating this principle of normative propriety, Hoffman then goes on to castigate and overturn a Court of Appeal decision in which the Judges had appraised and condemned the morality of the defendant's conduct as "commercial cynicism", as behaving "very badly" and as "wanton and unreasonable", where in his view it had merely been "discourteous."

Where law teeters on the brink of the abyss, when the judge is forced by novelty to make up the norm, then the fetish object, Equity as Complete Justice is marshalled to cover the tracks of invention and legal incompetence. At its baldest, the interests of capital dictate an economically driven mandate and outcome, irrespective of its human, organic and environmental costs. The fetish of equity is nothing more and nothing less than the theatrical device that transforms the drama of inequality into a performance of justice. The stupefaction of the fetishist is brilliantly delineated by Keston Sutherland in terms of the satirical narrative that Marx stages to show that de Brosses' racist account of African Sabinianism and Fetishism is in fact much more applicable to the bourgeoisie and the delusory *mysterium* of the commodity which is deemed "more nauseatingly intricate and Byzantine than anything in the playground of phantoms we were so proud to have grown out of." The fetish is not a theory, it is a dramatic performance, a staging and play between the *dramatis personae* of specific conflicts and cases. For Herian, following the Marxist critique of political economy, the juridical fetishization of equity is a creed, a giving of credit to the transubstantiation and metamorphosis of law, a process of stupefaction in which the lawyers can masquerade as having found answers, a Justice in which the players are written out of the play.

In a surprisingly revealing moment in *Cobbe v Yeoman's Row Management Ltd*, Lord Walker of Gestingthorpe picks up on a desideratum expressed in the leading judgement of Lord Scott of Foscote, that the remedial device of the constructive trust should not fall prey to "the indulgence of idiosyncratic notions of fairness and justice ...." Lord Scott would rather that "proprietary rights fall to be governed by principles of law and not by some mix of judicial discretion, subjective views about which party 'ought to win' ... and the formless void of individual moral opinion." A determination of proprietary estoppel should not be based simply upon a finding that a party had acted unconscionably. To this line of reasoning, restricting the remedy of a party who had relied upon oral assurances that were unenforceable if not evidenced in writing, Lord

Walker of Gestingthorpe intones: "My Lords, equitable estoppel is a flexible doctrine which the court can use, in appropriate circumstances, to prevent injustice caused by the vagaries and inconstancy of human nature. But it is not a sort of joker or wild card to be used whenever the court disapproves of the conduct of a litigant who seems to have the law on his side." Gestingthorpe rejects the theory of the joker but arguably jests in his turn by allowing a claim in *quantum meruit* for unjust enrichment, a different invocation, but an appeal to the mirror, to equity as complete justice nonetheless. "Mrs Lisle-Mainwaring's conduct was unattractive", and so "she was bound in honour only, and so in the eyes of equity her conduct, although unattractive, was not unconscionable". Equity will not intervene but then it immediately does so, in direct contradiction, which is to say in complete harmony, with what has been stated: "I would (in common, as I understand it, with all your Lordships) allow this appeal and direct an inquiry with a view to reimbursing Mr. Cobbe on a generous scale" not only for his expenditures but also "for his time and trouble" in seeking and obtaining planning permission". It is the disavowal of the joker, the dismissal of the wild card that signals the unconscious force of the fetish acted out in the neurosis of judging and the stupefaction or mysterium of hidden sources decked out as principles. The promise that law will not enforce or lack of formality, is enforced in equity, not as an estoppel but in *quantum meruit*, as a quasi-contract. Perhaps Gestingthorpe is hinting that equity is not a joker but rather a pack of wild cards.

The satirical analysis of the fetishistic performance is aimed at displacing the subject of criticism from the explicit object of astonishment or ridicule—the idol worshipper—to the actor who claims to understand and complete, in enlightened and rational form, the progress of civilization. In the mode of equity fetishism Lord Walker of Gestingthorpe denies the joker and pretends to put a rational and enlightened law in its place. Sutherland suggests that *détournement* is here the appropriate mode of critical response. It is Gestingthorpe, as adumbrated, who is playing the wild card, the trump, the joker. In so doing he substitutes his ethical beliefs, the fetishization of his own "formless void of individual moral opinion", promulgated here in the mode of the judicial faith in ECJ, the legitimate children of precedent completing, fulfilling, dressing the law, for those of the so-called clown and jester, the child who lacks reason and relies on the unconscious, upon chance and fate. It is important then to recollect that the fool is also the pataphysical herald of what cannot yet be imagined, the prodromus of uncomfortable truths, and not least the apperception that the King, or here Lord Walker, is without discursively discernible attire.

Returning to the spectre of equity and the haunting of the juristic scene, the fetish signals a text that is out of joint, that something is wrong in the state of law. The eerie presence of an outside, the signals from the beyond, mark the continued dependence of law upon the Idols of the Theatre, upon theological dogma and its arbitrium. What is at issue in the fetish is a question of agency, and most obviously a failure of presence, meaning that the forces that govern our lives are not fully available to sensory apprehension but rather are hidden by the image, the fetish object or word, idol or deity, ECJ in whatever guise, for it amounts to the same thing. The appeal of the wild card, the call of the joker, hides the force of law and the power of its effects. It is a failure of presence in that what moves the law is hidden from view. The eerie quality of equity is that of an unspoken outside referenced repeatedly here in the "unattractive" conduct of a woman and the paradoxical "generosity" that must be focused on calculating Mr. Cobbe's economic and psychic losses. Unconscious forces produce real effects in the psyche, the affect and the stiffled laughter of Gestingthorpe, the sleight of text that denies equity only to enforce equity, are precisely the eerie sound of equity plucking its harp and playing its role in law. It would be wrong, however, to end on such a point of the unthought and unsaid. There is a stronger historical and materialist message to divulge and explore and Herian elaborates upon this.

The notion of equity fetishism has its roots in ethnocentric anthropology. If subjected, as I think it must be, to *détournement*, to the mirror, and so displaced onto the critic rather than the subject criticized, then, as Herian is the first to acknowledge, he who casts the first aspersion of equity fetishism has to address the fetish within. As was made evident in *Hoffman v Porter*, law grasps at equity and brings an alien justice, an external spectral force to play in deciding the case in favour of the imputed wishes of the father. ECJ steps in to fill the legal void created by the absence of a name and the loss of paternity. What is most significant in theatrical terms is that the Judge could not abide uncertainty and felt compelled, *cum affectu*, to fill the gap, to cover the abyss, to provide an image of an absent presence to satiate the need for the genitive principle and the legitimacy of transmission. What the Judge seeks is certitude in a context of doubt, the name of the father in the bequest to the son, legitimacy of deed and donation that is to be mirrored in the legitimacy, which is to say the justice of the judgment. In dogmatic terms, the son is part of the father, and the father is in the son—*ego est in partre, et pater in me est*. The irony of this is the incertitude referenced earlier, the father cannot legitimate the son any more than the son can legitimate the father, because auto-affection is the opposite of rule. It also means that there is no *arche* or ground upon which equity can be founded, only *an-archos* or absence of a first principle. Complete and perfect justice is thus replaced by pain, dogma is the displaced expression of phantasmatic thinking, and only the work of history remains as the patient and material reconstruction of our fetishes, a working through of the spectres that haunt our judgement.

Peter Goodrich
Professor of Law
Cardozo School of Law
Yeshiva University
New York, USA

Acknowledgments This book is a revised version of my 2018 Ph.D. thesis. I would like to thank my supervisors, Professor Maria Aristodemou and Dr. Piyel Halder, for their assistance and encouragement. And my examiners, Professors Peter Goodrich and James Lee, for their incisive questions and rigorous challenge of my ideas. I would also like to thank friends and colleagues at The Open University Law School, Birkbeck Law School, and in the endlessly enlightening critical legal community.

CONTENTS

CHAPTER 1

Introduction

WHY EQUITY?

Textbooks on the law of Equity often begin with accounts from Ancient Greece and with Aristotle's particular interpretations (Burn and Virgo 2008; Haley and McMurty 2011; Virgo 2012; Martin 2012; Atkins 2013; Watt 2014; Hudson 2017).

> Equity bids us be merciful to the weakness of human nature; to think less about the laws than about the man who framed them, and less about what he said than about what he meant; not to consider the actions of the accused so much as his intentions; nor this or that detail so much as the whole story; to ask not what a man is now but what he has always or usually been. (Aristotle 2004, p. 50)

Jurists, legal commentators and scholars alike then trace or perhaps drag Equity into the present day via visitations to the musty enclaves of Roman and medieval law. In many respects, Aristotle's original formula is unavoidable, as long as it remains clear that 'this original formulation is but the point of departure for a free and unrestricted meditation on the possibilities of the concept' (Oppermann 2016, p. 118). For me, it is the latter half of this historical narrative trail and the conventional wisdom of Equity that continues to flow from it that marks an important point of departure. What it highlights is the residuum of sacred injunctions of Canon and Ecclesiastical Law intermingling with profane rules

© The Author(s), under exclusive license to Springer Nature   1
Switzerland AG 2021
R. Herian, *Capitalism and the Equity Fetish*,
https://doi.org/10.1007/978-3-030-66523-4_1

and doctrines of Common Law from the sixteenth century onwards as a response to new economic realities of property ownership, mercantilism, systems of credit and debt, and general shifts in socioeconomic existence these created; or, what we might tentatively refer to as modernity. That narrative can be summed up, in part, by the notion of Equity as a 'court of conscience', supplanted or 'repressed', as Peter Goodrich argues, by the systematization of the Common Law jurisdiction (1996, pp. 10–11; see also: Fortier 2005; Klinck 2010). In other words, if we care to look, then in the law of Equity we find a story as much about strategic change as we do about fixity or the often, seemingly slow, arthritic creep of ancient laws over time. Laws have always served particular masters. Capitalism has proven itself resilient and enduring, and laws have served it well. But masters seldom outlast the laws that benefit them, and new theories of justice help define new ways of thinking and working. Lessons from the past are crucial to understanding Equity in the present and future amid growing uncertainty and crisis wrought by powerful forces of political economy. And what is at stake for legal subjects governed by and reliant upon these laws is arguably more contentious than ever.

As a critique of Equity, and the civil justice system of which it forms a substantive and procedural part, I do not reproduce the standard legal histories and epistemologies found in textbooks and internalized legal logic and reason here. Instead, I account for the social, political, cultural, psychological, and economic relevance and situatedness of Equity. Briefly, and echoing Bernard Stiegler's formulation of critique, this book aims to engage in a polemical dialogue with the intellectual tradition(s) of Equity (2010, p. 14). I do not consider Equity anachronistic, redundant, or only relevant to niche groups of Chancery lawyers whether living or long since dead. As Riccardo Baldissone remarks, 'Neither the new common ground that we inherit from early modern times as the basis of contemporary science, nor the contemporary understanding of social practices as convention-based, support the traditional value-based legal notion of equity, which, because of this, may nowadays appear as a relic of a bygone era' (2016, p. 155). On the contrary, Equity is alive and vital to modern life, although more particularly, I argue, to societies as economic frontiers rather than communities as human ones. Equity fetishism as a modern phenomenon is, therefore, symptomatic of, and a defence to, what Freud referred to as the return of the repressed: 'The emotion that had disappeared re-emerges, transformed into social anxiety, tormented conscience, and unrelenting self-reproach, while the rejected idea undergoes a *substitution by displacement*, often on to something trivial or indifferent' (2005, p. 44). And Equity fetishism equally encompasses the fetish character proposed by Marx that Karl Polanyi regards as 'key to Marx's analysis of capitalist society' (2018, p. 160). As a bulwark of private property interests in Western capitalist societies, Equity is not *trivial* nor should we be indifferent to it. It is instead central to the psychology of modern commercial attitudes and practices.

With roots in the property basis of civil justice, I argue that Equity fetishism brings together political and economic dimensions of commodity fetishism under capitalism and the fetishism related to the fantasies and desires for complete justice also promulgated under capitalism. To reconcile these two positions requires discussion of the relationship between Marx and Freud's theories of fetishism, therefore, as much as it does the fundamentals of legal reason that describe the machinations of contemporary civil justice. What I propose here is not straightforward but a knotty problem involving several threads that require unravelling. Broadly, the story I tell in this book is one of complicity between stakeholders of law and capital in the shaping of modernity, and in telling that story I hope to highlight and articulate some of the internal workings of what Nancy Fraser and Rahel Jaeggi (2018) call the "black box" of capitalism. This complicity is no small claim on its own, but it is also one coloured by powerful psychological forces embodied in stakeholders— libidinal economy intertwined with political economy—that must be taken seriously if we are to better understand what is driving the lived practices of (Western) capitalist society and, at the same time, eroding community bonds.

STRUCTURE AND SCOPE

History matters, so I spend the first few chapters reviewing Equity during the eighteenth and nineteenth centuries and the wholesale reforms across law, politics, economics and social life in England and Wales that occurred in these periods. I also look at the younger settlor nations of America, Australia and Canada and the development and relative adaption of English law in these burgeoning jurisdictions. In England and Wales, the Equity reform agenda came to a head with the enactment of the *Judicature Acts* 1873–1875, which fused Equity and Common Law procedure in a new High Court system of civil justice with a notion of *complete justice* at its heart, a figurative yardstick of legal certainty undergirding capitalism and its relations, practices, and prejudices. The Judicature process did not cease with these Acts but continued to be reaffirmed in several pieces of legislation (1975, 1925 and 1981), and in the Rules of the Supreme Court ('RSC') (1883 and 1965) and Civil Procedure Rules ('CPR') in 1999. Other than the state of New South Wales, Australia followed the same course in the nineteenth century, and civil justice across various states of the United States not only reimagined and reconfigured the roles of Common Law and Equity courts and procedures, but, as with New York State, influenced the English reform process. I will explore the notion of complete justice during this period beginning with the influence of Jeremy Bentham both on law reform and on the complexion of civil justice during the drafting of and after the Judicature Acts. The conjunction of Common Law and Equity is, I argue, a product of beliefs and desires, specifically displacement in the form of fantastical belief that Equity as a means to complete justice ('ECJ') offers capitalism an answer to a lack that, for the stakeholder, always already lives elsewhere in their existence.

Hence, my formulation of the concept of Equity fetishism is symptomatic of the effects of the unconscious in the (re)production and mobilization of Equity's principles, rules and doctrines, and in the development of complete justice as a phenomenon during the rise of industrial and commercial capitalism. I map Equity fetishism across at least four stages of this capitalist evolution during the last two hundred years. First, the classical economics of Adam Smith, David Ricardo and Marx during the first half of the nineteenth century. Second, the neoclassical economics of Alfred Marshall, William Stanley Jevons, and Leon Walras in the latter half of the nineteenth century (arguably the direct ancestor of neoliberalism), which encompasses what I refer to here as the Judicature age. Third, the centre-left welfarism during the middle part of the twentieth century under the direction of John Maynard Keynes. Fourth and finally, the neoliberal upsurge from the latter part of the twentieth century under the tutelage of right-wing economists including Frederick Hayek, Ludwig Von Mises, and Milton Friedman that continues, in large part, today.

The consequence of this evolution, as Chapter 3 will begin to show, has been the establishment and growth of a form of *stakeholder*, one with a belief in civil justice adjudication and particularly concerned with the efficiency of justice administration. As D. M. Kerly remarked shortly after Judicature, the reunion of the jurisdictions of Equity and Common Law was, so it was believed, going to make the administration of civil justice both 'cheaper and more certain' (1889, p. 294). As the theory of the fetish will show, and in particular the role of the fetish in concealing a lack of perfectibility or certainty in the subjects, institutions, and systems, belief is key to understanding the dynamics of contemporary civil justice. Among other things, this includes the ultimate belief in what John Sorabji calls the 'triumph of equity over the common law' following the Judicature reforms and the subsequent implementation of ECJ by the justice system (2014, p. 56). And thus also the (re)emergence of Equity as a 'radically new commitment' to justice rooted in discretion and merit rather than via stringent formalism (Sorabji 2014, p. 47). And what Raymond Evershed called 'the necessary elasticity' of Equity that would 'add by way of complement or appendix to the enacted law what may be required to *perfect the system as a whole*' [emphasis added] (1954, p. 341). Following a historical review of Equity, Chapters 3, 4, and 5 will consider Equity within the field of political economy, and in particular, the relationship between Equity, private property and stakeholders of capitalism. This will, in turn, pave the way for an analysis of the theory of Equity fetishism and my new theory of civil justice introduced and defined across Chapters 6, 7, and 8. Finally, Chapters 9 and 10 will apply the theory of Equity fetishism to contemporary civil justice, focusing on the impact of neoliberalism on long-standing juridical institutions, attitudes, and practices.

Equity is, I suggest, neglected in contemporary critical legal scholarship, as a site to interrogate the intersectionality of law, economics and the political. This book is, therefore, in part, a rallying cry to those interested in and engaging with critical legal scholarship to look (again) at Equity. This involves seeing Equity at the centre of debates concerning the ideological influence of capital on the private property order. Further, it involves scrutinizing Equity's relationship to that ideology and the role its jurisprudence has in maintaining regimes of private property rights and commercialism, institutions and methods for growing financial capital, and in preserving personal and corporate wealth, notably through tax avoidance schemes underpinned by trusts law. Equity is not alone in its complicity to make capitalism work. As Alastair Hudson maintains, 'Capitalism requires class stratification on the basis of money. Property law, employment contract law and corporate law are central to the maintenance of that stratification because they fix ownership of assets within one class while organising the obligations of the other classes' (2018, pp. 58–59). Equity forms part of what Hudson calls a 'rigged system' (2018, p. 59). By highlighting and questioning the relationship between Equity, stakeholders, and capitalism, this book asks what is at stake politically from the operation of civil justice to meet these various ends, and thus contributes modestly to critical evaluations of law within capitalism.

I consider here the nature of Equity in capitalist modernity to be contingent upon a combination of materially historical, socioeconomic, political and psychological factors. My references to modernity throughout this book align with capitalism as systematic production broadly defined, although I will not examine the full expanse of capitalism here. We can also view modernity as a 'Western' phenomenon, where, to echo Anthony Giddens, references to the development of civil justice is a reference 'to institutional transformations that have their origins in the West' (1991, p. 174). This makes the nexus between Equity jurisprudence, notions of complete civil justice, and the private property order a site *par excellence* for analysing complex factors relating to capitalist and neoliberal capitalist subjectivities, and why I consider overlaps between the work of Marx and Freud on fetishism as instructive. For example, I do not fully accept Marx's claim that, 'it is not the consciousness of men that determines their existence, but on the contrary, it is their social existence which determines their consciousness' (1859). Rather, as Freud's insistence on castration as a requirement for entrance into society attests, we can make a claim for certain psychic conditions in the subject's production that prefigure the existence of the very 'men' that Marx refers to (McGowan 2013, p. 4). Together the two theories provide a thorough analysis of the subjects in question.

I recognize the discussion in this book will follow a path worn thin in places by discussants, enthusiasts, and critics of the relationship between law and capitalism. Whether considering the classic liberal capitalist fervour for individualism, entrepreneurialism and free trade in Victorian Britain—something that has re-emerged under contemporary forms of neoliberalism in the late twentieth century—or imperialist capitalism and heavy industry built around cartels, trusts, and monopolies that have sought to conquer the world and often achieved this aim, Equity has been part of the 'rational' legal apparatus of civil justice that maintains the social order. Underscoring the key ideas presented by this book is a critique of the influence of capitalist economic reason on the management and organization of public (State) institutions of civil justice. This influence continually manifests itself through, for example, legitimation of reforms of civil justice justified in terms of cost and efficiency. In recent decades this has led to questions relating to access to justice, legal aid, and the everyday ability of the courts to handle workloads, to name but three (Lord Woolf 1996). Yet issues such as these, and many others, remain unresolved, and this book does not have solutions or answers to them. What this book maintains, however, is that capitalism is a root cause of inequity and inequality, and, therefore, we must challenge it.

METHOD

Finally, it is important to describe some key elements of this book's critical method. As a theory of civil justice, Equity fetishism contrasts with conventional interpretations, analyses, and wisdom on Equity, but necessarily so if a critical vocabulary of ECJ is to emerge. Conventional wisdom is, I claim, found in across legal narratives, speeches, lectures, academic articles, case reports, commentary, and even to some extent work that self-identifies as criticism of positive law and the *status quo*. To be clear, I do not fix the backdrop from which Equity fetishism emerged and against which it exists. Mostly, I define Equity fetishism based on the pervasive influence of economic ideas, rituals and practices that make up capitalist subjectivity and its recent 'mutant' neoliberal form (Han 2017, p. 5). Conventional wisdom is useful as an objective insight into particular events or states of affair that make up the *status quo*—the Hansard Parliamentary reports referred to in later chapters is an example. However, I see this wisdom reflecting and reproducing privilege and command of a particular class over legal discourse. 'Conventional' is a normative qualification, therefore, and it stems from the status of legal wisdom and conduct being self-referential, self-perpetuating and resolvable on its own internal logic. Roger Cotterrell points to the role of legal critique to deal precisely with claims that law is a 'self-justifying edifice' rather than a 'social construct', which denies and seeks to denude the political status of law in contemporary capitalism (1987, p. 79).

In their contrasting definitions of *general* and *restrictive jurisprudence*, where the latter resonates with the definition of conventional wisdom here, Costas Douzinas and Adam Gearey define restrictive as an 'endless interrogation of the essence or substance of law' resulting in 'a limited number of institutions, practices and actors' being included and 'considered relevant to jurisprudential inquiry' and therefore a 'large number of questions' going unanswered (2005, p. 10). Similarly, Wendy Brown and

Janet Halley see law and legal institutions and systems stemming from
the problematic of law figuring as 'technically neutral within liberalism'
(2002, p. 6). For them, this requires a 'left critique' of the conventional
wisdom of liberal and conservative jurisprudence and legal institutions
that begins 'with a critique of liberalism itself as well as an explicit focus on
the *social powers* producing and stratifying subjects that liberalism largely
ignores', including, most notably, capital's domination of the social and
political (Brown and Halley 2002, p. 6). This book largely agrees with
the need for left critique of this sort.

Discussion in later chapters examines conventional wisdom from the
nineteenth century and more recently to determine what is both said and
left unsaid in discourse about the socioeconomic and political landscape
that both fermented Judicature reform, and from which, I argue, Equity
fetishism ultimately emerged. Equity fetishism speaks to the notion of a
jurisdiction of conscience that has been both absorbed into the Common
Law, repressed and lost but also preserved and valorized, not least, Peter
Goodrich argues, by contemporary critical legal studies when it invokes
'the ethical dimensions of judgment and justice' (1996, p. 4). This point
is important for two principal reasons. First, because of what it says about
my fetishism of Equity—I will return to this matter in the following
chapter. Second, naming Equity fetishism makes possible a general legal
critique of the type described by the likes of Douzinas, Gearey, Brown
and Halley. It exposes Equity not only to students within law schools (*qua*
schools of divinity 'devoted to the preservation of the faith'), but to a critical legal education that journeys 'beyond the university walls into society
at large' (Watt 2012, p. 42). Naming Equity fetishism treats Equity as
a *major* jurisprudence within the Common Law tradition, and invites
consideration of tensions between the social, legal, economic, psychological and political. And it is because critical legal scholarship posits a 'great
paradox of justice […] clouded in controversy, uncertainty and disputa-
tion' that, I argue, Equity or more particularly the notion of ECJ demands
interrogation (Douzinas and Gearey 2005, p. 28).

CONCLUSION

Equity fetishism is symptomatic of complicity and collusion between
civil justice and capitalism. Common Law and Equity share responsibility in supporting capitalism to undertake its full array of practices.
Equity does not enjoy exclusive dominion over private property, contract,

nor in affording stakeholder's restitution or remedies if the social relations that both property and contract involve cannot function as they ought to, notably within the boundaries of capitalist reason and logic. But through the theory of Equity fetishism, this book shows the importance of the *peculiarities* of Equity's contribution to the goals of capital and the specific structure in fantasy Equity gives to capitalist stakeholders. Further, civil justice is not just a site for settling stakeholder property disputes, for calls to financial accountability, or paths to remedy and restitution within the logic of capitalism. It is a way to (re)produce capitalist class power and ideology and guarantee, latterly, neoliberal capitalism as a primary, prevailing social aim and standard for contemporary societies *contra* community. In structuring society this way, capitalism both relies upon and generates psychological effects displaced onto the institutions, systems, networks, and so on that make up and maintain the structure. 'Law and legal reasoning not only give form to the economic, but economize new spheres and practices', argues Wendy Brown, and in this way 'law becomes a medium for disseminating neoliberal rationality beyond the economy, including to constitutive elements of democratic life' (2015, p. 151). What Brown is highlighting here, I claim, is the complexity of the conjunction between (neoliberal) capitalism and law (and Equity), the political, the economic, and psychological. This is a reality of overlapping fictions, illusions, fantasies, rituals and symbolism of which Equity is a part, and one, I argue, which demands attention.

REFERENCES

BOOKS & ARTICLES

Aristotle. *Rhetoric.* Translated by W. Rhys Roberts. 2004. New York: Dover Publications.

Atkins, S. *Equity and Trusts.* 2013. London: Routledge.

Baldissone, R. From Helen's Pharmacy to the Multiverse of Equities: Difference, Opposition, *Différance. Pólemos*, Vol. 10, No. 2 (September 2016), pp. 137–157.

Brown, W. *Edgework: Critical Essays on Knowledge and Politics.* 2005. Princeton: Princeton University Press.

Brown, W., Halley, J. (eds.). *Left Legalism/Left Critique.* 2002. Durham: Duke University Press.

Burn, E.H., Virgo, G.J. *Maudsley & Burn's Trusts & Trustees, Cases & Materials.* 7th Edition. 2008. Oxford: Oxford University Press.

Cotterrell, R. Power, Property and the Law of Trusts: A Partial Agenda for Critical Legal Scholarship. *Journal of Law and Society*, Vol. 14, No. 1 (Spring 1987), pp. 77–90.

Douzinas, C., Gearey, A. *Critical Jurisprudence: The Political Philosophy of Justice*. 2005. Oxford: Hart.

Evershed, R. Reflections on the Fusion of Law and Equity After 75 Years. *The Law Quarterly Review*, Vol. 70 (July 1954), pp. 326–341.

Fortier, M. *The Culture of Equity in Early Modern England*. 2005. Farnham: Ashgate.

Fraser, N., Jaeggi, R. *Capitalism: A Conversation in Critical Theory*. 2018. Cambridge: Polity Press.

Freud, S. *The Unconscious*. Translated by Graham Frankland. 2005. London: Penguin Modern Classics.

Giddens, A. *The Consequences of Modernity*. 1991. Cambridge: Polity Press.

Goodrich, P. *Law in the Courts of Love: Literature and Other Minor Jurisprudences*. 1996. London: Routledge.

Haley, M., McMurty, L. *Equity & Trusts*. 3rd Edition. 2011. London: Sweet & Maxwell.

Han, B.C. *Psycho-Politics: Neoliberalism and New Technologies of Power*. Translated by Erik Butler. 2017. London: Verso.

Hudson, A. *Equity and Trusts*. 9th Edition. 2017. London: Routledge.

Hudson, A. Law as Capitalist Technique. *King's Law Journal*, Vol. 29, No. 1 (2018), pp. 58–87.

Kerly, D.M. *An Historical Sketch of the Equitable Jurisdiction of the Court of Chancery: Being the Yorke Prize Essay of the University of Cambridge for 1889*. 1889. Leopold Classic Library.

Klinck, D.R. *Conscience, Equity and the Court of Chancery in Early Modern England*. 2010. Farnham: Ashgate.

Martin, J.E. *Modern Equity*. 19th Edition. 2012. London: Sweet & Maxwell.

Marx, K. *A Contribution to the Critique of Political Economy*. 1859. https://www.marxists.org/archive/marx/works/1859/critique-pol-economy/preface.htm.

McGowan, T. *Enjoying What We Don't Have: The Political Project of Psychoanalysis*. 2013. Lincoln: University of Nebraska Press.

Oppermann, J.P. Tending the Garden: Equity and Exscription. *Pólemos*, Vol. 10, No. 2 (September 2016), pp. 117–136.

Polanyi, K. *Economy and Society: Selected Writings*. 2018. Cambridge: Polity Press.

Sorabji, J. *English Civil Justice After the Woolf and Jackson Reforms: A Critical Analysis*. 2014. Cambridge: Cambridge University Press.

Stiegler, B. *For a New Critique of Political Economy*. 2010. Cambridge: Polity Press.

Virgo, G. *The Principles of Equity & Trusts*. 2012. Oxford: Oxford University Press.

Watt, G. *Equity Stirring: The Story of Justice Beyond Law*. 2012. Oxford: Hart Publishing.

Watt, G. *Trusts & Equity*. 6th Edition. 2014. Oxford: Oxford University Press.

Wolff, J. *An Introduction to Political Philosophy*. 1996. Oxford: Oxford University Press.

Setting the Scene

INTRODUCTION

'One reason why modern life is so uncomfortable is that we have grown self-conscious about things that used to be taken for granted', states economist Joan Robison, 'Formerly people believed what they believed because they thought it was true, or because it was what all right-thinking people thought. But since Freud exposed to us our propensity to rationalization and Marx showed how our ideas spring from ideologies we have begun to ask: Why do I believe what I believe?' (1964, p. 7). This book analyses the law of Equity ('Equity') within Western (Anglo-American) Common Law, capitalist and neoliberal capitalist civil justice systems through a Marxist Freudian reading of fetishism. I understand contemporary Equity and civil justice to be institutions, concepts, and practices within neoliberal capitalism, but also historically rich imprimaturs of the evolving trends and desires of capital over several centuries. Both are also products of a fusion of law and economics fermented in Western Common Law jurisdictions, and of notions of competition, free-market efficiency standards, and the legal utilitarianism that neoliberalism promotes.

The character of contemporary Equity is much the same as it was at its medieval inception, 'albeit in a much-diluted form', as Irit Samet argues, with a focus on 'open texture norms ("principles"), court discretion element, penchant for *ex post* adjudication, and concern with the

13
R. Herian, *Capitalism and the Equity Fetish*,
https://doi.org/10.1007/978-3-030-66523-4_2

conscionability of the defendant's action' (2020, p. 6). Equity and civil justice systems in Western Common Law jurisdictions have a long working relationship with capital and have long aided in the management of the vagaries and crisis of capitalism. Many species or breeds of capitalism have existed since its earliest inception, yet we can point to a number of features and propensities baked into its general structure, underpinned by law, which amount to legitimized flaws. As Paddy Ireland describes,

> Capitalism purports to be a system based on competitive free markets in which consensual contractual exchanges take place between private agents seeking personal material gain. These market exchanges are secured and guaranteed by a neutral state which protects private property rights and freedom of contract. There is no ceiling on the size of the material gains that these market actors might secure as long as they play by the rules; nor should there be. Market competition and this absence of limits also underpin capitalism's dynamism and ability to deliver material wealth. Moreover, as any large accumulations of wealth arising out of market processes are the products of voluntary and consensual exchanges, they are prima facie legitimate. They are further legitimised by the fact that the self-interested pursuit of unlimited material gain in competitive markets operates in the wider public interest by ensuring the efficient allocation of resources and the maximisation of aggregate social wealth: private vice yields public benefits. (2018, p. 6)

Meanwhile, characteristics of neoliberal capitalism's impact upon law and legal systems in Western Common Law jurisdictions emerge in several ways. Jeanne Schroeder highlights that 'the legal utilitarian [...] views all human relations in terms of individual self-interest' (2004, p. 14); David Harvey maintains that 'To live under neoliberalism also means to accept or submit to that bundle of rights necessary for capital accumulation. We live, therefore, in a society in which the inalienable rights of individuals to private property, and the profit rate trump any other conception of inalienable rights you can think of' (2005, p. 181); Jodi Dean talks of 'the emergence of a new legal regime that strengthens the power and reach of the state by securing and protecting corporate, financial, and market interests', and that 'neoliberalism designates a particular strategy of class domination that uses the state to promote certain competitive dynamics for the benefit of the very rich. Pursued through policies of privatization, deregulation, and financialization, and buttressed by an ideology of private property, free markets, and free trade' (2009, p. 132; 2012, pp. 122–123). Wendy Brown argues that 'More than simply securing the rights of capital and structuring competition, neoliberal juridical reason recasts political rights, citizenship, and the field of democracy itself in an economic register' (2005, pp. 151–152). Thus, when Man Yip and James Lee talk of the 'commercial pragmatism of simplifying legal standards for commercial actors, as well as wider commercial concerns' underlying contemporary judicial reasoning that places equitable principles in 'jeopardy', this book interprets that as symptomatic of neoliberal capitalist effect on law and procedures of civil justice (2017, p. 648).

The (Ir)Rational Structure of Law

As juridical institutions, concepts, and practices within capitalism in its broader historical setting, Equity and civil justice and have long helped to define what Max Weber called, 'the rational structure of the law' (2002, p. 365). Capitalism and capitalist interests, Weber claims, 'undoubtedly smoothed the path for the legal profession [Juristenstandes], with its specialist training in rational law, to dominate the administration of justice and other forms of administration' (2002, p. 365). Chancery practitioners, for instance, have long contributed to the capitalist legal system and profession that Weber highlights. The civil justice system has contributed to the evolution of jurisprudence (rules, principles, and doctrines) tailored towards maintaining exclusionary regimes of private property, corporate and commercial interests, and institutions such as trusts valued as core interventions within 'modern rational' capitalism for the management of wealth and assets (Weber 2002, p. 365). And as a system with 'contract at its centre', capitalism relies on the remedies that equity provides to ensure contracts perform reasonably and efficiently (Hodgson 2015, p. 116). As pillars of capitalism, private property and the safeguarding of private property rights and interests to develop financial capital, have benefited and guaranteed the success of a few capitalist stakeholders, leading to inequalities. Inequality, as a description of capitalism's limited benefit, is not a theme that will be specifically discussed during this book. It is a powerful undercurrent to the critique I offer however, encompassing several concepts and ideas that are relevant to Equity, civil justice, and private property, including how civil justice reaches and enforces decisions about what is just and fair. Therefore, some sign of how we might understand inequality is necessary and how it is a reflection not so much on laws rational structure but its irrational affects.

Ardent advocates of capitalism still recognize its ability to produce inequality and inequity. But in contrast to centrist, left socialist, and communist critique, right-wing and libertarian viewpoints explain inequality as a necessary function of capitalism that still, they will argue, leads to widely held social benefits. As Joseph A. Schumpeter maintains, 'no social system can work which is based exclusively upon a network of free contracts between (legally) equal contracting parties and in which everyone is supposed to be guided by nothing except his own (short-run) utilitarian ends' (2010, p. 377). Similarly, Ludwig von Mises states, 'the preservation of these feudal intuitions was incompatible with the system of capitalism. Their abolition and the establishment of the principle of equality under the law removed the barriers that prevented mankind from enjoying all those benefits which the system of private ownership of the means of production and private enterprise makes possible' (2009, pp. 6–7). Or inequality as a liberal requirement to resist the incursion of government on private interests, as Milton Friedman agues, 'Much of the actual inequality derives from imperfections of the market. Many of these have themselves been created by government action or could be removed by government action. There is every reason to adjust the rules of the game so as to eliminate these sources of inequality' (2002, p. 176).

Meanwhile centrist and centre-left commentators recognize flaws in capitalism, but not irredeemable failures. Angus Deaton claims that 'Economic growth is the engine of the escape from poverty and material deprivation. Yet growth is faltering in the rich world. Growth in each recent decade has been lower than in the previous one. Almost everywhere, the faltering of growth has come with expansions of inequality' (2013, p. 327). Thomas Piketty maintains that 'the resurgence of inequality after 1980 is due largely to the political shifts of the past several decades, especially in regard to taxation and finance. The history of inequality is shaped by the way economic, social, and political actors view what is just and what is not, as well as by the relative power of those actors and the collective choices that result' (2014, p. 20). And Joseph E. Stiglitz maintains that 'Countries around the world provide frightening examples of what happens to societies when they reach the level of inequality toward which we are moving. It is not a pretty picture: countries where rich live in gated communities, waited upon by hordes of low-income workers; unstable political systems where populists promise the masses a better life, only to disappoint. Perhaps most importantly, there is an absence of hope. In these countries, the poor know that their prospects of emerging from poverty, let alone making it to the top, are minuscule. This is *not* something we should be striving for' (2013, p. 4).

In Chapter 5, I discuss the concept of private property in depth. For now, however, I can define it as contingent on notions of resource *scarcity* that give form to social relations (and market relations in a neoliberal capitalist schema) through bundles of legal, moral, and customary rights, concepts and practices including those of use, possession, ownership, enjoyment, and exclusion (Marx and Engels 1970, pp. 79–81; Penner 1997; Honoré 2013, pp. 563–574; Schroeder 2004, pp. 179–182; Alexander and Peñalver 2012; Pierson 2016). 'Property is a legal and social institution governing the use of most things and the allocation of some items of social wealth', J. W. Harris maintains, and social wealth 'comprises all those things and services for which there is a greater potential total demand than there is supply' (1996, p. 1). For Joseph Singer a definition can be made even more succinct, 'Property is about rights over things and the people who have those rights are called owners' (2000, p. 2). In private property contexts, these mechanisms can assume a particular quality as *safeguarding* functions that guarantee assignment of separate objects (things) to individuals. Meanwhile, libertarian and utilitarian approaches to private property foreground liberal policies that underscore forms of morality based on private ownership, including through the greater contractual determination of property rights (a *contractarian* perspective) (Nozick 1974; Von Mises 2005; Hayek 2013). Suman Gupta (2001) calls Hayek's and Nozick's conceptualization of private property within the libertarian tradition 'anti-political'. In contrast, I argue that social and power relations *make up* private property and property rights and that they are, therefore, *political* concepts and not, as Graham Virgo suggests, 'neutral' (2015, p. 15). Contract meanwhile maintains a close association with private property and 'presupposes the institution of property' and is of special concern within capitalism for enabling the 'wealth-allocating function' of property by dissociating it from a use-control function (Harris 1996, p. 50).

Private property is the principal mode of bourgeois socioeconomic desire, aspiration and organization in Western Common Law jurisdictions under capitalism, not least, as Marx and Engels claim, because of a 'juridical illusion' of reducing law to the private will that underscores the selfish nature of much civil justice litigation (1970, p. 81, see also,

Jolowicz 1983, p. 298). Within capitalism, argues Nikolas Rose, individuals 'are forced into a profound inwardness, and cling for comfort to a belief in their own uniqueness, in the process elaborating a complex inner world of self' (1999, p. 66). As a result, Rose concludes that 'the fundamental dialectic of modern society—maximum individualization and maximum "freedom" is developed only at the price of maximum fragmentation, maximum uncertainty, maximum estrangement of individual from fellow individual' (1999, p. 66). Certainty and coherence in the substance and procedure of civil justice becomes a necessary counterweight to the realities of existence within capitalism, therefore. Tempered by a flexibility and responsiveness that allows rules to bend to novel social and economic demands, the mode of existence Equity provides is enjoyable and desirable to stakeholders, especially regarding business and commercial activities. I *will* discuss the flexibility that Equity brings to Common Law and civil justice at several points throughout this book and consider it especially vital to understanding the role of Equity within neoliberal capitalism.

We find an abundance of expressions of Equity's flexibility and responsiveness in judicial statements. Lord Cottenham L.C. in *Taylor v. Salmon* (1838) 4 My. & Cr. 134 states that, 'I have before taken occasion to observe that I thought it the duty of this court to adapt its practice and course of proceeding as far as possible to the existing state of society, and to apply its jurisdiction to all those new cases which, from the progress daily making in the affairs of men, must continually arise, and not, from too strict an adherence to forms and rules established under very different circumstances, decline to administer justice, and to enforce rights for which there is no other remedy' (at 14). Devlin LJJ in *Ingram v Little* [1961] 1 QB 31 claims that 'The true spirit of the common law is to override theoretical distinctions when they stand in the way of doing practical justice' (at 73); Millett J in *Lonrho plc. v Fayed and Others (No. 2)* [1992] 1 WLR 1 states 'Equity must retain what has been called its "inherent flexibility" and capacity to adjust to new situations by reference to mainsprings of the equitable jurisdiction' (at 9). Lord Hoffmann in *Co-Operative Insurance Society Ltd. Respondents and Argyll Stores Ltd. Appellants* [1997] 2 WLR 898, dealing with remedies, urged that 'A decree of specific performance is, of course, a discretionary remedy and the question for your Lordships is whether the Court of Appeal was entitled to set aside the exercise of the judge's discretion. *There are well-established principles which govern the exercise of the discretion but these, like all equitable principles, are flexible and adaptable to achieve the ends of equity, which is, as Lord Selborne L.C. once remarked, to "do more perfect and complete justice"* than would be the result of leaving the parties to their remedies at common law: *Wilson v. Northampton and Banbury Junction Railway Co.* (1874) L.R. 9 Ch App 279, 284' [my emphasis] (at 901). 'Equity's place in the law of commerce, long resisted by commercial lawyers', argued P.J. Millett., 'can no longer be denied' (1998, p. 214). Whilst Lord Reed and Lord Neuberger in *Zurich Insurance plc UK v International Energy Group Ltd* [2015] UKSC 33 agreed that 'There is often much to be said for the courts developing the common law to achieve what appears to be a just result in a particular type of case, even though it involves departing from established common law principles. Indeed, it can be said with force that that precisely reflects the genius of the common law, namely its ability to develop and adapt with the benefit of experience' (at 209).

It is important to note that I put no definitive dates on the origin of capitalism, which remains a complex question much debated by economic historians (Heilbroner 2000; Weber 2002; Hodgson 2015; Wood 2017). I understand the emergence of capitalism, however, as involving a series of sociocultural, legal (including determinations of an evolution in the jurisprudence of property and contract), and political shifts in Britain, France, and other European nations that started in the fifteenth century. These shifts gathered pace during the sixteenth century and matured during the Enlightenment and post-Enlightenment with the onset of Revolution in England, America, and France and the rise of industrialization and urbanization (Hobsbawm 1992, pp. 13–16; Lippit 2005, p. 1; Scott 2011; Hodgson 2015, p. 17; Pierson 2016). I will explore the evolution, systemization, and calibration of Equity and civil justice to capitalism and forms of commercialism symptomatic of capitalist reason and logic at key stages in history including the nineteenth century and late twentieth century, notably the same periods that Thomas Piketty identifies with the 'prodigiously inegalitarian' '"first globalization" of finance and trade (1870-1914)', and 'the "second globalization", which has been under way since the 1970s' (2014, p. 28). And via figures of note who have been influential in shaping legal thinking, reform, and the relationship and tensions between law and economics, including Jeremy Bentham, Frederick Hayek, and Richard Posner.

Equity fetishism is symptomatic of the influence on the subject, and on the systems and institutions that organize the society in which the subject exists, of ideology, fantasy, and desire founded on logics of economic reason. What Karl Polanyi called 'atomistic and individualistic' organic forms and Louis Althusser referred to as 'interpellated subjects', I reconsider here as *stakeholders* (Polanyi 2001, p. 171; Althusser 2008). The overlap between theories of ideology and fetishism is productive of critical insight of the stakeholder who exists within what Lorenzo Chiesa and Alberto Toscano have called the 'ideological force-field of contemporary capitalism' (2007, p. 118). Stakeholders also, through that same combination of ideology and fetishism, enjoy and find pleasure in existence rooted in the fantasies that ideology and fetishism together offer. 'Fantasies can make life bearable, though they can also lead us to error', argues Bernard Harcourt, but they are sometimes 'so extravagant or unrestrained that the person fantasizing should know, herself, that they are unreal. In that sense, the person may be complicit in the act of fantasizing' (2012, p. 2418). Stakeholders are economic subjects complicit in the fantasy Harcourt describes. Individuals willing to answer the call of capitalism to engage in, among other things, free-market logics of competition and efficiency. Stakeholders always seek to accumulate, exploit, and seize opportunities to exercise self-interest, economic advantage and gain, even where it might involve calling the bargaining and conduct of others foul, unfair, or unequal.

As a theory of civil justice Equity fetishism first highlights the encounter of economic subjects within capitalism with the 'fact of castration as the requirement for entrance into society', and then the nature of the stakeholder construction in fantasy of a fetish to conceal the threat of castration, which takes the form of demands, needs, and desires directed at the institutions, concepts, and practices of Equity and civil justice (McGowan 2013, p. 4). Equity fetishism points to the fact of the unconscious as a vitiating factor within Equity jurisprudence and its place in civil justice procedure predicated on the stakeholder's encounter with the trauma of castration, the paradigm negativity endured by all subjects that Maria Aristodemou calls the 'trope of insufficiency, of loss, of absence [...] "lack"', which 'instigates and permeates not only our cultural products, but our social, legal, and political practices' (2014, p. 7). Jeanne Schroeder, in her book on the erotics of markets, discusses the gendered aspects of castration that resonate with the present book, although gender is not a theme that I will cover here. 'The two sexes are two positions one can take with respect to castration', claims Schroeder, 'denial and acceptance. The masculine, which feels that he has lost a precious part of himself, falsely claims to possess and exchange the object of desire.

The feminine, which feels that she has lost her selfhood, accepts the role of identification with the enjoyment of the object of desire' (Schroeder 2004, p. 241).

Although gender is not an explicit theme in this book, on Schroeder's account the masculine form of castration is of primary concern here. Not because it tells us anything about capitalism than the account of feminine castration cannot, but because the masculine reflects the privileging of wealth maximization within capitalism, and the dominance of patriarchy in shaping the conjunction between law and economics, including the civil justice system that the stakeholder utilizes to maintain their self-interest (Schroeder 2004, p. 243). Following Schroeder's account of masculine castration as the dominant mode in societies underscored by wealth maximization, namely those within capitalism, she describes how the 'masculine must lie to himself and pretend nothing has been lost. *He must deny the existence of the real and act as though the symbolic were complete*' [emphasis added] (2004, p. 241). This last statement is crucial to understanding the encounter stakeholder's within capitalism have with castration: it is an encounter that signals an insufficiency, loss, or absence that the *fetishistic* stakeholder refuses to acknowledge, one they disavow and conceal via substitutes in fantasy. The substitute I am highlighting here is Equity as a means to complete justice ('ECJ').

AM I AN EQUITY FETISHIST?

Fetishism is central to this book because of what I claim it reveals about Equity and ECJ as socioeconomic, institutional, systemic, and encoded symbolic forms. I agree with Lord Denning and Gary Watt, where both claim the 'essential educational nature of Equity' (Denning 1952, pp. 1–10; Watt 2012, p. 42). As a body of jurisprudence in Chancery and throughout civil justice, Equity holds a notable place and *application* in law. This book will analyse and interrogate Equity as a text, explore the language used to describe and apply it. I will examine how lawyers and non-lawyers alike speak Equity, narrate, report, valorize, and criticize it. The aim is to treat Equity as an object of educational intrigue and academic curiosity. This does, however, raise a potential problem that I need to address before moving on: am I fetishizing Equity?

To talk of Equity or ECJ rather than law or civil justice problematizes Althusser's claim that such a distinction is merely 'internal to bourgeois law, and valid in the (subordinate) domains in which bourgeois law exercises its "authority"' (2008, p. 18). This book agrees with Althusser's observations as to the fundamental nature of the distinction in terms of political economy but does not view it as credible from the point of view of critical method. This is because to overlook Equity or reduce it into any of the levels to which it is ultimately subservient (Common Law, civil justice, or even the broader superstructure of capitalism) risks overgeneralization. To particularize is not to accept the authority of bourgeois law but to aim for a more precise criticism of it. Because the emphasis here is on Equity's jurisprudential and procedural peculiarities and distinctiveness from the general or Common Law and argues that it is necessary to do so to facilitate a more precise analysis of the law, suggests an innate fetishism.

Is this a problem? Baudrillard noted that the 'term "fetishism" almost has a life of its own. Instead of functioning as a metalanguage for the magical thinking of others, it turns against those who use it and surreptitiously exposes their own magical thinking' (1981, p. 90). Based on Baudrillard's account, I admit to some fetishism here. We can see this as a general problem for modern theory to escape self-contradiction and constantly problematize itself (Douzinas and Gearey 2005, p. 305). For Baudrillard, psychoanalysis is the only mode of critique able to escape the 'vicious circle' inaugurated by a surreptitious exposure to one's own magical thinking (1981, p. 90). 'Psychoanalysis has escaped this vicious circle', says Baudrillard, 'by returning fetishism to its context within a perverse *structure* that perhaps underlies all desire', hence it 'avoids any projection of magical or transcendental animism, and thus the rationalist position of positing a false consciousness and a transcendental subject' (1981, p. 90).

That this book focuses on Equity amid a far broader field of law is undoubtedly a fetishism of sorts. This is because it affords Equity *devotion* (a key indicator of fetishism) that I do not extend, for example, to other areas of civil justice. Treating Equity in this way is to consider it a discrete gloss on the law and thus to elevate it to a fetishisitic prerequisite. To (re)claim Equity as a subject of criticism and inquiry, it is necessary to stray into levels of objectification and to concede that Equity is an object worthy of special devotion within the broader spectrum of law and civil justice. Finally, as later chapters will discuss, the following book engenders some level of neuroticism as a legal academic project. Neuroticism within the legal community means directing expertise, knowledge, and meaning to placing limits and constraints, seen as necessary, on economic existence, by defining laws that counterbalance and give particular form to economic existence within capitalism. Freud defines neurosis as key to notions of civilization and the creation of social utility that resonates, in some respects, with the ideas of Jeremy Bentham that I will discuss in Chapter 3. 'It was discovered that a person becomes neurotic', claims Freud, 'because he cannot tolerate the amount of frustration which society imposes on him in the service of it cultural ideals, and it was inferred from this that the abolition or reduction of those demands would result in a return to possibilities of happiness' (2001, p. 87). The neuroticism of the legal community is, therefore, an important complement to the perverse enjoyment sought by stakeholders, and, I argue, the two structure Equity fetishism as a fantasy of civil justice within the capitalist juridical-economic imagination.

REFERENCES

BOOKS AND ARTICLES

Alexander, G.S., Peñalver, E.M. *An Introduction to Property Theory.* 2012. Cambridge: Cambridge University Press.
Althusser, L. *On Ideology.* 2008. London: Verso.
Aristodemou, M. *Law, Psychoanalysis, Society: Taking the Unconscious Seriously.* 2014. Abingdon: Routledge.
Baudrillard, J. *For a Critique of the Political Economy of the Sign.* Translated by Charles Levin. 1981. St. Louis: Telos Press Ltd.
Brown, W. *Edgework: Critical Essays on Knowledge and Politics.* 2005. Princeton: Princeton University Press.
Chiesa, L., Toscano, A. Agape and the Anonymous Religion of Atheism. *Angelaki Journal of Theoretical Humanities,* Vol. 12, No. 1 (April 2007), pp. 113–126.
Dean, J. *Democracy and Other Neoliberal Fantasies: Communicative Capitalism and Left Politics.* 2009. Durham: Duke University Press.
Dean, J. *The Communist Horizon.* 2012. London: Verso.
Deaton, A. *The Great Escape: Health, Wealth, and the Origins of Inequality.* 2013. Princeton: Princeton University Press.
Denning, A. The Need for a New Equity. *Current Legal Problems,* Vol. 5, No. 1 (January 1952), pp. 1–10.
Douzinas, C., Gearey, A. Critical Jurisprudence: The Political Philosophy of Justice. 2005. Oxford: Hart.

Freud, S. *Moses and Monotheism, an Outline of Psycho-Analysis and Other Works: The Standard Edition Volume XXIII (1937–1939)*. Translated and Edited by James Strachey. 1964. London: The Hogarth Press.

Freud, S. *The Future of an Illusion, Civilization and Its Discontents and Other Works: The Standard Edition Volume XXI (1927–1931)*. Translated and Edited by James Strachey. 2001. London: Vintage.

Friedman, M. *Capitalism and Freedom*. 2002. Chicago: University of Chicago Press.

Gupta, S. *Corporate Capitalism and Political Philosophy: Corporate Capitalism and Political Philosophy*. 2001. London: Pluto Press.

Harcourt, B.E. Fantasies and Illusions: On Liberty, Order, and Free Markets. *Cardoza Law Review*, Vol. 33, No. 6 (August 2012), pp. 2413–2428.

Harris, J.W. *Property & Justice*. 1996. Oxford: Oxford University Press.

Harvey, D. *A Brief History of Neoliberalism*. 2005. Oxford: Oxford University Press.

Hayek, F.A. *Law, Legislation and Liberty*. 2013. London: Routledge Classics.

Heilbroner, R. *The Worldly Philosophers*. 2000. London: Penguin Books.

Hobsbawm, E. *The Age of Revolution 1789–1848*. 1992. London: Abacus.

Hodgson, G. M. *Conceptualizing Capitalism: Institutions, Evolution, Future*. 2015. Chicago: University of Chicago Press.

Honoré, A. M. Ownership. *Readings in the Philosophy of Law*. Edited by Jules L. Coleman. 2013. New York: Routledge, pp. 563–574.

Ireland, P. From Lonrho to BHS; The Changing Character of Corporate Governance in Contemporary Capitalism. *King's Law Journal*, Vol. 29, No. 1 (2018), pp. 3–35.

Jolowicz, J. A. General Ideas and the Reform of Civil Procedure. *Legal Studies*, Vol. 3, No. 3 (November 1983), pp. 295–314.

Lippit, Victor D. *Capitalism*. 2005. London: Routledge.

Marx, K., Engels, F. *The German Ideology*. Edited by C.J. Arthur. 1970. London: Lawrence & Wishart.

McGowan, T. *Enjoying What We Don't Have: The Political Project of Psychoanalysis*. 2013. Lincoln: University of Nebraska Press.

Millett, P.J. Equity's Place in the Law of Commerce. *Law Quarterly Review*, Vol. 114 (April 1998), pp. 214–227.

Nozick, R. *Anarchy, State and Utopia*. 1974. New York: Basic Books.

Penner, J.E. *The Idea of Property in Law*. 1997. Oxford: Oxford University Press.

Pierson, C. *Just Property, Volume Two: Enlightenment, Revolution, and History*. 2016. Oxford: Oxford University Press.

Piketty, T. *Capital in the Twenty-First Century*. Translated by Arthur Goldhammer. 2014. Cambridge: The Belknap Press of Harvard University Press.

Polanyi, K. *Great Transformation: The Political and Economic Origins of Our Time*. 2001. Boston: Beacon Press.

Rose, N. *Powers of Freedom: Reframing Political Thought*. 1999. Cambridge: Cambridge University Press.

Samet, I. Equity. *Research Handbook on Private Law Theories, Hanoch Dagan & Benjamin Zipursky eds., Forthcoming*. 2020. https://papers.ssrn.com/sol3/papers.cfm?abstract_id=3600193.

Schumpeter, J.A. *Capitalism, Socialism and Democracy*. 2010. London: Routledge Classics.

Schroeder, J.L. *The Triumph of Venus: The Erotics of the Market*. 2004. Berkeley: University of California Press.

Scott, B.R. *Capitalism: Its Origins and Evolution as a System of Governance*. 2011. Berlin: Springer.

Singer, J. *Entitlement: The Paradoxes of Property*. 2000. New Haven: Yale University Press.

Stiglitz, J.E. *The Price of Inequality*. 2013. London: Penguin Books.

Virgo, G. *The Principles of the Law of Restitution*. 3rd Edition. 2015. Oxford: Oxford University Press.

Von Mises, L. *Liberalism: The Classical Tradition*. Edited by Bettina Bien Greaves. 2005. Indianapolis: Liberty Fund.

Von Mises, L. *The Anti-Capitalist Mentality*. 2009. Mansfield Centre: Martino Publishing.

Watt, Gary. *Equity Stirring: The Story of Justice Beyond Law*. 2012. Oxford: Hart Publishing.

Weber, M. *The Protestant Ethic and the "Spirit" of Capitalism and Other Writings*. Edited and Translated by Peter Baehr. 2002 London: Penguin Books.

Wood, E.M. *The Origins of Capitalism: A Longer View*. 2017. London: Verso.

Yip, M., Lee, J. The Commercialisation of Equity. *Legal Studies*, Vol. 37, No. 4 (2017), pp. 647–671.

CASE-LAW AND LEGISLATION

Co-Operative Insurance Society Ltd. Respondents and Argyll Stores Ltd. Appellants [1997] 2 WLR 898.

Ingram v Little [1961] 1 QB 31.

Lonrho plc. v Fayed and Others (No. 2) [1992] 1 WLR 1.

Taylor v Salmon (1838) 4 My & Cr 134.

Zurich Insurance plc UK v International Energy Group Ltd [2015] UKSC 33.

CHAPTER 3

Reform Economics and the 'Plucked Rib' of Equity

INTRODUCTION

'If chancellors were Cardinals and Archbishops before the Reformation, and common lawyers afterward, it is easy to see that the theory and practice of equity had to change', argues Timothy Endicott (1989, p. 557). And whilst nineteenth-century chancery judgements 'bear no reference to the safety of the plaintiff's soul', Endicott concludes, 'the change demands closer examination, and particularly an answer to the question of how equity survived at all as a system outside the common law. Why was the institutional reconciliation delayed until 1873?' (1989, p. 557). The following chapter develops the theory of Equity fetishism by examining it as a phenomenon occurring within broader philosophical, sociocultural, economic and political changes during the eighteenth-and nineteenth centuries, notably because of the work of Jeremy Bentham. I will assess Judicature and Chancery reform as it was set out in the Parliamentary reports and records from the time, to further develop my argument that the reforms signalled a closer alignment between civil justice and the needs, desires and fantasies provoked by capitalism.

Two pieces of legislation bookend the theory of civil justice this book proposes, and the source of that legislation was the reform agenda constructed in Parliament during the nineteenth century. The first being the *Supreme Court of Judicature Act* 1873 ('the 1873 Act'), followed by the *Senior Courts Act* 1981 (initially called the *Supreme Court Act*)

R. Herian, *Capitalism and the Equity Fetish*, https://doi.org/10.1007/978-3-030-66523-4_3

('the 1981 Act'). These and other pieces of legislation, including the *Supreme Court of Judicature Act* 1875 and the *Supreme Court of Judicature (Consolidation) Act* 1925 ('the 1925 Act'), act as stepping stones in the history of Equity fetishism. Also relevant are the Rules of the Supreme Court ('RSC'), which, following the Woolf Reforms, became the Civil Procedure Rules after 1999. These rules fleshed out the procedural role and place of Equity set out in the Judicature legislation. Together this legislation and the formation of the RSC signal important stages in the evolution of civil justice since the nineteenth century. My examination of the Judicature period here is less for explaining the tension between the stringent rule compliance and formalism of Common Law and the liberal approach of Equity as the basis of complete justice, than to explain what made perfectibility and complete justice such powerful and necessary ideals in the minds of civil justice reformers during the nineteenth century and in the decades thereafter. If, as William Davies following Karl Polanyi states, the 'achievement of nineteenth-century liberalism was to produce a sense of economic activity as separate from and external to social and political activity', a point on which this book largely agrees, then highlighting the resurgence of capital as grounds for Equity fetishism shows how the civil justice reforms and ultimately ECJ fitted into this 'achievement' (2017, p. 21).

The Pleasure, Pain, and *Pannomion* of Jeremy Bentham

I view Jeremy Bentham's influence on this book's subject in two ways. First, Bentham's influence over law reform and thus Chancery reform as a species of it—'the founder of all legal reform' as Bentham was enthusiastically referred to during the Parliamentary law reform debates in the 1830s (HC Deb 29 April 1830 Vol. 24 cc243-89 at 263). Second, and specific to Equity and thus Equity fetishism, the influence of Bentham's idea of 'complete law' or pannomion on the excretion of uncertainties (if not always a corresponding guarantee of certainties) from the substance and processes of the law, which has led commentators to speculate on whether he was the progenitor of Judicature reform and the fusion of Common Law and Equity (Dinwiddy 1989, pp. 283–289; Holdsworth 1929, pp. 20–21; Crimmins 2018). 'The standard account of Chancery', argues Mark Fortier in his assessment of Equity and the law in Restoration and eighteenth-century England, 'is one of a Restoration regularization of principles and procedures after the wild and woolly early modern period before the inefficiency, stultification, and stagnation decried by Jeremy Bentham [...] became endemic' (2015, p. 15). Further, Bentham's influence is important here because of what it tells us about the tensions produced by principles and ideology imposed upon the fundamental institutions and procedures of law. Specifically, the exposure of civil justice (at this point in time still the bifurcated system of Common Law and Equity courts) to Bentham's ideas of utilitarianism and political economy and the tensions this created between conservative protectionism of law's institutions and a shifting liberal political class intoxicated by the promises of capitalism, and increasingly subservient to the influence and the will of business and commerce.

Michael Lobban points to a particular instance between Lord Abinger and Lord Langdale during the 1830s and the first serious moments of the nineteenth-century reform programme directed at Chancery, in which Abinger dismissed Langdale's ideas for reform of the office of Chancellor 'as Benthamite theory out of tune with practice' (2004a, p. 419). More pointedly, in the Parliamentary speech Lobban is referring to, Lord Abinger, in what Lobban says is a reference to Bentham, claims that, 'ingenious gentleman [Bentham] maintained that speedy justice was so essential, that no system of judicature could be perfect unless there was one judge eternally sitting, so that when one was fatigued another should take his place. That certainly was the very perfection of theory. But human affairs would not admit of its application; he, therefore, must request his noble and learned Friend to mix up with his theory a little more of his experience in practice' (HL Deb 13 June 1836, Vol. 34, cc413-86 at 475). The reference to 'perfection of theory' is of note regarding Bentham's particular vision of complete justice and, as this book claims, integral to the notion of perfection in terms of fantasy and fetishism.

Certainty and perfection were themes Bentham explored rigorously throughout his work, in part as a rebuttal to Blackstone's vision and 'mapping' of a system of laws in the *Commentaries of the Common Law and English Constitution*, which Bentham saw as expansive, flexible, yet elitist and overly focused on the demands of the King and of the aristocracy (1864, p. 71; see also, Letwin 1998). But also because of the growing perception of Chancery as dysfunctional. Thus the tendency outside of Chancery towards generalizing and universalising 'common equity was helping further political and social causes with which any progressive-minded person might sympathize', argues Fortier, 'within Chancery the movement was to delimit and order general equity for the sake of enclosing it within precedent and rule-based jurisprudence' (2015, p. 16). Gerald Postema maintains that in contrast to critics like Bentham, others followed Blackstone too closely even as systemic issues with the Common Law troubled them. 'Unlike Bentham, these critics treat this bred-in-the-bone resistance to theory and system not as sufficient cause to raze the obsolete structure and replace it with a fully modern, rational, built-from-scratch code', states Postema, 'but rather, like Blackstone, to festoon its ancient, ramshackle ramparts with celebratory banners' (2014, p. 70). Blackstone followed Grotius in his interpretation of Equity considering Aristotelian flexibility and adaptability based on that idea that, 'since in laws all cases cannot be foreseen or expressed, it is necessary, that when the general decrees of the law come to be applied to particular cases, there should be somewhere a power vested of excepting those circumstances, which (had they been foreseen) the legislator himself would have excepted' (2009, at 61).

As the following passage shows, Bentham reserved a special level of vitriol for Blackstone's ideas, and for Equity:

> In regard to the Law of England in particular, it is here that he gives an account of the division of it into its two branches (branches, however, that are no ways distinct in the purport of them, when once established, but only in respect of the source from whence their establishment took its rise) the *Statute* or *Written law*, as it is called, and the *Common* or *Unwritten*: an account of what are called *General Customs* or institutions in force throughout the whole empire, or at least the whole nation; of what are called *Particular Customs*, institutions of local extent established in particular districts; and of such *adopted* institutions of a general extent, as are parcel of what are called the *Civil* and the *Canon* laws; all three in the character of so many branches of what is called the *Common Law*: in fine, a general account of *Equity*, that capricious and incomprehensible mistress of our fortunes, whose features neither our Author, nor perhaps any one is well able to delineate; of *Equity*, who having in the beginning been a rib of *Law*, but since in some dark age plucked from her side, when sleeping, by the hands not so much of God as of enterprizing Judges, now lords it over her parent sister. (1891, pp. 95–96)

'Bentham directed this analysis against a host of ethical propositions he sought to eliminate as competing alternatives to the utility principle', claims James Crimmins, 'such as "moral sense", "common sense", "law of reason", "natural justice", and "natural equity". All are dismissed on the grounds that they are merely empty phrases that express nothing beyond the sentiment of the person who advocates them' (2018). Roger Cotterrell also points to Bentham's fervent dislike of natural law, which he considered a 'formidable nonentity' and a 'labyrinth of confusion' (1989, p. 122). Bentham's dislike of the uncertainty of language, including the language of Equity, as a contributory factor to a lack of coherence in Common law system, was central to his motivation for a complete law and complete code. This insistence on systemization, and especially its relationship to the problematic of Equity, in particular, remained a powerful theme some two hundred years later in the work of Peter Birks (Lobban 2014; Watts 2014). We will discuss Birks in more detail later regarding Equity and property, but for now it is worth noting the lineage between Bentham and Birks as advocates for clarity and order as bulwarks of certainty in law, a position that placed Equity as a jurisprudence of discretion and conscience on the wrong side of both men (Postema 2014, pp. 69–70).

For Bentham, certainty and perfection of the law had to be in line with economic and social expediency and improvement. In his introduction to Bentham's *A Fragment on Government*, F.C Montague states that Bentham's ideal of codification of the law *qua* complete law was twofold: 'an advantage in assisting the study of the law and an advantage in assisting the administration of the law' (1891, p. 50). He continues:

> First, as regards the study of the law, Bentham believed that law once codified would be brought within the grasp of laymen as well as of lawyers; that every person of sound mind would be able to understand and to remember the provisions of the law. Secondly, as regards the administration of the law, Bentham believed that law once codified could be administered with certainty, with speed and with economy, since there would be little for judges to do when the application of law had been made so simple, and less for lawyers to do when every man would be able to conduct his own case. Codification, therefore, would make the knowledge of the law attainable by all, and the remedy for wrong endured accessible to all, and thus in one word perfect the legal development of society. (1891, p. 50)

The preface to *A Fragment on Government* begins with Bentham's assessment of the post-Enlightenment age through which he was living, on the cusp of the meteoric rise of industrial capitalism, as 'a busy age; in which knowledge is rapidly advancing towards perfection' (1891, p. 93). And, therefore, Bentham's idea of complete law matters here because of the conjunction of law, property and economics that it represents—a theme that we will see developing in-step with the evolution of capitalism throughout the nineteenth, twentieth and twenty-first centuries.

Bentham recognized that power, and political power in particular, was as much over things (property) as it was persons (1891, p. 186). That both had profound effects on subjective being (psychology), notably portrayed as an insistence on *pleasure, happiness*, and a striving for the reduction of *pain* in Bentham's utilitarianism and his ultimate regard for law and the political will (Bentham 1864; Wolff 1996; Kelly 2003, pp. 307–323; Sorabji 2014, p. 76). The avoidance of pain that concerns Bentham is notable here because it echoes the role, I claim, in the avoidance for the economic subject (stakeholder) of the trauma of castration that occurs within capitalism via Equity fetishism. This does not make Equity fetishism a utilitarian theory but reveals the *utility* inherent in fetishism and fantasy. Equity fetishism is symptomatic of the pain alleviation Bentham envisaged, as Paul Kelly maintains: 'In terms of his [Bentham's] psychology, pain and pleasure are intimately connected, but in terms of his practical application of this psychology to the science of legislation and government, pain is by far the more important consideration. *Whatever else it is that people want, they all want to avoid pain*' [emphasis added] (2003, p. 311).

Franceso Ferraro points to the mitigation of pain in Bentham's theory being directly associated with mitigation of disappointment (2010, p. 2). The legal system, as one branch of the utilitarian infrastructure maintaining the happiness of the individual, must provide means of overriding the strictness of laws where it is necessary to do so for the welfare of the individual. This notion of welfarism is important to note prior to the later discussion relating to the influence of Bentham on the law and economics models of neoliberal capitalism, because of its influence on that school of thought and, in particular, the work of Ronald Coase and Richard Posner. 'It is because Law and Economics combines Benthamite empiricism with a particular (Coasian) idea of free competition that it preserves a central feature of neoliberalism, and remains hostile to state interventions', argues Davies, 'it strives to square the circle between liberalism and utilitarianism, through an idiosyncratic appeal to the rationality of individual decision making' (2017, p. 77). Bentham was, according to Amanda Perreau-Saussine, 'a legal positivist who would count as a paradigm rationalist' (2004, p. 348).

I maintain that Bentham's *pannomion* is symptomatic of an alignment of legal reason to what Morris R. Cohen calls 'the Benthamite hedonistic psychology', a 'classical economic optimism that there is a sort of pre-established harmony between the good of all and the pursuit by each of his own self economic gain' to forge a complete civic juridical ideal (1982, pp. 77–75). In his outline of the development of complete law in the English civil justice system from the nineteenth century onwards, John Sorabji gives particular attention to the effects of Bentham's 'utilitarian, consequentialist theory of ethics, known as welfare-hedonism' (2014, p. 76). Bentham understood law as establishing an 'expectation' regarding property and its exploitation that accords fully, I suggest, with Cohen's portrait of 'economic optimism' as euphemistic of a resurgent capitalism (1864, p. 112). 'Property and law are born together, and die together' states Bentham, and F. C. Montague remarks that for Bentham, 'when the law has once sanctioned expectations it is bound to uphold those expectations' (1864, p. 113; Bentham 1891, p. 39). In what functions both as a literal interpretation of the evolution of capitalism that Bentham would have been witness to in the eighteenth century, and a metaphor of the inherent exploitability of property that its privatization facilitated, he remarks on the protection the law provides in order for him to 'inclose [*sic*] a field, and to give myself up to its cultivation with the sure though distant hope of harvest' (1864, p. 112). Enclosure, understood as lost access to the commons, was paradigmatic of the shifts in law and property ownership that the expansion of capitalism demanded, and one that the methods and systems of private civil justice and governance enabled. 'Enclosure (when all the sophistications are allowed for) was a plain enough case of class robbery', argues E. P. Thompson, '*played according to fair rules of property and law laid down by a parliament of property-owners and lawyers*' [emphasis added] (2013, pp. 237–238). Thompson further notes that, 'what was "perfectly proper" in terms of capitalist property relations involved, none the less, a rupture of the traditional integument of village custom and of right', a new morality rooted in the ideals and laws of private property ownership that supplanted traditional social and political relations (2013, p. 238). If Equity, therefore, had as Irit Samet claims 'always seen itself as appealing to objective moral judgement that is shared by all reasonable people (if they think sincerely about the issue at hand)', then the morality with which Equity would come to deal with and judge at this time was the new morality of capital Thompson highlights (2020, p. 8).

Cohen attributes the influence of Bentham to shaping a political theory of contractualism, 'that in an ideally desirable system of law all obligation would arise only out of the will of the individual contracting freely', a system supported in part by remedial counterpoints such as specific performance that Equity offers to shore-up such agreements and arrangements (1982, p. 74). I will examine contract law, along with private property, as the key to Equity's influence within capitalism in greater depth in later chapters. But for now we are able, at least, to recognize that with his enthusiasm for law reform, Equity was necessarily central to Bentham's broader social and philosophical ideas. And, therefore, as with the work of Peter Birks at the end of the twentieth century, Bentham's arguably overstated his aversion to Equity. Bentham might have found Equity and encumbrance to his *pannomion,* but he equally recognized that Equity was far too embedded in the landscape of the Common Law to dislodge, something nineteenth-century reformers, many of whom celebrated Bentham's ideas, would also discover.

THE AGE OF REFORM AND CAPITAL

Following the erosion of ancient feudal hegemonies and the absolute and divine authority of monarchs across Europe, a nascent middle class with increasing authority in Parliament on its side saw a retreat in 'the forces of conservatism, privilege and wealth', who latterly had to 'defend themselves in new ways', and the 'defenders of the social order had to learn the politics of the people' (1997, p. 39). Confronted by members of a new liberalizing socioeconomic class who refused to submit to the economic limitations of conservatism and the last vestiges of feudal traditions, led to uncertainty for the establishment forces. Uncertainty concerning their future dominance of the social order and many of its institutions and, equally, a degree of confusion with regard to their sociopolitical affiliations and identities. Whilst a significant growth in property ownership especially by the middle classes since the nineteenth century suggests the erosion of feudal-like traditions concerning property, where question marks remain regarding the extent to which such traditions have actually been undone is in terms of land. In particular, the ownership of land by private stakeholders versus the amount of acreage. For example, it has been suggested that whilst seventy per cent of land in the United Kingdom is subject to a private stake, this still only amounts to three out of sixty million acres (Cahill 2011).

The politics of the people during this time evolved a spectrum of interests unmatched by any prior period in British politico-economic history as the restrictive yoke of limited suffrage was lifted and old entrenched lines dividing the social classes were rendered permeable due to the authority that opportunities for private property ownership afforded the liberal middle classes. It was not, however, as Frederick Hayek following John Locke argues, simply the material aspect of property that was of importance but 'life, liberty and estates' that each individual had the right to pursue (2013, p. 102). Hayek looks to the seventeenth century and John Milton for his confirmation of the deep and well-founded traditions of liberal property rights and ownership, as well as the rights to exploit that ownership for personal advantage. As Milton, quoted by Hayek, puts it: the 'liberty to dispose and economise in the land which God has given them, as masters of family in their own inheritance' (2013, p. 159). Jeremy Bentham, as we have seen, further underscored the onus on private property and its inherent exploitability for the fortunes of the burgeoning liberal middle classes in the eighteen and nineteenth centuries, through his framing of the 'established expectation' to be able to 'draw such and such an advantage from the thing possessed' (1864, p. 112).

A politics of plurality became, for a time, the norm in nineteenth-century society, ranging from mass revolutionary stirrings of a new urban working class (proletariat); to the socialist and cooperative experimentations of Owenism and Chartism that followed in the wake of the French Revolution and other radical philosophies, notably the work of Saint-Simon; to cries from libertarians keen to impose their individualism and entrepreneurialism on the world and for greater shares of wealth through exploitable property rights. No matter how substantively divergent these points on the spectrum were, they were united in opposition to long-standing conservative values and traditions that were the preserve of a relatively small and highly privileged class of aristocratic landowners. For centuries this class had exclusive dominion over Chancery Equity, inasmuch as Chancery dealt, to a large extent, only with the interests, feuds and so on of those with enough property to warrant it. But when the liberal bourgeoisie demonstrated property interests and substantial claims of their own it became clear, at least to the bourgeoisie, that the prevailing system of civil justice comprised of separate sites of Equity and Common Law adjudication did not work in their favour. As we will see later in the chapter, the prevailing system of civil justice simply did not offer sufficient support to emerging forms of commercialism nor the increasing desire of the bourgeoisie to accumulate and secure rights and claims to property, money and therefore also power. Displeasure at the perception that Chancery was not commercially viable in its structure and function manifested in a variety of ways. For instance, in the view of the Chancery Commission established during the mid-nineteenth century to determine areas of reform, orders regulating Chancery's proceedings were considered 'ill-adapted to the type of business generated in a modern commercial society' (Lobban 2004a, p. 411).

At the highest levels of legislative and executive power the taste for reform in order to dislodge the old order manifested itself during the early 1850s as the influence of the conservatives in Parliament began to wane and the imposition of progressive liberal ideas took root. As historian Sir Llewellyn Woodward suggests: 'The very names of parties were unstable for a time. The terms "conservative-liberal" and "liberal-conservative" came into use', and the 'allegiances of party leaders was as uncertain as that of their followers' (1962, pp. 160–161). In the wake of this liberal ascendancy tensions over the most propitious form of economic organization that society ought to adopt arose, and in particular how new streams of wealth generation both private and commercial ought to be governed, regulated and administered. This was dealt with at length in the House of Commons regarding the proposal to implement plans for social organization that has been championed by the social reformer Robert Owen. Defending the motion for wider implementation of what Robert Owen had achieved at his socialist utopia in New Lanark, Sir William Crespigny maintained that: 'At the period when Adam Smith wrote his treatise on the Wealth of Nations, the great object was to increase the wealth of the country. This object had been since achieved by the increase of machinery, so as almost to increase the production of some articles much beyond consumption. Now, Mr Owen's plan, to remedy this—to render the production of the necessaries of life fully adequate to the increase of population—would effect a reorganization, and a re-memorializing of the lower classes, which there was no man of virtue who would not, he was persuaded, be most glad to see' (HC Deb 16 December 1819 Vol. 41 cc1189-217 at 1193 and 1194). A major obstacle to these liberal aims was, as Bentham had argued, the prevailing civil justice system, which was perceived to be wholly inadequate to the task of improving economic conditions for the bourgeoisie despite a number of attempts at reform between the 1820s and 1870s in which the appointed Commissions sought shorter, cheaper and more certain justice (Sorabji 2014, p. 13).

Following in the wake of Adam Smith's *Wealth of Nations* the nineteenth century marked a definitive moment in the ascendancy of progressive economic thinking (what today is referred to as classical economics), which increasingly found fault and dysfunction in many of the social institutions of the State and, correspondingly, proffered remedies in the form of mass, largely liberal, reforms that relied on greater competition and markets. To establishment forces the rapid and influential growth of middle-class industrialists and capitalist stakeholders signalled a threat, as this class, intent, as Marx argued, on 'having', especially with regard to property rights and ownership, grew in strength and authority. 'Private property has made us so stupid and one-sided', says Marx, 'that an object is only *ours* when we have it ... In the place of *all* physical and mental senses there has, therefore, come the sheer estrangement of *all* these senses, the sense of *having*' (Marx and Engels 1975, p. 300). Nouveau riche social climbers, parodied by the likes of the conservative Benjamin Disraeli in his 1828 novel *The Voyage of Captain Popanilla*, represented to those who clung to conservative notions and pseudo-feudal traditions a vulgar intrusion in society. And yet this bourgeois middle class managed to accumulate increased levels of property and wealth in their various domains of enterprise, driven in part by the fear born of competition and markets, whereby 'one accumulates or one gets accumulated' (Heilbroner 2000, p. 156). Bourgeois stakeholders demanded more cost-effective and efficient civil justice that would be capable of securing and making certain private property rights, therefore, freeing them to invest, to buy and sell, with greater confidence. Against this backdrop of the growing interest in and influence of Equity's domain over private and commercial trusts in the nineteenth century, Chantal Stebbings maintains that: 'Efficient trust administration and the recruitment of trustees required certainty in trusts law. Uncertainty led to litigation, expense and deterrence. The essential question facing trust lawyers of this new age was the extent to which the law would go to guarantee the safety of the trust fund, and whether potential trustees were willing or able to follow' (2002, p. 16).

The aggressive but increasingly creative *use* of capital by the bourgeois middle classes via newly formed markets for commodities stood in stark contrast to the stagnant notions of settlements in perpetuity enjoyed by the likes of the aristocracy. As Karl Polanyi makes clear, 'If there is one concept firmly established in middle class thinking it is that of Capital as a primary factor of production' (2018, p. 161). Where feudal property interests had relied on inertia, capitalism demanded liquidity and a constant circulation of capital and commodities in markets, the new engines of progress that would, so it was (and still to large extent is) believed, provide a foundation upon which to build prosperity for all (Heilbroner 2000, p. 102). The shift from the predominance of land as a basis for capital accumulation and wealth that had begun in earnest during the Reformation, represented a shift from fossilized and un-useful status symbols that were incapable of sufficient liquidity and financial equity. As a result, there was a rise in commodification and exploitation of forms of wealth, such as shares, as an outgrowth of incorporation in order to maximize capital gains. '[T]he means of production and of exchange, on whose foundation the bourgeoisie built itself up', claimed Marx and Engels, 'were generated in feudal society'; but 'the feudal relations of property became no longer compatible with the already developed productive forces; they hindered production rather than advancing it [...] Into their place stepped free competition, accompanied by a social and political constitution adapted to it, and by the economical and political sway of the bourgeois class' (1998, p. 8). Further, with the rising tide of liberal middle class socioeconomic and political power came a proliferation of voices and discourse intent on shaping the direction society. Reform during this period, as the Great Reform Acts are a testament to, was a major social and cultural project, as well as an economic, political, and legal one.

Positing capitalism as a self-destructive system greatly distanced Marx and Engels from many prominent commentators, socialist and non-socialist alike, before them, including those, such as the influential economist David Ricardo, who had supported the practicalities of Robert Owen's socialism, even though he did not support the theory behind it. In the 1819 Parliamentary debate concerning a motion to support Robert Owen's ideas, David Ricardo was recorded as stating that 'he was completely at war with the system of Mr Owen, which was built upon a theory inconsistent with the principles of political economy, and in his opinion was calculated to produce infinite mischief to the community' (HC Deb 16 December 1819 Vol. 41 cc1189-217). Nevertheless, Ricardo went on to support the motion, adding to the small minority of sixteen members against a majority of one hundred and twenty-five who voted not to support Owen. 'For Adam Smith, the capitalist escalator climbed upward, at least as far as the eye could see', maintains Heilbroner,

> For Ricardo that upward motion was stalled by the pressure of mouths on insufficient crop land, which brought a stalemate to progress and a windfall to the fortunate landlord. For [John Stuart] Mill the vista was made more reassuring by his discovery that society could distribute its product as it saw fit, regardless of what "economic laws" seemed to dictate. But for Marx, even that saving possibility made it untenable. For the materialist view of history told him that the state was only the political ruling organ of the economic rulers. The thought that it might act as a referee, a third force balancing the claims of its conflicting members, would have seemed sheer wishful thinking. No, there was no escape from the inner logic, the dialectical development, of a system that would not only destroy itself but, in so doing, would give birth to its successor. (2000, p. 161)

In the dialectical tradition that ultimately sought to criticize it, capitalist class power forged new syntheses between politics and economics. Stakeholders invested financially but also psychologically in the new horizons of capitalism that were beginning to arise as the nineteenth century unfurled, were keen to cement their interests. And just as Frederick Hayek would claim during the middle of the twentieth century, stakeholders were conscious of the importance of securing a favourable legal framework that would give structure and support to profitable enterprise and the growth of capitalism, as well as help disseminate capitalist ideology, thus bringing it into harmony with conceptions of justice through the concept of property rights and ownership. The deliberate aim of stakeholders, as Marx's materialist view of history discussed by Heilbroner in the passage above maintains, was to ensure that law and civil justice were brought under the influence of economic reason *qua* capitalist ideology.

It was clear and perhaps no more so than in the accusations directed at the Court of Chancery, that civil justice in England and Wales was not in rude health when it came to the demands placed on it by stakeholders. In a telling commentary on civil justice in the mid-Victorian era, John Stuart Mill makes a deliberate point of distinguishing Equity as 'the best substantive law' from its problematic home in Chancery (2008, p. 261). The reforms mentioned by Mill were aimed at modernizing Chancery and by extension the civil justice system as a whole that appeared to be struggling under the sheer weight of the business it had to increasingly contend with. Michael Lobban argues that:

After 1830, debates over Chancery reform were dominated by disputes over detail, rather than disagreements on principle. If there was general political agreement on the need for law reform in general, there was much technical disagreement about what could be achieved and how. Debates were generally dominated by expert and professional opinion, and the reforms that were made were piecemeal and often lacked coherence. So it was with the Chancery: reform of the court was not ideology-driven and was not informed by principled goals such as Benthamite codification or substantive fusion. Reformers were more concerned with promoting efficiency by responding to practical problems identified in the working of the court. Reforms were experimental, building on the lessons of the Chancery commission and attempting to solve the problems of the litigant and the practitioner. (2004b, pp. 565–566)

To return briefly to the influence of Bentham as raised here and by Lobban: whilst it is the case that Bentham's name is not mentioned with regularity in the later years of the law and Chancery reform process according to Hansard, it is not true that Bentham was entirely vacant from the minds of reformers during the period of reform as a whole (HC Deb 29 April 1830 Vol. 24 cc243-89 at 263 and 286). Further, Lobban's notion of Chancery reform not being ideologically driven (in the mould of Bentham or otherwise), but instead focused on efficiency is, I suggest, to underplay the significance of efficiency as an ideological trope within capitalism. The day-to-day concerns of and problems faced by litigants and practitioners that reformers need to address may well have been to do with the finer details of Chancery operations, of what it did well, what it achieved, as well as what it failed to achieve. But litigants were especially concerned about what the court ought to achieve for them with regard to property rights, which is self-evident given litigants came to Chancery at all. They were not, in other words, gratuitously or abstractly interested in Chancery as an institution nor efficiency as an end in itself as implied by Lobban. Instead, Chancery provided access to, vindication within, and influence over the burgeoning liberal economic system. What the Judicature Commission appointed in 1867 set out to do therefore was effect fundamental change through a more efficient and cost-effective court structure that was ideological because it was inescapably embedded in the political economy of the capitalist age. If reforms were concerned with notions of justice as a universal good, the aim was, nevertheless, first and foremost cost and efficiency savings that would satisfy the demands of economic reason and, therefore, of capitalism.

The Age of Judicature

As the previous section argued, Equity fetishism is symptomatic of a bourgeois stakeholder mindset that, by the end of the nineteenth century, had become accustomed to commercialism and economic reason as benchmarks for being in the world. 'The global triumph of capitalism is the major theme of history in the decades after 1848', claims Hobsbawm, it was 'a triumph of a society which believed that economic growth rested on competitive private enterprise' (1997, p. 13). Frederick Engels describes these conditions further,

> The struggle of capital against capital, of labour against labour, of land against land, drives production to a fever-pitch at which production turns all natural and rational relations upside-down. No capital can stand the competition of another if it is not brought to the highest pitch of activity. No piece of land can be profitably cultivated if it does not continuously increase its productivity. No worker can hold his own against competitors if he does not devote all his energy to labour. No one at all who enters into the struggle of competition can weather it without the utmost exertion of his energy, without renouncing every truly human purpose. (Marx and Engels 1975, p. 435)

I argue that stakeholders concerned with commercial certainties and guaranteeing economic futures constructed a fantasy of civil justice with complete justice at its core and applied it systematically, it was, for instance, the fantasy that lay behind what Kerly referred to as a 'cheaper' administration of civil justice (1889, p. 294). A fantasy, however, that posits complete justice as stakeholder denial of the trauma of castration, the paradigm negativity that capitalist ideology blinds stakeholders to by demanding immersion in a 'logic of success' that maintains that the lost object is always (re)obtainable, and the symbolic (law) perfectible (McGowan 2016, p. 241). The result, as this chapter section will describe, was Sect. 25(2) *Supreme Court of Judicature Act* 1873 and the creation of a 'unified code of procedure' that brought Common law and Equity together as a complete form of justice. D. M Kerly described Judicature on the following terms,

> The division of the systems of Equity and Common Law which it was now decided to abandon was peculiar to England and the colonies and states descended from her. The inconveniences it created, and the additional cost and risk, and the unnecessary delays it occasioned had steadily

increased with the elaboration and development of the law, and the great improvements effected in procedure, which had attracted and admitted into the Courts an enormously increased mass of judicial business, had only made the evils incidental to the separation less easy to be borne. (1889, pp. 291–292)

Echoing Robert Heilbroner, during the nineteenth century 'the time for the economists had arrived', and the civil justice system represented a target for rationalization, which according to Max Weber was long overdue in comparison with the civil systems of Continental Europe (Heilbroner 2000, p. 41; Weber 2002, p. 27). To perfect justice using economic calculation meant the ultimate 'triumph over the threat of castration and protection against it' (Freud 2001, p. 154). But what precisely constituted the Judicature reforms and how and why did the notion of ECJ emerge from them?

Passed in a spirit of economic rationalization, I argue that the 1873 Act was the legislative tail end of a significant period of systemic legal reform which began under the sponsorship of the Parliamentarian M.A. Taylor during the early decades of the nineteenth century.[1] Judicature, some say, prompted a need to tidy up a legal 'field littered with the most venerable survivals from the Middle Ages', and this notion concerned not only laws that appeared ill-adapted to the needs of the modern economy, but to the whole edifice of civil justice (Ensor 1936, p. 17). The Judicature process, a process that Parliament and legal reformers were pursuing earnestly and in larger numbers from the 1850s onwards, fitted the general economic strategies being adopted and applied to systems and institutions of State elsewhere (Woodward 1962). Reflecting on the court system as it existed pre-Judicature (King's/Queen's Bench; Chancery; Admiralty; Exchequer etc.), advocates of reform couched reform as a public interest and the claim that society would, as a result, enjoy a civil justice system that was more efficient and cost-effective (Holdsworth 1929, p. 27). For example, the statement made in Article XII of the Chancery Reform Association plan that, 'there is a determination on the part of a large portion of the public, and of their representatives in Parliament, to have cheaper law procedure'; quite what made up a 'large portion' is, however, unknown (1850, p. 194). In reality, civil justice was the preserve of a privileged

---

[1] See for example: *Appeals in the House of Lords—and suitors in Chancery.* HC Deb 7 March 1811 Vol. 19 cc260-9

and wealthy few who owned much of the private property and focused on *their* rights as a priority over satisfying the demands of public interest. Michael Lobban claims that, mostly, law reform did not excite the public imagination. Instead, he continues, 'law reform did interest the mercantile and trading communities, who were especially concerned about developments in the law of debtor and creditor, bankruptcy and company law' and therefore often the 'chamber of commerce and mercantile associations played a major role in promoting reforms in these areas' (2004b, p. 567).

Reform interested stakeholders who were intent on legal certainty to facilitate accumulation (the concentrating of wealth in order to further concentrate wealth) and grow the economy. As Ursula Le Guin suggests, 'It seems that the utopian imagination is trapped, like capitalism and industrialism and the human population, in a one-way future consisting only of growth' (1989, p. 85). Stakeholders lobbied heavily to ensure they could achieve growth. Whether reforms ever targeted an inclusive social good and public interest is, however, far less certain. Given limited, albeit incremental suffrage, the 'public' referred to in the reform debates in Parliament could not have reflected society. Much like capitalism today, political decisions benefited a class of privileged property-owning stakeholders with lobbying power and private interests to protect and exploit. They did not benefit the bulk of a property- and power-less society for who debt rather than credit was fast becoming the norm, and for whom civil justice had limited relevance (Wood 2017, pp. 2–3).

The perceived 'evils' in the civil justice system, therefore, reflected, I argue, the experience and individual interests of private and commercial stakeholders; it was a mirror held up to the proliferation of bourgeois ideology in nineteenth-century, but one that has not retreated. In keeping with the more contemporary capitalist notion of so-called 'trickle-down' economics that dominated economic policy development in Western capitalist societies in the aftermath of World War II, the reform agenda fitted notions of providing a rising tide of prosperity that would raise the fortunes of all members of society (Arndt 1983, pp. 1–10). Judicature was a politico-economic issue for those in Parliament keen to show that Britain was a progressive and powerful industrial nation that respected and celebrated its past. But for some, notably members of the judiciary, Judicature represented progress in the wrong direction. For example, Sir Roger Bowyer speaking in Parliament at the second reading of the Bill that would become the 1875 Act: 'How the Act of 1873 was passed through Parliament no one could tell. He did not sit in that Parliament and therefore was not responsible. At the time there was a Government which prided itself very much on what was called progress. They did not, he thought, draw a distinction between progress and change. They did not see that though progress was good when you were going in a good direction, it was bad when you were going in a bad direction; or that a man going over a precipice might reasonably be glad of what had been stigmatized as a retrograde movement. The Act of 1873 was brought in as a measure of progress. A great portion of the other side of the House thought it necessary to follow suit. He would venture to say there was scarcely a member of the legal profession of any position or experience who did not regret that the Act of 1873 was passed' (*HC Deb 10 June 1875 Vol. 224 cc1631-68*). To conclude this stage of my history of Equity within capitalism, I maintain that Judicature reflected key psycho-political desires of capitalist class power in the nineteenth century projected and displaced onto the civil justice system. This led to a civil justice synonymous with economic logics and reason, means of accumulation and growth that aimed to fill a lack in the psychic make-up of the stakeholder and, ultimately, the Equity fetish.

REFERENCES

BOOKS AND ARTICLES

Arndt, H.W. The 'Trickle Down' Myth. *Economic Development & Cultural Change*, Vol. 32, No. 1 (1983), pp. 1–10.
Bentham, J. *Theory of Legislation*. Translated from the French of Etienne Dumont by R. Hildreth. 1864. London: Trüber & Co.
Bentham, J. *A Fragment on Government*. 1891. Oxford: Clarendon Press.
Blackstone, W. *Commentaries on the Laws of England Book I*. 2009. https://www.gutenberg.org/files/30802/30802-h/30802-h.htm.
Cahill, K. The Great Property Swindle: Why Do So Few People in Britain Own So Much of Our Land? *The New Statesmen*. 11 March 2011. http://www.newstatesman.com/life-and-society/2011/03/million-acres-land-ownership.
Cohen, M.R. *Law and the Social Order: Essays in Legal Philosophy*. 1982. New Brunswick: Transaction Books.
Cotterrell, R. *The Politics of Jurisprudence: A Critical Introduction to Legal Philosophy*. 1989. London: Butterworths.
Crimmins, James E. Jeremy Bentham. *The Stanford Encyclopedia of Philosophy*. Edited by Edward N. Zalta. 2018. [Online] Available at: https://plato.stanford.edu/archives/sum2018/entries/bentham/.

Davies, W. *The Limits of Neoliberalism: Authority, Sovereignty and the Logic of Competition*. 2017. London: Sage.

Dinwiddy, J.R. Adjudication Under Bentham's Pannomion. *Utilitas*, Vol. 1, No. 2 (October 1989), pp. 283–289.

Endicott, Timothy O. The Conscience of the King: Christopher St. German and Thomas More and the Development of English Equity. *Toronto, Faculty of Law Review*, Vol. 47, No. 2 (1989), pp. 549–570.

Ensor, R. *England 1870–1914*. 1936. Oxford: Clarendon Press.

Ferraro, F. Direct and Indirect Utilitarianism in Bentham's Theory of Adjudication. *Journal of Bentham Studies*, Vol. 12 (2010), pp. 1–24.

Fortier, M. *The Culture of Equity in Restoration and Eighteenth-Century Britain and America*. 2015. Farnham: Ashgate.

Freud, S. *The Future of an Illusion, Civilization and Its Discontents and Other Works: The Standard Edition Volume XXI (1927–1931)*. Translated and Edited by James Strachey. 2001. London: Vintage.

Hayek, F. A. *Law, Legislation and Liberty*. 2013. London: Routledge Classics.

Heilbroner, R. *The Worldly Philosophers*. 2000. London: Penguin Books.

Hobsbawm, E. *The Age of Capital 1848–1875*. 1997. London: Abacus.

Holdsworth, W.S. Blackstone's Treatment of Equity. *Harvard Law Review*, Vol. 43, No. 1 (November 1929), pp. 1–32.

Kelly, Paul. Bentham. *Political Thinkers from Socrates to the Present*. Edited by David Boucher and Paul Kelly. 2003. Oxford: Oxford University Press, pp. 307–323.

Kerly, D.M. *An Historical Sketch of the Equitable Jurisdiction of the Court of Chancery: Being the Yorke Prize Essay of the University of Cambridge for 1889*. 1889. Leopold Classic Library.

Le Guin, U. K. *Dancing at the Edge of the World: Thoughts on Words, Women, Places*. 1989. New York: Grove Press.

Letwin, S.R. *The Pursuit of Certainty: David Hume, Jeremy Bentham, John Stuart Mill, Beatrice Webb*. 1998. Indianapolis: Liberty Fund.

Lobban, M. Preparing for Fusion: Reforming the Nineteenth-Century Court of Chancery, Part I. *Law and History Review*, Vol. 22, No. 2 (Summer 2004a), pp. 389–427.

Lobban, M. Preparing for Fusion: Reforming the Nineteenth-Century Court of Chancery, Part II. *Law and History Review*, Vol. 22, No. 3 (Fall 2004b), pp. 565–599.

Marx, K., Engels, F. *Collected Works, Volume 3 1843–1844*. 1975. London: Lawrence & Wishart.

Marx, K., Engels, F. *The Communist Manifesto*. Edited by David McLellen. 1998. Oxford: Oxford World Classics.

Mill, J.S. *Principles of Political Economy and Chapters on Socialism*. Edited by Johnathan Riley. 2008. Oxford: Oxford University Press.

Perreau-Saussine, A. Bentham and the Boot-Strappers of Jurisprudence: The Moral Commitments of a Rationalist Legal Positivist. *Cambridge Law Journal*, Vol. 63, No. 2 (July 2004), pp. 346–383.

Polanyi, K. *Great Transformation: The Political and Economic Origins of Our Time*. 2001. Boston: Beacon Press.

Polanyi, K. *Economy and Society: Selected Writings*. 2018. Cambridge: Polity Press.

Postema, G.J. Law's System: The Necessity of System in Common Law. *New Zealand Law Review*, Vol. 2014, No. 1 (2014), pp. 69–105.

Samet, I. Equity. *Research Handbook on Private Law Theories, Hanoch Dagan & Benjamin Zipursky eds., Forthcoming*. 2020. https://papers.ssrn.com/sol3/papers.cfm?abstract_id=3600193.

Sorabji, J. *English Civil Justice After the Woolf and Jackson Reforms: A Critical Analysis*. 2014. Cambridge: Cambridge University Press.

Stebbings, C. *The Private Trustee in Victorian England*. 2002. Cambridge: Cambridge University Press.

Thompson, E.P. *The Making of the English Working Class*. 2013. London: Penguin Modern Classics.

Watts, P. Taxonomy in Private Law—Furor in Text and Subtext. *New Zealand Law Review*, Vol. 2014, No. 1 (2014), pp. 107–144.

Weber, M. *The Protestant Ethic and the "Spirit" of Capitalism and Other Writings*. Edited and Translated by Peter Baehr. 2002 London: Penguin Books.

Wolff, J. *An Introduction to Political Philosophy*. 1996. Oxford: Oxford University Press.

Wood, E.M. *The Origins of Capitalism: A Longer View*. 2017. London: Verso.

Woodward, L. *The Age of Reform 1815–1870*. 1962. Oxford: Clarendon Press.

CASE-LAW AND LEGISLATION

Supreme Court of Judicature Act 1873 (c.66).
Supreme Court of Judicature Act 1875 (c.77).

CHAPTER 4

The Road to Complete Justice

INTRODUCTION

On the eve of the first Judicature Act, the Attorney General, Lord Coleridge, in a tentative defence of the outgoing Court of Chancery, was reported as stating in Parliament that,

> Without entering into a lengthened history of the subject, or a defence of the law of England as at present administered, or of the tribunals which administered that law, he might say, as one who had passed a large portion of his life in its study, that he had formed a strong opinion that, whatever might be the defects in the law, they were to be attributed, not to the learned Judges who administered it, but to the fact that the system on which it was founded, having grown up during the Middle Ages, was incapable of being adapted to the requirements of modern times. While saying, on the whole, that whatever might be its defects, it was founded on substantial justice and common sense, yet it was beyond controversy, that in many instances our procedure was impracticable and inconvenient, for no one practically conversant with its details could deny that there were certain great defects in them which ought to be remedied. First of all, there was the broad distinction which had become inveterate between what was called in this country Law and Equity. In other countries, the distinction existed, and must always exist; but in this country alone, Law and Equity were made the subject of separate and even conflicting jurisdiction. (HC Deb 09 June 1873, vol. 216, col. 640)

© The Author(s), under exclusive license to Springer Nature Switzerland AG 2021
R. Herian, *Capitalism and the Equity Fetish*,
https://doi.org/10.1007/978-3-030-66523-4_4

Lord Coleridge's statement is part lament and part progressive edict, and notable for his reflection on the tension between past practices and allegiances and the needs and desires of 'modern times' stirred up by the period of reform because of the growing influence of capitalist stakeholders in Parliament. Coleridge is reflecting on a period which, as per Marx and Engels' incendiary indictment of the age, had seen the transformation of the modern State into little more than a 'committee for managing the common affairs of the whole bourgeoisie' (1998, p. 5). The outgoing court system and Chancery, in particular, may have been 'founded on substantial justice and common sense', yet Coleridge's reference to the Middle Ages betrays a sense that the earlier practices and allegiances were being swept aside by a burgeoning middle-class intent, at least in terms of civil justice, on individualism through ownership and proprietary rights (West 2003, pp. 20–42). This emphasis on property ownership and rights forged a new ethics and a particular form of stakeholder morality that derived its power and authority from the fetishization of economic idolatry. 'Once property had been officially deified', says Hay, 'it became the measure of all things' (1975, p. 19).

The spirit of capitalism channelled through wealth and private property signalled the emergence of a belief in a new God and puritanical belief, what Weber calls a 'specifically *middle-class ethic of the calling*', which the Church of England, as an old religion, could not compete with (2002, p. 118; Heilbroner 2000, p. 35). 'In the consciousness of living in the full grace of God and being visibly blessed by him', Weber claims, 'the middle-calls businessman was able to pursue his commercial interests. Indeed, provided he conducted himself within the bounds of formal correctness, and as long as his moral conduct was beyond reproach and the use to which he put his wealth gave no offence, it was his *duty* to do so' (2002, pp. 118–119). Hence, the 'modern times' of which Coleridge spoke on the eve of Judicature were those informed by the growth of commerce, business, and markets, all of which had resolved no use for the 'supernatural sanctions' of religion, yet mirrored religion as an eternal edifice built on faith, fealty, obligation, and duty (Tawney 1990, p. 192). ECJ, if it would meet the demands of stakeholders and satisfy the 'moral' cause of which Weber speaks, thus needed to be recognizable as a secularized system of justice whose spiritualism and Godly inferences were no longer those of Christendom but of capitalism.

Coleridge did not so much predict as show a commitment to the new economic order emerging in the nineteenth century (Pugsley 2004). 'A time always comes at which the moral principles originally adopted have been carried out in all their legitimate consequences', claims Sir Henry Maine, 'and then the system founded on them becomes as rigid, as unexpansive, and as liable to fall behind moral progress as the sternest code of rules avowedly legal' (1972, p. 40). Maine locates this moment at the start of the nineteenth century and the Chancellorship of Lord Eldon, who dominated the Equity jurisdiction as Lord Chancellor for the better part of a quarter of a century. Eldon, Maine argues, was 'the first of our equity judges who, instead of enlarging the jurisprudence of his court by indirect legislation, devoted himself through life to explaining and harmonising it' (1972, p. 40). Maitland sees Eldon as the tail end of a process of systemization under a series of Chancellors during the eighteenth century (1969, pp. 10–11). Lord Eldon, as Lord Chancellor from 1801 to 1806 and then again from 1807 to 1827, was in a prime position to shape Equity under the rising tide of economic efficacy. Lord Eldon's influence politically, as Lord Chancellor, in shaping a politico-economic landscape favourable to the rise of bourgeois capitalism extended beyond his work in Chancery. Some argue, for example, that he was a notable opponent of the trade union movement, and that, had he been more diligent, would have opposed the repeal of the *Combination Act* 1799 following the Hume Report in 1824, an Act which prevented workman from forming unions and engaging in collective bargaining, the repeal of which formally legalized trade unionism (Williams 1954, pp. 46–47). Further, it was arguably Eldon's particular contribution to the formalization of trusts jurisprudence that aligned Equity so well with the individualistic and *laissez-faire* instincts of stakeholders for wealth accumulation and built so effectively on the mentality of the previous century that had eroded the 'older moral economy as against the economy of the free market' (Thompson 2013, p. 73).

Yet the story begins even before this, with a noteworthy transformation in Equity practice beginning as early as the Tudor period and under the Stuart monarchy via the high-powered proclamations of Lord Ellesmere in the *Earl of Oxford's Case* (1615) 1 Ch Rep 1. Although not comparable to the wholesale secularization of belief under capitalism from the nineteenth century onwards, the earlier changes demand mention because they shift Equity towards a 'common set of progressive principles and practices based in natural law and rights', and away from 'Christian antinomianism and radical assertions of the free Christian conscience' (Fortier 2015, p. 6). As a result, by the time the taste for reform under the banner of capitalist economic reason took hold in the mid-nineteenth century, Equity's basis as a contemporary body of law in Canon Law had diminished and its notion of conscience transformed from an ecclesiastical to a civil one (Sorabji 2014, p. 40). Paraphrasing the words of Marx and Engels, Equity's 'most heavenly ecstasies of religious fervour' had all but been drowned 'in the icy water of egotistical calculation' (1998, p. 5). Equity was, therefore, primed and ready to serve an emerging economic, moral order, and a bourgeois middle-class intent on having private property and using it to generate personal and commercial forms of wealth.

Even as a practical philosophy of complete justice was forming in the minds of reformers, therefore, it was against a backdrop of Equity as 'the servant of justice' (Sorabji 2014, p. 43). 'As it matured', says Sorabji, 'equity adopted as strict an approach to rule-compliance as the common law. It did so not because such an approach was inevitable, as it was at common law due to the nature of the forms of action, but rather, because such an approach was understood to be the optimum means to ensure that the Chancery Court was able to achieve complete justice' (2014, p. 43). Further, for the requirements of stakeholders in the private property order, to make the day-to-day function of the private property order appear just and fair to and for stakeholders, civil justice needed to possess flexibility and judicial discretion. 'Equity's inquisitorial processes for taking accounts', argue Michael Bryan and Vicki Vann, 'were superior to the common law's accounting methods in adjusting rights and liabilities' (2012, p. 19). Equity signified the law's commitment to fairness and a superior wisdom that engendered 'a pure and flexible restraint on the lumbering beast of the common law' (Chesterman 1997, p. 355). For Graham Virgo, the matter is one of imagination and imaginativeness, and therefore whereas 'the Common law has a tendency to be rigid and unimaginative in its application, Equity is much more imaginative in its application and development', and Virgo points in particular to Equity's intervention in contract through rescission (Virgo 2012, pp. 35–36; *Cheese v Thomas* [1994] 1 WLR 129; *Mahoney v Purnell and others (Baldwin and another, third parties)* [1996] 3 All ER 61). Chesterman, meanwhile, maintains that to consider Equity an imaginary other 'is to engage in self-deception' because the earlier systemization of Equity had already made it resemble Common Law (1997, p. 355). Somewhat contrary to Chesterman's conclusion, I argue that self-deception was precisely the point and that Equity fetishism shows the significance of fantasy in shaping the civil justice stakeholders wanted, and the civil justice they wanted to project onto society.

Following a contemporary critique of Judicature and the so-called fusion of Equity and the Common Law, Chesterman argues that it is 'not only impossible but undesirable to provide a complete programme for future decisions', and instead points to displacing the ossification of doctrine by 'a new ethic of *responsibility to justice*' (1997, p. 364). The logic of Equity fetishism maintains however that this is not what happened following the Judicature reforms. And Chesterman is critiquing fusion because he reaches a similar conclusion. Instead, the ossification of ECJ centred on the doctrine of unconscionability as a means of flexibility, agility, and responsiveness across the civil justice system allowing 'equity to temper the harsh application of the common law and the counter-vailing need for certainty in the adjudication of legal rights', but equally to sustain a fantasy of an economic and moral world-order based, at least in the stakeholder's mind, on complete justice (1997, p. 354). 'Seen through the eyes of one whom the enactment of the Judicature Acts is part of history', claims J. A. Jolowicz, 'the most important of the ideas contained in the phrase "complete justice" is the creation of a single juris-diction for the administration of both law and equity so that, in a single set of proceedings, *the remedies of both should be available and the need for the parties to have recourse to more than one court should be eliminated, thereby achieving considerable savings of both time and expense*' [emphasis added] (1983, p. 298).

A Problem Called Chancery

By the time of the Judicature Commission in 1867, to make progress in civil justice reform, the necessity of the Court of Chancery was in question. As John Stuart Mill highlighted,

> Of all parts of the English legal system, the Court of Chancery, which has the best substantive law, has been incomparably the worst as to delay, vexation, and expense; and this is the only tribunal for most of the classes of cases which are in their nature the most complicated, such as a case of partnership, and the great range and variety of cases which come under the denomination of trust. The recent reforms in this Court have abated the mischief, but are still far from having removed it. (2008, p. 261)

It is important to note that what I refer to as 'a problem called Chancery' brought together several concerns for reformers and stakeholders alike, some of which were very long-standing. Chancery was not merely a court, it was a pillar of the civil justice system and the exclusive domain of Equity. Chancery embodied a heady mix of rules, principles, and ideas that were a direct consequence of Equity's roots in Canon Law and the Christian intellectual tradition, thus informing the popularity of Equity jurisprudence. Sorabji points to 'the means by which litigants could obtain documentary evidence from their opponents', also called 'discovery', as an example of the legacy of Canon Law practice on the shape of Equity and Chancery in particular (2014, p. 41).

Chancery reform began in the first half of the nineteenth century, predicated on the need for speed, efficiency, and cost-effectiveness, three things the Court was said to lack. The failings of Lord Eldon's Chancellorship were key reasons cited for triggering the calls for reform. Sir Henry Maine disagreed with these criticisms of Eldon's Chancellorship. 'If the philosophy of legal history were better understood in England', argues Maine, 'Lord Eldon's services would be less exaggerated on the one hand and better appreciated on the other than they appear to be among contemporary lawyers' (Maine 1972, p. 40). In contrast D. M. Kerly maintained that 'The last years of Lord Eldon's Chancellorship were marked by the commencement of a persistent and determined attack upon the abuses which had grown up in Chancery, or, inherent in its practice from the first, had developed until they could no longer be tolerated' (1889, p. 264). But whilst some may have believed Eldon could make the process of reform cleaner and more straightforward, the flaws in the court were far more complex. As the Judicature Commission later in the century would eventually concede, these perceived flaws could not be remedied at a granular level nor did the various matters of principle 'generate a coherent reform strategy', instead wholesale change was needed at the very level of civil justice (Lobban 2004a, p. 390). For example, Michael Lobban maintains that 'the years up to 1873 saw frequent discussion over whether the various functions of the Lord Chancellor should be separated out, though the matter remained unresolved. Equally, Lobban continues, 'there was periodic discussion of whether there were enough judges to handle the court's caseload, or whether new ones should be appointed' (2004a, p. 390).

Notwithstanding a lack of personnel during the eighteenth and early nineteenth centuries, Chancery's problems in processing the increased levels of business it faced were arguably a product of growing commercial interest and the demands of capitalism as much as, if not more than issues internal to the civil justice system. Chancery Equity provided stakeholders with the means, for example, to define and enforce commercial partnerships and 'a central forum for both property disputes and property management', which reflected, as Chantal Stebbings maintains, the emergence 'of the new professional and commercial middle class' that was 'confident, articulate and independent' and the 'new wealth of the country' (2002, p. 13). Commercial litigants continued to rely on Equity in growing numbers even when Chancery, condemned as flawed by various nineteenth-century reform associations, was creaking under the weight of a conspicuous caseload. There was a notable contradiction between the popularity of the Court of Chancery and the laws it administered; the virtues of Equity were enthusiastically extolled, especially regarding property and trusts jurisprudence, whilst the evils of Chancery, litigant vexation at the court's arcane structures and procedures, long delays and high costs, and corruption by the court masters, lingered and provided both the rationale and motivation to bring an end to the bifurcated civil justice system (Lobban 2004a, pp. 391, 395).

Justice, whilst desirable in principle, needed to function for stakeholders as a support for economic activities and reason, not the other way around. Sorabji argues that, under equity, 'truth could not but be loved too well or obtained at too high a price' (2014, p. 42). That, at least, was the determination of a prevailing cohort of Chancery judges, Equity lawyers, and those narrow segments of society with wealth enough to sustain prolonged and often obtuse litigation. If complete justice was to carry a price following Judicature, it would have to be one that was acceptable to broader sections of society, namely bourgeois stakeholders. Not that voices from within the edifices of Equity or Common Law were silent on the matter. Chancery's survival post-Judicature as a Division of the newly formed High Court system and homology of the lost Court was a decision made prior to the passing of the Judicature legislation and championed by the legal profession. As Lobban maintains: 'On the basis of the recommendations of the commission, Lord Chancellor Hatherley introduced a bill in March 1870. It sought to create a single High Court of Justice with separate divisions but left the details of the distribution of business between the divisions and of procedure to be determined by rules made by a majority of the judges' (2004b, p. 594). The fears of the legal professionals trained only in the ways and means of Equity (the Chancery bar and judges), although a secondary influence in the Judicature reform process behind stakeholders, were apparent in its agenda.

Given the desire for Equity but increasing attacks on Chancery, an inevitable question was how Equity's future without its Court would unfold. What would it mean to deprive Equity of its independent basis in law and dilute the special knowledge held by members of the Chancery bar and its judges? 'Chancery reformers', states Lobban, 'responded to the common law changes, and vice versa, generating a mutual movement towards fusion', a dialogue that helped to both distinguish Equity and ensure subsumption into a monolithic legal discourse (2004b, p. 587). With fusion an increasing reality, Equity judges and lawyers pressed the case to preserve 'their special knowledge' in order to 'prevent it being eroded by greater powers being granted to the common law' (Lobban 2004b, p. 593). There was resistance to the reform agenda, therefore, especially from members of the Chancery bar but equally from other members of the legal community. This was because they saw the unification of the courts and the corresponding notion of complete justice being pursued as contentious if not impossible, given the potential for conflict between the rules of doctrines of Equity and those of the Common Law.

Viewed through the lens of psychoanalysis the resistance by members of the legal community to the stakeholder drive for complete justice revealed a neurotic attachment to certain laws and forms of procedure that continues in doctrinal approaches to law and legal reason that regard it as essential to modern society 'that the law be closely and cogently reasoned', not least because access to courts 'is hugely expensive' (Watts 2014, pp. 107–144). Evidence from the legal community's discourse concerning ECJ reveals individual and broader community tendencies towards the neurotic defence of the existing legal edifice, crystallized in the office of Chancellor for instance, and the self-justification of Chancery's rules, doctrines, and principles. As Michael Lobban maintains: 'For Chancery men, who felt under siege, given the numerical predominance of common law judges, the Chancellor's position was vital to ensure the ultimate supremacy of the principles of equity' (Lobban 2004a, p. 426). 'The equity judges scarcely wanted to promote a code that would bring about substantive fusion', Lobban further argues, rather theirs were 'essentially defensive positions: to protect their knowledge and prevent its being eroded by greater powers being granted to the common law' (Lobban 2004b, p. 593). This in stark contrast to the perverse belief of stakeholders of the importance of complete justice as an ally of economic reason, and thus the inevitable elision of law and economics. The neuroses of the legal community described here is symptomatic of legal expertise and reasoning founded on a fantasy of law's inherent logic, law *without*, *above*, or *beyond* the (traumatic) reality of capitalist influence bearing down upon it and its institutions. 'Neurotics are dominated by the opposition between reality and phantasy', argues Freud, if 'what they long for the most intensely in their phantasies is presented to them in reality, they none the less flee from it; and they abandon themselves to their phantasies the most readily where they need no longer fear to see them realized' (2001, p. 110). We will explore these ideas in more depth in later chapters.

For commercial interests demanding certainty from the law and improvements in civil justice, the Court of Chancery appeared to represent all that was rotten in the prevailing system. John Smith made plain in a Parliamentary debate in 1825 on delays in Chancery that, businessmen perceived Chancery to be so bad they used to threaten one another with filing a bill as leverage in disagreements over commercial transactions (HC Deb 31 May 1825 Vol. 13 cc960-1008 at 982). The growing bourgeois middle class, as the new stakeholders of capitalism hungry for improvements in both social and fiscal status, found themselves increasingly influential in shaping institutions able to benefit them. No longer, for example, was Chancery Equity the sole preserve of the aristocracy or feudal lords who could afford to suffer the inefficiencies and 'diseases of the Court' of Chancery—inefficiencies that would eradicate the fortunes of less well-off middle classes (Kerly 1889, p. 154). Equity, with its procedural mechanisms, jurisprudence, and forms of reasoning, suited and satisfied the needs of those stakeholders who were set on *having* and *using* property and capital as a way of indulging self-interests. As Maitland so vociferously proclaimed, 'Of all the exploits of Equity, the largest and the most important is the invention and development of the Trust. This is perhaps the most distinctive achievement of English lawyers. It seems to us almost essential to civilization, and yet there is nothing quite like it in foreign law' (1969, p. 23). The Court of Chancery, with its many layers of administration and bureaucracy, and its arcane systems of practice and pleading, elicited quite the opposite reaction.

Chancery had many critics. Beginning with M. A. Taylor as reported in the 1820s: '... as it existed at present, this Chancery jurisdiction was perfectly detested throughout the country; and, in an age like this, such cumbrous forms of proceeding could not much longer be endured'; to

Lord Hatherley, Lord Chancellor at the first reading of the doomed High Court of Justice Bill (the immediate precursor to Judicature) in 1870, who was reported as saying: '... it had long been the opinion that we had suffered grievously in our whole system of judicature—nay, in our whole system of jurisprudence—from the unhappy separation of our Courts into two distinct branches, administering law on totally distinct principles' (HC Deb 31 May 1825, Vol. 13, cc960-1008 at 995). The pressing question for reformers repeatedly, therefore, was what to do about the dysfunction in and persistent failures of Chancery. 'The growing wealth of the country and its increasing trade', claims Kerly, 'brought forcibly home to every man of business the need for Courts where rights could be plainly declared and speedily secured' (1889, p. 265). He continues,

> During the last century the great estates of the country had at irregular intervals struggled slowly through Chancery, and their proprietors had come to regard the delays and expenses of the process as inevitable, if unpleasant incidents of ownership, but the merchant and middle classes were less patient, and, moreover, the Court was even less fitted for the decision of disputes in which they were likely to be interested than for the administration of estates. (1889, p. 265)

When reformers spoke of the 'evils', 'melancholy evidence of the mischief and misery inflicted upon society by the Court of Chancery', and of the 'Poverty, pauperism, madness, suicide produced by the torturing delays, the inquisitorial proceedings, and the ruinous costs of a suit in Chancery', these were not problems faced by a privileged few (The Chancery Reform Association 1850, pp. 193–208). Although, as I argued earlier, neither was it a problem faced by the public at large for whom the justice under debate, linked to private property and transactions of personal and commercial wealth, was a distant reality. It was the burgeoning bourgeois class that believed Chancery was failing them, or, rather, was maladjusted to serve. So unpopular had Chancery become by the middle of the century among those who relied on it for adjudication that an article on Chancery reform talked of a procession of advertising vans roaming London and denouncing the Court of Chancery as the British Inquisition (The Chancery Reform Association 1850, p. 193).

With an aim of reconfiguring civil justice to better suit commercial and business interests, Chancery reformists drew on the experience of other Common Law jurisdictions to inform their decision-making. In particular, reformists looked for thinking that could lift the burden of custom and tradition that at once glued the British social order together and encumbered its progress. The systemic reform of the New York justice system and its civil procedure code during the first half of the nineteenth century proved influential. This was especially so given the United States was directing much of its energy towards meeting successful commercial ends and promoting markets to organize and manage society in ways attractive to stakeholders in Britain. Alexis de Tocqueville noted that, America was a country where 'individual entrepreneurship was the dominant norm', and these were precisely the conditions favoured by the upwardly mobile stakeholders of the middle classes in Britain who were busy lobbying for civil justice reform throughout the nineteenth century (Wolin 2001, p. 347). 'The key political impetus for fusion came from America', states Lobban, 'LAS [Law Amendment Society] members had followed with great interest the process of reforming New York's civil procedure after 1847. At the end of 1850, the society invited David Dudley Field to address them on these reforms and, having met the great reformer, set up a committee chaired by Robert Lowe to consider whether law and equity could be fused in England' (2004b, p. 584). The Field Code of Civil Procedure established the basis for civil procedure across America and linked the worlds of law, business, and finance. The Code deliberately accounted and thus made space for the imposition and growth of capitalist ideology through the administration of civil justice, rather than treating commercial interests as an afterthought to legal abstractions as the basis for defining justice.

'The common law courts have from time immemorial administered equity law. The only embarrassment that has attended it, has arisen from the imperfect machinery of the courts of law', declaimed the authors of the New York Civil Code considering the shortcomings in its sister State Pennsylvania (New York (State) 1850, p. 268). 'If they had enlarged their forms, as our code has enlarged them', it continues, 'their system would have been excellent' (1850, p. 268). What the New York experience showed to reformers in Britain was that it was possible for Equity or Common law to administer the rules and doctrines of the other as justice (attuned to economic reason) required. The unification of the courts would mitigate uncertainty, derived from the inconvenience and expenditure of having to shuttle between different courts in the hope of a final judgement. The ambition of Judicature was to manage a crisis in civil justice out of existence. At a technical level, it was a very particular interpretation of justice that the reformers had in mind. One founded on rights in succession, inheritance, acquisition by contract and warrantable conveyances. The ambition of Judicature is questionable because it aimed at benefitting stakeholders for whom these technicalities mattered rather than the public at large. Any residual impact from the reforms that might benefit the public was, I argue, a secondary concern for reformers.

The important message for stakeholders from American civil justice reform remained the benefits of and therefore the need to align law more closely with economics. 'Field's democratic politics [...] intersected with New York's commercial culture at the heart of his procedural reform', argues Kellen Funk, 'the "plain speaking" valued by Jacksonian Democrats had become the language of the marketplace and was now made the language of the law' (2015). A highly motivated belief in capitalism and the economic rationales of competition and efficiency it promoted already existed in England by the time of Field's visit, not least because of Bentham's influence. Unlike America, however, it did not reveal itself so readily on the surface of all social life in England in the ways de Tocqueville had described in the 'New World'. Given the fiscally liberal political context, however, capitalist ideals marked the rationale for the fusion of Equity and the Common Law and the decision regarding the primacy of complete justice. And they maintained a constant and progressive tension in the Common Law to ensure harmony with society on these terms. Michael Lobban disagrees with this view, and especially the influence of Bentham. He maintains that 'reform of the court was not ideology-driven and was not informed by principled goals such as Benthamite codification or substantive fusion', instead reformers 'were more concerned with promoting efficiency by responding to practical problems identified in the working of the court' (2004b, p. 566). However, Lobban errs in this analysis, I suggest, because it implies efficiency is non-ideological, when efficiency is a socioeconomic and political problem capitalism sees as a problem to solve, and, therefore, a core concern for capitalist ideology.

The decision of reformers to follow the experience of American civil justice reform is, I argue, a key moment in the fantasy of complete justice *qua* Equity fetishism. The message from New York was that Equity could not easily be excluded from the machinery of justice. The British Parliament reflected this sentiment in the lead up to Judicature where the Attorney General Sir John Coleridge referred to Equity as possessing a 'superior breadth and wisdom' compared to the Common Law (HC

Deb 09 June 1873 Vol. 216 cc640-86). They therefore saw the role that Equity was to play in achieving the desired completeness of justice as vital.

Equity as a Means to Complete Justice

The wager this book makes is that within capitalism, stakeholder's desire to avoid the traumatic reality of castration encourages complete justice as a juridical mode, institution, and ideal of certainty and coherence capable of making the capitalist economy work more efficiently and effectively. Equity is key to this, I argue, because of the latitude and options it can provide for stakeholders within capitalism, as described by Roscoe Pound,

> Before the law, we have justice without law; and after the law and during the evolution of law we still have it under the name of discretion, or natural justice, or equity and good conscience, as an anti-legal element. [Although] equity is a stage in the growth of law whereby it is expanded and liberalized after the period of fossilization, as it were, that inevitably follows primitive struggles toward certainty and definite statement, we must not forget that it is also a necessary reaction in certain periods of growth towards justice without law. (Pound 1905, pp. 20–21)

In return for this expenditure of desire, capitalism provides the stakeholder with pleasure through its guarantees of rewarding self-interest and satisfaction with wealth and private property, and, simultaneously, a means of denying and disavowing the traumatic reality of castration. Later we shall explore in more depth the role fantasy plays in the bargain between stakeholder and capitalism, and in particular the role of Equity fetishism in mediating desire and satisfaction within capitalism.

The extent to which the failure of complete justice to be *complete* is crucial to the psychic life of the law, to legal practitioners, and stakeholders because it maintains unmet demand as desire. But this constant striving for perfection of justice also makes the law neurotic. For example, we find Lord Romilly in the Parliamentary debates regarding a High Court of Justice Bill in the 1870s—an immediate precursor to Judicature—lamenting but not denying the possibility of complete justice: 'You will never get a perfect union of Law and Equity unless you make a code of laws which will, to a considerable extent, alter the character of the laws that now exist. You are now making a prodigious alteration in English law, with which many persons will be shocked. The fusion of Law and Equity will require great care and time - it is a matter not to be done speedily, it cannot be done by altering the procedure merely, and I hope some delay will be given that the subject may be duly and more fully considered' (HL Deb 29 April 1870, Vol. 200, cc2034-57 at 2039). The Lord Chancellor, Lord Selborne, speaking immediately prior to the passing of the first Judicature Bill in 1873 stating that, 'This Bill had been carefully framed [...] in order to clear the platform, to unite jurisdictions, to bring together the Courts, to abolish all technical and legal impediments to the perfect and complete action of the Courts upon every matter within their cognizance, but so to do this that the immediate transition should be made without violence, without danger to the rights of persons or property, or to the interests of the public at large' (HL Deb 11 March 1873, Vol. 214, cc1714-39 at 1732).

I have introduced complete justice as influential to the reform agenda of Jeremy Bentham and explained the role of complete justice in the fusion of Common Law and Equity following the nineteenth-century Judicature Acts. Spencer Walpole discussing the Judicature Bill, 30 June 1873, was reported as stating that: 'Let the House consider what the fusion of Law and Equity meant. It was a system of jurisprudence under which any Court should administer complete justice from the beginning to the end of a suit or cause' (HC Deb 30 June 1873, Vol. 216, cc1561-605 at 1599). Complete justice, as we have seen, was a phrase that appeared in parliamentary debates in the lead up to Judicature in 1873, as did similar notions of 'unification' and 'perfection' that, whilst stated as part of an agenda for 'practical' and 'public interest' reform engender the fetishistic prerequisite that I claim explains complete justice within the private life of self-interested stakeholders. Complete justice has long been associated with a combination of activities between Common Law and Equity and represented a desirable outcome of the two working together. We can view complete justice as predating the Judicature reforms and having a long association with Equity as a body of laws and an idea of justice (Sorabji 2014). The association with Equity is especially pertinent when distinguishing the former methods and practices of Equity in the Court of Chancery from those of the Common Law courts, with the latter representing a formalist mode of rule compliance that ECJ supplemented with more discretionary approaches to adjudication following the Judicature reforms. Walpole's statement echoes the earlier definition of complete justice made by Sir John Mitford (Lord Redesdale) at the end of the eighteenth century which appears throughout his *Treatise on the Pleadings in Suits in the Court of Chancery by English Bill*, a text that would define understandings of Equity adjudication during the nineteenth century in both Britain and America,

> It is the constant aim of a court of equity to do complete justice by deciding upon and settling the rights of all persons interested in the subject of the suit, to make the performance of the order of the court perfectly safe to those who are compelled to obey it, and to prevent future litigation. For this purpose all persons materially interested in the subject ought generally to be parties to the suit, plaintiffs or defendants, however numerous they may be, so that the court may be enabled to do complete justice by deciding upon and settling the rights of all persons interested, and that the orders of the court may be safely executed by those who are compelled to obey them, and future litigations may be prevented. (1876, p. 256)

Key to understanding the significance of complete justice is that we do not limit it in definition to Equity but as a product of the relationship and the tensions between Equity and Common Law adjudication. Since Judicature notions of complete justice have informed a civil justice system comprising Equity *and* Common Law as concurrent jurisdictions, and it is more accurate to describe Equity as *a* means to complete justice, therefore, rather than *the* means to complete justice. The reforms in the nineteenth century cemented complete justice in mainstream legal discourse by implementing the rules governing the new Supreme Court system (the Rules of the Supreme Court, or 'RSC'). The effect of ECJ has led to 'the development of procedural devices distinct from those at common law; a strong commitment to rectifying errors in decision-making'—notably via a more robust appellate jurisdiction—'and a strict approach to rule-compliance married to a liberal approach to relief from adverse consequences for non-compliance' (Sorabji 2014, p. 41).

But what of the influence of capitalist ideology on civil justice and how the influence of unconscious desires and fantasies promulgated by capitalism both through the property concept and the civil justice system designed to administer it might contribute to 'an image of ordinary plenitude that the subject has lost?' (McGowan 2013, p. 199). As a product of capitalist fantasy, complete justice fits squarely within the definitional role of fantasy articulated by psychoanalysis. It enables the conversion of the subject's traumatic experience of lack [a product of castration] into 'a more acceptable experience of loss in order to produce the illusion that there is somewhere a satisfying object of desire' (McGowan 2013, p. 199). Besides conventional accounts of civil justice that view its role purely to facilitate the knowledge and performance of rights that civil law gives us, the assertion here is that ECJ has, as Aristodemou states regarding legal discourse, an *'other side'* supported by ideologies, fantasies, and unconscious desires (2014, p. 3). Notwithstanding the balancing act played by the legislative determination of concurrency in bringing Equity and the Common Law together, complete justice is a direct reflection both of a 'triumph of equity over the common law' and a justice system that was, following the Judicature reforms in the nineteenth century, recast 'in equity's image' (Sorabji 2014, pp. 56–57). Equity's relationship with and contribution to the contemporary civil justice system since the nineteenth century is, if not exactly unique, both fundamental and defined by what it means to complete justice.

Complete justice is not a niche or marginal concern for critical analyses of civil justice. It is vital to considerations of law and justice within the prevailing socioeconomic system, namely capitalism. And, importantly, for considerations of how subjects exist within that system from the point of view of the effects that civil justice engenders. If the civil justice system has an incontrovertible role and place in contemporary socioeconomic life as the means of organizing knowledge of and claims to the rights that the civil law gives us, then the importance of the reasoning that fuels that system, namely ECJ, is clear. The following description of the civil justice system is instructive,

> The civil justice system exists in order to enable individuals, businesses, and local and central government to vindicate and, where necessary, enforce their civil legal rights and obligations, whether those rights are private or public. It exists to ensure that the mere assertions of the civil law are 'translated into binding determinations'. Equally, it provides the basis for individuals to resolve disputes concerning their civil legal rights and obligations consensually through any of various informal and formal means of alternative dispute resolution procedure, as well as, the means to enforce consensual resolution. In this way, the system provides a secure framework through which social and economic activity takes place, property rights, civil rights and liberties are secured and government is rendered subject to the due process of law. In delivering justice in this manner, the civil justice system provides a public good by giving life to the rule of law. (Sorabji 2014, p. 10)

Sorabji's account of complete justice reveals several aspects I claim are central to its appeal. For example, vindication of property rights, as the application of prescribed personal or proprietary remedies that enable a claimant to secure a proprietary interest. Graham Virgo explains that once 'a claimant has established that he or she has a legal or equitable proprietary interest which can be followed [in law] or traced [in equity] into the property which has been received by the defendant, the claimant can establish a restitutionary claim to vindicate his or her proprietary rights' (2015, p. 631). In Equity this can include constructive trusts that enable a full transfer of the property to the claimant through trusts in which the defendant holds the property as trustee for the claimant as beneficiary, or a proportionate share by the same mechanism (Virgo 2015, pp. 632–633).

Equity was and is a vital component of the civil justice system, both procedurally and jurisprudentially. This is notable in the administration of property, including the creation and vindication of proprietary and personal rights, and especially the influence that the doctrine of unconscionability has had on shaping the rights regime within the ambit of civil justice. 'The use of unconscionability as a rationale for intervention', as Nicholas Hopkins has remarked, 'has enjoyed an apparent revival not only in English law but throughout the common law world' (2007, p. 3). Mark Pawlowski talks of the expansion of unconscionability via proprietary estoppel signalling a considerable flexibility' in the court's reasoning highlighted in several cases including *Jennings v Rice* [2002] EWCA Civ 159 (CA), *Campbell v Griffin* [2001] W & TLR 981 (CA), *Ottey v Grundy* [2003] EWCA Civ 1176 (CA), *Uglow v Uglow* [2004] Civ 987 (CA), and *Murphy v Burrows* [2004] EWHC 1900 (2001, p. 79). 'Equity', as Dennis Klinck maintains in his survey of Equity and the notion of complete justice in the Ontario Court of Chancery, 'not only restrains the common law where its strict application might be unjust, but *it makes whole or perfect the justice of the common law*' [my emphasis] (2006, p. 48). John Sorabji meanwhile notes that 'complete justice' was the terminology favoured in the nineteenth century, whilst 'substantive justice' became the favoured terminology during the twentieth century, but, he continues: 'despite these terminological differences, the idea they expressed was the same: justice was achieved when an individual claim or dispute concluded with a court judgment that was "substantively accurate"' (2014, p. 2). As a result, ECJ marries formal rule compliance with 'a liberal approach to procedural amendment or the grant of relief from the adverse consequences of procedural error' (Sorabji 2014, p. 68). Or what we might view as a *flexibility* that Equity brings to the administration of civil justice.

The notion and problematic of Equity's flexibility, regarding doctrines such as estoppel and unconscionability, is a potent and consistent theme throughout legal case law and orthodoxy. For example, Millett maintains that 'Resistance to the intrusion of equity into the business world is justified by concern for the certainty and security of commercial transactions [...] This is often repeated like a mantra. But it is inaccurate and its influence has been harmful' (1998, p. 214). Lord Walker in *Cobbe v Yeoman's Row Management Ltd and another* [2008] 1 WLR 1752 stated that 'equitable estoppel is a flexible doctrine which the court can use, in appropriate circumstances, to prevent injustice caused by the vagaries and inconstancy of human nature. But it is not a sort of joker or wild card to be used whenever the court disapproves of the conduct of a litigant who seems to have the law on his side. Flexible though it is, the doctrine must be formulated and applied in a disciplined and principled way' (at 46). Meanwhile, Lord Neuberger urged that 'it is simply not for the courts to go galumphing in, wielding some Denningesque sword of justice, to rescue a miscalculating, improvident or optimistic property developer from the commercially unattractive, or even ruthless, actions of a property owner, which are lawful at common law' (2009, p. 541). Whether Equity is *more* flexible than Common Law is, however, open to debate. Douglas Laycock, for example, argues 'The most general distinction between law and equity in the early days was in the attitudes of the two systems toward formalism and discretion. Law was formal and rigid; equity was flexible, discretionary - a court of conscience [...] I suspect that this historical stereotype is exaggerated, because we also say that the genius of the common law was in its flexible stability and its capacity for growth within a tradition' (1993, p. 71).

A key issue surrounding ECJ as fetish is that it takes the place not of some actual or perfect form of justice awaiting discovery by the subject, but masks the traumatic reality that there is no complete justice at all. Instilling the civil justice system with ECJ in the Judicature's aftermath, the stated aims of reformers were improvements in efficiency in terms of time, by reducing delays in court business and costs. The aim of the RSC was to cement this economic reasoning and ensure it became standard practice to adhere to efficiencies in all civil justice proceedings. This, many believed, would lead to 'complete justice' between parties most times, including in the cases, *Prestney v Corporation of Colchester* (No 2) (1883) 24 Ch D 376 at 380; *In re Sussex Brick Company* [1904] 1 Ch 598 at 609; *Cloutte v Storey* [1911] 1 Ch 18 at 35; and *In Re Colgate (A Bankrupt), Ex parte Trustee of the Property of the Bankrupt* [1986] Ch 439 at 44. As a fetish ECJ at once fills and disguises a *lack* of complete justice predicated on the Aristotelian legacy of ideas concerning Equity's role regarding general theories of justice. Much like Sorabji's definitions, Aristotelian inspired narratives always remain vague as to precisely how Equity *completes* justice. Any insistence that Equity is a means to complete justice that the general law cannot complete—Maitland's 'gloss' on the law is another version of this—whilst instructive as to the areas of law in which Equity ought to serve, tells us very little about completion or perfection of the law (1969, p. 18). What these accounts have in common with my argument, however, is an acknowledgement of a lack, most often in the form of a gap in justice; the same gap that, at least in mainstream thought, explains the logical basis for a corresponding law or set of laws (namely Equity) required to fill the gap.

J. Walter Jones offers just such an account: 'The unwritten law, in its aspect of what equity or fairness requires in the case [...] can be accorded an element of generality in that the attitude of approach represented by it towards special problems expresses *a fundamental human striving to fill the gap* which constantly opens between enacted law and the call of justice' [my emphasis] (1956, p. 9). Jones' account is interesting because it appears to go further than most commentators by asking questions of sociology (if not exactly psychology). For Jones, the gap that requires filling is not necessarily institutional, systematic, or even philosophical, but human. What Jones' account does not acknowledge is the gap, I suggest, that the desiring subject strives to fill is in itself. The gap never exists in Equity or civil justice, but in the subject, who conceives of those laws and justice. I cannot stress this point enough because it goes to the heart of my argument and the theories of Equity and civil justice relating to castration that I will develop during the book.

The distinct and pronounced features of Equity's completion of civil justice are notable in the Australian Common Law tradition, and specifically the state of New South Wales (NSW) where Equity remained separate (un-fused) from Common Law until 1972 following enactment of the *Supreme Court Act* 1970 (NSW), one hundred years after England and Wales. The jurisdiction of Australia is not the focus of this book, but as a jurisdiction within the broader Western Common law capitalist tradition, the fact NSW kept a separate court of Equity long after comparable jurisdictions had fused their own civil justice systems raises important questions. For instance, whether the experience of Equity and the reasoning that flows from NSW reveals any more detail as to civil justice unification and thus the desire to perfect the system than comparable jurisdictions because of the recent, living memory of the separate court. The answer, it would appear, is mixed. There was merely a failure to attempt fusion in NSW for one hundred years following Judicature in England and Wales and rest of Australia because of 'legislative inertia' (Bryan and Vann 2012, p. 12). On the other hand, the 'influential opposition to postpone the enactment of the judicature legislation for the best part of a century' played a role, with judicial resources rooted in a tradition that 'permitted equity specialisation', and the specialization in turn reflected the growing 'volume of commercial and property litigation in Sydney which ensured a heavy workload for the equity judge' (Bryan and Vann 2012, p. 12). Equity in NSW, therefore, survived as a discrete body of law because of demand by commercial stakeholders.

The longer and more specialized training for Equity lawyers in NSW reaped its rewards. In his recognition of Meagher, Gummow, and Lehane, three prominent Australian lawyers from NSW, Peter Birks saw 'the greatest masters of equity in the modern world' (1996, p. 3). And the three provide incisive analyses of the interventions of Equity into the business of Common law,

> The equitable jurisdiction, of enormous importance, comprised [...] *(ii)* the enforcement of contracts on principles unknown to the common law – for example, sometimes recognizing contracts not under seal, long before the simple contract was accorded recognition at law; *(iii)* interference with the rigidity of the law in cases where the presence of fraud, forgery or duress would render the enforcement of strict legal rights unconscionable; *(iv)* the giving of remedies unavailable at law, for example, injunction or specific performance; *(v)* the development in the equitable action of account of a much more flexible and beneficial instrument than its common law counterpart; and *(vi)* the giving of common law remedies where they theoretically existed at law, but in practice were not available – owing, for example, to local rebellion, bias and "the violence" (as it was put in many petitions) of the defendant. (Meagher et al. 1992, p. 5)

In this passage, Meagher et al. bring into play many discrete aspects of Equity, but they are equally those of importance to complete justice, for example, the emphasis on flexibility and unconscionability. As discussed previously here, unconscionability and the flexibility it delivers relative to the strict application of Common Law rules or insistence upon rights is key to Equity's contribution to civil justice. In his analysis of the development of ECJ in the civil justice system, Sorabji shows how these conscientious roots (unconscionability) of Equity as an alternative to the formal rule compliance of the Common Law have directly informed the notion of complete justice,

> Unlike at common law, procedural compliance was not a factor that equity had to consider when assessing the substantive merits of a case [...] That difference stemmed from its development out of a form of canon law procedure, which required the Chancery Court to act as a Court of Conscience and thereby secure the reformation of sin through correcting a litigant's corrupt conscience. To achieve this is placed a positive duty on the court not to act unconscionably. While equity over the course of time would transform an ecclesiastical concept of conscience into a civil one, it maintained its commitment to ensuring that it would, in the words of Lord Nottingham LC, 'never [...] confirm an award against conscience' [...] It did so through ensuring that it would pursue, as Lord Talbot LC described it in Knight v Knight, 'complete justice'. (2014, pp. 39–40)

Following the theme of unconscionability briefly, I argue that as a facet of complete justice unconscionability ultimately functions as a field of representation that aims to fill a gap not in cases involving civil justice—as Jones or Meagher et al. believe—but in subjects who both conceive of and seek complete justice. The source of this 'gap' is not precisely as Walter Jones claims, but as Freud tells us, castration. But whilst castration 'is the nothing that generates the subject, and the encounter with it traumatizes the subject' this does not mean that all confrontations and encounters with this paradigmatic form of negativity are universal (McGowan 2013, p. 113). Fetishism, as later chapters will outline in more detail, is a perverse form that the subject's encounter with castration assumes. Although fetishism, like other forms of subjective deflection of traumatic experience, is far from a guarantee that the subject will avoid the traumatic realization of castration. 'The fetish merely appears to substitute something that could potentially or actually exist', argues Samo Tomšič, 'its main function is to reject castration from the symbolic, but this move always backfires and the fetish turns from a prosthetic organ into a monument of castration' (2015, p. 15). On this account, ECJ assumes a very different form: a 'monument' to a *lack* of justice. One, for example, laid bare through extensive vindication of the many fallacies that supposedly make up complete justice, and the stakeholder belief that complete justice is the clearest example of what is flexible and fair.

Conclusion

The nineteenth century 'was a period of great developments for the equitable jurisdiction' (Martin 2012, p. 15). 'The enormous industrial, international and imperial expansion of Britain in this period', says Jill Martin, 'necessitated developments in equity to deal with a host of new problems. The accumulation of business fortunes required rules for the administration of companies and partnerships; and the change in emphasis from landed wealth to stocks and shares necessitated the development of new concepts of property settlements' (2012, p. 15). Whilst a politically expedient settling in the body of laws started before the start of the century, Lord Eldon ensured in the opening decades of the nineteenth century that the process of Equity's systemization was both brought up to the standards of the Common Law and ultimately reconfigured to meet the demands of capitalism.

Between the establishment of the Judicature Commission in 1867 and enactment of the first piece of Judicature legislation in 1873, reformers made the case for unification and perfection of the civil justice system *qua* complete justice. With Chancery gone, it only remained necessary to translate ECJ into the civil justice system. This was the role for the Rules of the Supreme Court (RSC) in the aftermath of Judicature. 'From the 1820s to 1873 there was a decisive shift away from the common law's formalist approach to securing substantive justice towards equity's complete justice approach', explains Sorabji, 'a shift', he concludes, 'that was finalised by the introduction of the RSC post-1873' (2014, p. 48). Jolowicz echoes the significance that resulted from Judicature on justice. 'Probably the most significant achievement of the Judicature Acts, and the most fundamental aspect of 'complete justice' was the ultimate separation of substantive law from procedure', argues Jolowicz, 'this alone made possible the belief, now almost universally accepted as self-evident, that legal rights and obligations are one thing, the machinery and procedures for their recognition and enforcement another' (1983, p. 300).

Equity procedure and jurisprudence were central to the civil justice that commercial and private stakeholders alike demanded and showed a just and unyielding devotion to. This helped secure the victory of Equity over the Common law regarding complete justice and made ECJ a standard of civil justice underlying the vast expansion in private property ownership and wealth during the twentieth century, for a few stakeholders. Equity fetishism ties the fantasy of capitalism, the (il)logic and belief that it is possible to locate one's ultimate desire, to a legal means of investing in and engaging with that fantasy. Equity and ECJ allowed stakeholders access to and control over private property rights, it vindicated their belief as it vindicated their rights, and furnished stakeholder existence with a sense of inevitability that the lost object was (and is) always near and castration a lie. Complete justice *qua* Equity fetishism fixed the gaze of the stakeholder and lured them with the promise of something special, something they would not give up.

REFERENCES

BOOKS AND ARTICLES

Aristodemou, M. *Law, Psychoanalysis, Society: Taking the Unconscious Seriously.* 2014. Abingdon: Routledge.

Birks, P. Equity in the Modern Law: An Exercise in Taxonomy. *Western Australian Law Review*, Vol. 26, No. 1 (July 1996), pp. 1–99.

Bryan, M.W., Vann, V.J. *Equity & Trusts in Australia.* 2012. Cambridge: Cambridge University Press.

Chesterman, S. Beyond Fusion Fallacy: The Transformation of Equity and Derrida's 'The Force of Law'. *Journal of Law and Society*, Vol. 24, No. 3 (September 1997), pp. 350–376.

Fortier, M. *The Culture of Equity in Restoration and Eighteenth-Century Britain and America.* 2015. Farnham: Ashgate.

Freud, S. *A Case of Hysteria, Three Essays on Sexuality and Other Works: The Standard Edition Volume VII (1901–1905).* Translated and Edited by James Strachey. 2001. London: Vintage.

Funk, K. Equity Without Chancery: The Fusion of Law and Equity in the Field Code of Civil Procedure, New York 1846–76. *Journal of Legal History*, Vol. 36, No. 2 (2015). http://ssrn.com/abstract=2600201.

Hay, D. *Albion's Fatal Tree: Crime and Society in Eighteenth-Century England.* 1975. London: Pantheon.

Heilbroner, R. *The Worldly Philosophers.* 2000. London: Penguin Books.

Hopkins, N. How Should We Respond to Unconscionability? Unpacking the Relationship Between Conscience and the Constructive Trust. *Contemporary Perspectives on Property, Equity and Trusts Law.* Edited by Martin Dixon and Gerwyn LL H Griffiths. 2007. Oxford: Oxford University Press, pp. 3–18.

Jolowicz, J.A. General Ideas and the Reform of Civil Procedure. *Legal Studies,* Vol. 3, No. 3 (November 1983), pp. 295–314.

Jones, J.W. *The Law and Legal Theory of the Greeks.* 1956. Oxford: Clarendon Press.

Kerly, D.M. *An Historical Sketch of the Equitable Jurisdiction of the Court of Chancery: Being the Yorke Prize Essay of the University of Cambridge for 1889.* 1889. Leopold Classic Library.

Klinck, D.R. Doing "Complete Justice": Equity in the Ontario Court of Chancery. *Queens Law Journal,* Vol. 32, No. 1 (Fall 2006), pp. 45–81.

Laycock, D. The Triumph of Equity. *Law and Contemporary Problems,* Vol. 56, No. 3 (Summer 1993), pp. 53–82.

Lobban, M. Preparing for Fusion: Reforming the Nineteenth-Century Court of Chancery, Part I. *Law and History Review,* Vol. 22, No. 2 (Summer 2004a), pp. 389–427.

Lobban, M. Preparing for Fusion: Reforming the Nineteenth-Century Court of Chancery, Part II. *Law and History Review,* Vol. 22, No. 3 (Fall 2004b), pp. 565–599.

Maine, H. *Ancient Law.* 1972. London: J.M. Dent & Sons Ltd.

Maitland, F.W. *Equity: A Course of Lectures.* 1969. Cambridge: Cambridge University Press.

Martin, J.E. *Modern Equity.* 19th Edition. 2012. London: Sweet & Maxwell.

Marx, K., Engels, F. *The Communist Manifesto.* Edited by David McLellen. 1998. Oxford: Oxford World Classics.

McGowan, T. *Enjoying What We Don't Have: The Political Project of Psychoanalysis.* 2013. Lincoln: University of Nebraska Press.

Meagher, R.P., Gummow, W.M.C., Lehane, J.R.F. *Equity Doctrines & Remedies.* 3rd edition. 1992. Sydney: Butterworths.

Mill, J.S. *Principles of Political Economy and Chapters on Socialism.* Edited by Johnathan Riley. 2008. Oxford: Oxford University Press.

Millett, P.J. Equity's Place in the Law of Commerce. *Law Quarterly Review,* Vol. 114 (April 1998), pp. 214–227.

Mitford, J. *A Treatise on the Pleadings in Suits in the Court of Chancery by English Bill.* 1876. New York: Baker, Voorhis & Co. Publishers. http://www.mindserpent.com/American_History/reference/equity/1876_mitford_by_jeremy_equity_pleading.pdf.

Neuberger, L. The Stuffing of Minerva's Owl–Taxonomy and Taxidermy in Equity. *Cambridge Law Journal,* Vol. 68, No. 3 (November 2009), pp. 537–549.

Pawlowski, M. Unconscionability as a Unifying Concept in Equity. *The Denning Law Journal*, Vol. 16 (2001), pp. 79–96.

Pound, R. The Decadence of Equity. *Columbia Law Review*, Vol. 5, No. 1 (January 1905), pp. 20–35.

Pugsley, D. Coleridge, John Duke, First Baron Coleridge (1820–1894). *Oxford Dictionary of National Biography*. 2004. Oxford: Oxford University Press. http://www.oxforddnb.com/view/article/5886.

Sorabji, J. *English Civil Justice After the Woolf and Jackson Reforms: A Critical Analysis*. 2014. Cambridge: Cambridge University Press.

Stebbings, C. *The Private Trustee in Victorian England*. 2002. Cambridge: Cambridge University Press.

Tawney, R.H. *Religion and the Rise of Capitalism*. 1990. London: Penguin Books.

Thompson, E.P. *The Making of the English Working Class*. 2013. London: Penguin Modern Classics.

Tomšič, S. *The Capitalist Unconscious: Marx and Lacan*. 2015. London: Verso.

Virgo, G. *The Principles of Equity & Trusts*. 2012. Oxford: Oxford University Press.

Virgo, G. *The Principles of the Law of Restitution*. 3rd Edition. 2015. Oxford: Oxford University Press.

Watts, P. Taxonomy in Private Law—Furor in Text and Subtext. *New Zealand Law Review*, Vol. 2014, No. 1 (2014), pp. 107–144.

Weber, M. *The Protestant Ethic and the "Spirit" of Capitalism and Other Writings*. Edited and Translated by Peter Baehr. 2002. London: Penguin Books.

West, Edwin G. Property Rights in the History of Economic Thought: From Locke to J.S. Mill. *Property Rights: Cooperation, Conflict, and Law*. Edited by Terry L. Anderson and Fred S. McChesney. 2003. Princeton: Princeton University Press, pp. 20–42.

Williams, F. *Magnificent Journey: The Rise of the Trade Unions*. 1954. London: Odhams Press.

Wolin, S.S. *Tocqueville Between Two Worlds: The Marking of a Political and Theoretical Life*. 2001. Princeton: Princeton University Press.

MISCELLANEOUS ONLINE RESOURCES

Art. XII—The Chancery Reform Association reporting on and quoting, H.W. Weston, Secretary to the Chancery Reform Association. *Chancery Infamy, or a Plea for an Anti-Chancery League; Dedicated to All Chancery Suitors and Reformers*. 2nd Edition. 1850. London: Effingham Wilson.

New York (State). Commissioners on Practice and Pleadings. *The Code of Civil Procedure of the State of New-York*. 1850. Albany: Weed, Parsons & co., public printers. https://archive.org/details/codecivilproced00fielgoog.

CHAPTER 5

Stakeholders of Capitalism

INTRODUCTION

The following chapter focuses on many substantive and doctrinal elements that I will later discuss in relation to Equity fetishism. As the title of the chapter shows, the focus here is on stakeholders, and especially their use and reliance upon features of Equity, civil justice, and private property, including the law of trusts ("trusts"), contractual remedies, and the law of fiduciaries ("fiduciaries"), to undertake economic activity within capitalism. 'I think that we can safely say', argued Holdsworth in the first half of the twentieth century, 'that, without the evolution of a system of equity, English law could not have been made adequate to meet the social and economic needs of the modern state' (1925, p. 202). To determine what is at stake from Holdsworth's claims of adequacy, this chapter will examine the role of Equity in the balance of power between law and economics within capitalism.

Whilst Equity provides rules and procedures with Common Law, informing frameworks of civil justice through which stakeholders operate commercially and engage financially, including in the form of personal and commercial asset management, exchange and transaction, law does not as a general rule command economics within capitalism. On the contrary, law is beholden to economic reason and this manifests in a variety of ways. For example, the moulding of regulations to be market-complementing,

© The Author(s), under exclusive license to Springer Nature Switzerland AG 2021
R. Herian, *Capitalism and the Equity Fetish*,
https://doi.org/10.1007/978-3-030-66523-4_5

or, as Yip and Lee maintain, to ensure 'primacy of commercialist pragmatism' within the field of Equity jurisprudence and competence (2017,
p. 657). The focus here is on the property concept and private property as mandated sites that capitalism and neoliberal capitalism *uses* to its
advantage. Equity derives a great deal of authority and legitimacy as a
body of private laws from the property concept, and with the property
regime constructed by the Common Law at large. As Peter Birks maintains, 'There are legal property rights and equitable property rights, and
there are legal obligations and equitable obligations. There is not really
anything else' (1996, p. 19). Further, Bryan and Vann describe some key
aspects of Equity's peculiar contribution, including,

> The creation of special rules governing the assignment of property interest.
> An assignment is the immediate transfer of an interest in property. Prop-
> erty, for this purpose, includes intangible property, such as a chose in
> action, for example, the right to enforce a contract. Common law and
> statute prescribe formalities for the transfer of most forms of property.
> Equity enables property to be assigned where the method of assignment
> does not comply with these rules. It also enables 'future property', meaning
> property to which the transferor does not at present have title, to be
> assigned. (2012, p. 17)

Equity is relevant within capitalism because it offers these sorts of mechanism for stakeholders within the Common Law, to manipulate and
manage private property, extract value, and generate usable wealth. In the
form of trusts this manipulation is even more acute, as Jonathan Garton
explains regarding the purposes a stakeholder may have for establishing
a trust, 'These purposes include concealing ownership, facilitating land
conveyancing and other types of dealing in property, holding and control-
ling property for the sake of large groups of people (particularly in the
fields of collective investment and charitable and other non-profit orien-
tated activity), providing for the founder's family in various ways over
long periods of time (both before and after his or her death), protecting
property from creditors and from the extravagance of individual members
of the family, and cutting down tax liabilities, particularly on the transfer
of private capital' (2015, p. 12).

Following Garton, we can also note Sarah Worthington's view of Equity's 'manipulation of traditionally accepted concepts of property', and that
'Equity would sometimes regard certain assets as property even when

the Common Law did not' (2006, p. 51). As a species of private law, Equity, as Peter Birks explains, 'concerns the persons who bear rights, the rights which they bear, and the actions by which they protect those rights' (1996, p. 8). Further, Graham Virgo claims that Equity is 'even more imaginative in its recognition of property rights' than Common Law, because 'Equity is able to recognize rights to assets and the use of property, but also the value of property and rights that may arise in the future' (2012, p. 18). With Equity, therefore, stakeholders have a rich tapestry of ways with which to establish and manage private property interests, rights in assets such as debts, and securities, and make them tradeable forms of wealth. With these mechanisms and interactions, stakeholders do not manage assets or undertake transactions as neutral practices. Rather, they create and exploit ('leverage' to use the parlance of modern business), what Virgo refers to as, 'particular events' that create equitable property rights (2012, p. 18). 'Equitable proprietary rights need to be created specifically', argues Virgo, with 'a variety of events that will operate to create equitable interests in property', and he lists what he views as the major examples of these,

> By far the most significant is the express creation of that interest, as occurs where an express trust is created. Secondly, this may arise by virtue of a presumed intent that property should be held by the legal owner on behalf of the claimant [e.g. resulting trusts]. Thirdly, the equitable proprietary interest may arise by operation of law, often because the defendant can be considered to have acted unconscionably. (2012, p. 19)

Virgo also describes the role of Equity's creation of *personal* rights as 'of real significance to the development of the law', and notably that of fiduciaries, which we will examine in more depth later (2012, p. 21).

'It is all very well to identify a body of judge-made law, give it a name, identify certain vague characteristics, and then seek to justify this by reference to constitutional, political and legal developments many hundreds of years ago', argues Virgo, concluding that the 'crucial question is whether Equity remains relevant today' (2012, p. 8). This book agrees with Virgo on the need to determine the relevance of Equity today, moreover that Equity 'clearly is' still relevant 'in terms of explaining long-established doctrines of private law and also as a mechanism for providing new solutions to contemporary problems' (2012, p. 8). What I can add to these evaluations of Equity is, however, an analysis of its contribution to stakeholder adherence to the ideological principles of capitalism by providing alternative solutions to contemporary problems, as Virgo would have it. Equity fetishism, as my psychoanalytical interpretation of the role and function of law, sees Equity reinforcing and reproducing capitalist ideology through its defence of the fairness of transactions and the flexibility required to perform them within, for instance, commercial contexts involving the law of contract. In doing so, Equity does not represent a universal ideal of fairness or transcendent morality but one that functions and has relevance to stakeholders within the closed circuits of capitalism, what Mark Fortier refers to as 'the moral narrowing of equity in the development of its imperatives' (2005, p. 186). And yet the social and political pervasiveness of capitalism and in its neoliberal form means the narrow deontological imperatives of Equity have become normative standards in the wider field of subjective existence. 'Every legal relation is a relation between subjects', argues Evgeny Pashukanis, the 'subject is the atom of legal theory, its simplest, irreducible element' (1989, p. 109). Therefore, before looking at private property in more detail, it is necessary to examine the particular interpretation of economic subjectivity Pashukanis describes and one that underscores this book, *the stakeholder*.

THE STAKEHOLDER

The stakeholder is an economic subject defined by a certain primacy they give to private property interests. Marx called these subjects 'the adherents of the monetary and mercantile system, who look upon private property *only as an objective* substance confronting men' (Marx and Engels 1975, p. 290).[1] Following Althusser, in this book's introduction I described the stakeholder as one who willingly answers the call or 'hail' of capitalism and is thus 'interpellated' as a capitalist subject. We can now expand on this initial outline. The stakeholder is one who engages in competition and the 'free-market' logics of property distribution, regulation and efficiency, where the latter denotes allocation of resources to maximize value. Further, the stakeholder seeks to accumulate, exploit and seize opportunities for economic advantage and gain, even where that

---

[1] Given the parity of dates, Marx's view of mercantilism can usefully be compared to Michael Lobban's reference to the significant influence on and 'major role' of 'the mercantile and trading community' in law reform during the nineteenth century (Lobban 2004, p. 567).

might or involves calling foul, unfair or unequal the bargaining practices and conduct of other stakeholders. On this basis, the stakeholder defined here corresponds with what Karl Polanyi called 'atomistic and individual-istic' organic forms (2001, p. 171). Whilst the stakeholder is historically contingent and socially varied, they are always already beholden to the authority and hegemony of economic reason, what Antonio Gramsci calls 'economism' (1971, pp. 158–168).

I do not define the stakeholder as passive in the face of the economic logic and reason brought about by capital's domination of social life, but by a complex of economic, legal and psychological referents. As the name suggests, stakeholders commit to a certain mode of being in the world centred on capitalist logic, reason and ideology, and a belief in the fantasies promulgated by capitalism. At heart, the stakeholder *enjoys* capitalism. They adhere, slavishly so, to the ways and means of capitalism by coveting private property and indulging in self-interest. The fundamental fantasy of the stakeholder is, therefore 'that of an individual existence that owes nothing to the larger social structure in which it resides', making the stakeholder a private, perverse, and narcissistic figure who seeks meaning and understanding of the self in the materialism of private property and the opportunism it affords them (McGowan 2013, p. 204). In contrast to psychosocial 'subject', the stakeholder is a particular form of economic and legal subjectivity defined by the private property order within capitalism who uses civil justice to access and navigate that order. The stakeholder is a category of subjects whose property and financial interests are substantial, according to the Ministry of Justice. This includes stakeholders deemed sufficiently 'important, complex or substantial' to warrant being dealt with by the High Court rather than the county courts (Ministry of Justice 2016, p. 3). My definition of the stakeholder is not only theoretical, therefore, but reflects an economic subject for whom complete justice between the parties in civil cases is a viable proposition *only* because they have the financial means and sociopolitical privilege to access the civil justice system. I argue that stakeholders thus engender the fetishisitic prerequisite of Equity and ECJ through an encounter with civil justice because they can, broadly speaking, afford it.

These stakeholders might be asset-rich, maybe even high net worth individuals or corporations, and enjoy a powerful position in terms of property rights. In questioning the privilege enjoyed by stakeholders, however, psychoanalysis points not at fulfilled subjects, but the inverse.

Capitalist ideology instead 'aims at producing subjects who experience their existence as dissatisfied and simultaneously invest themselves completely in the ideal of happiness or complete satisfaction' (McGowan 2013, p. 60). The completeness of the 'investment' sought by stakeholders manifests itself *in* material and abstract financial investments (forms of which I will discuss in more detail later in this chapter), but, importantly, also via a visceral engagement with capitalist ideology itself as the hoped-for means through which to actualize a complete, non-castrated self. Investment thus encompasses the banality of bureaucracy and the perversity and ecstasy of risk and competition, allowing stakeholders to seek what they desire and find enjoyment in bureaucratic systems of justice and property.

The theory of Equity fetishism extrapolates to the wider 'theoretical' population of as yet under- or unprivileged bourgeoisie stakeholders that exist within what Lorenzo Chiesa and Alberto Toscano call the 'ideological force-field of contemporary capitalism' (2007, p. 118). This population of bourgeois stakeholders *want* to be the privileged adherents of a juridical demarcation of substantial claims and of transactions defined by the Ministry of Justice, and in many respects Equity and the flexibility it brings to Common law and civil justice is there to help achieve that goal. As Mark Pawlowski maintains, with particular regard to the flexibility of Equity through the doctrine of unconscionability,

> Although the jurisdiction to set aside unconscionable bargains was originally confined to reversioners and expectant heirs, it has since been extended to poor and ignorant persons and where the transaction in question was made at a considerable undervalue without the benefit of independent legal advice. More recently, it has been held that the modern equivalent of "poor and ignorant" is "a member of the lower income group [...] less highly educated." This broadening of the class of claimant eligible for relief has increased considerably the potential availability of the doctrine to a wider range of transactions where the terms are unconscionable and the victim does not receive independent legal advice. The essential elements of the doctrine were set out by Mr Peter Millett QC (sitting as a deputy judge of the High Court) in *Alec Lobb (Garages) Ltd v Total Oil (Great Britain) Ltd*:
>
> First, one party has been at a serious disadvantage to the other, whether through poverty, or ignorance, or lack of advice, or otherwise, so that circumstances existed of which unfair advantage could be taken [...] Second, this weakness of the one party has been exploited by the other in

some morally culpable manner [...] And third, the resulting transaction has been, not merely hard or improvident, but overreaching and oppressive. (2001, p. 80)

Within neoliberal capitalism the nineteenth-century notion of the stakeholder as a 'man of property' in the vein of Soames Forsyte in John Galsworthy's *Forsyte Saga* (2001) has largely broken down. This does not mean the capitalist stakeholder has vanished. Instead neoliberalism induces a wider popular desire for economic privilege, the result of, what Jodi Dean calls, 'the extent of the class power that has gotten us to think in terms of competition, efficiency, stock markets, bonuses, and financial success' (2012, p. 73). For all stakeholders, investment and maintaining high levels of economic engagement is key because this provides the means to disavow castration as the lack that psychoanalysis maintains is at the core of the subject. They do so by committing the stakeholder not to the limited scope of the personal fetish, but more completely to the fantasies aroused by capitalism of attaining a certain perfection or complete satisfaction in or through private property and other capitalist institutions, including markets. Further, the stakeholder's investment includes a commitment to as many of the ways and means necessary to maintain this fantasy. Hence ECJ, cast in this context, underscores a devotion whereby the notion of complete justice is itself a sublimation of stakeholder desire caught in providing an object of pure belief.

Equity drives or induces stakeholder engagement through different mechanisms and instruments, some of which the economist Anthony Atkinson describes,

When politicians talk of Britain becoming a "property-owning democracy", they often mean property in the sense of housing. This is, however, a rather special asset, generating a return in the form of imputed income. Other forms of popular wealth, such as savings and bank accounts or pension funds, are held via financial institutions. The latter hold the share certificates. One consequence is that part of the capital income now accrues to the financial-services sector that manages these funds. There is a wedge between the rate of return to capital and the income received by savers. The growth of popular wealth has contributed to the increased "financialization" of the economy. (This, in turn, has implications for the separation of beneficial ownership and control...). (2015, p. 71)

Housing, share certificates, capital income from intangibles, and, perhaps most revealingly, 'the separation of beneficial ownership and control' that is the *sine qua non* of trusts, all feature within Equity's jurisprudence. Engagement with these areas suggests that stakeholders do not passively or reluctantly answer the ideological 'hail' of capitalism. They unreservedly put themselves at the centre of economic rationalizations conducted in the name of capital. It reveals that Equity is a crucial tool enabling stakeholders in their enjoyment of and belief in capitalism.

PRIVATE PROPERTY POWER

There can be no mistaking the relationship between what I call here the private property order and the fact that such an order comprises what Marx called commodities. As the lens through which to describe and understand the point at which capitalism, the stakeholder, and Equity meet, therefore, Equity's administration of the private property order is of crucial importance. As Todd McGowan maintains, 'enjoyment of the commodity in contemporary capitalist society requires a delicate balancing act between ignorance and knowledge', and the suggestion here is, that regarding the private property order, Equity facilitates enjoyment in this way (2016, p. 103). This involves dealing with the influence of capitalist class power on the property concept, and that concept as peculiarly *private* and thus determined legally via, for example, the dictate of ownership rather than mere possession, as the source of what J. A. Jolowicz calls 'selfish litigation': 'litigation in which the actual concern of the parties is to promote or to protect only their own "private" interests' (1983, p. 305).

'Private', Raymond Williams explains, 'is still a complex word but its extraordinary historical revaluation is for the most part long completed' (1988, p. 242). Of the great number of instances of the term Williams traces, it is private as a 'conventional opposition to what is public' that is significant here (1988, p. 242). In her discussion on the contrast between public and private realms, Hannah Arendt suggests a similar definition. For Arendt, privacy is given meaning by its opposition to the public realm, one in which everything 'can be seen and heard by everybody and has the widest possible publicity' (2000, p. 199). Further, 'the term "public" signifies the world itself, in so far as it is common to all of us and distinguished from our privately owned place in it [...] The Public realm, as the common world, gathers us together and yet prevents our falling over each other' (Arendt 2000, p. 201). Both Arendt and Williams point to an important factor in property: we take what is private from things in a fundamental state of openness, and we subsequently enforce that taking through rights, hence Jolowicz's contrast between private and public relating to the difference between 'selfish' and 'unselfish' litigation, where the former reflects a defence of private interests brought voluntarily by the plaintiff or claimant (1983, pp. 305–312). Private property, even when it exists in a public domain which allows non-owners some form of access to it is always already in a state of withdrawal or opposition that drives non-owners away and prevents access or forms of adverse control or possession. For Frederick Hayek, the private nature of property, in terms of rules of demarcation, makes possible 'the delimitation of protected domains of individuals or groups' and is 'as well as scientific truth as any we have attained in this field' (2013, p. 103). Whilst serving a deliberate ideological purpose in Hayek's thinking, private property was also funda-mental to Hayek's 'inseparable trinity' along with law and liberty (2013, p. 102). 'There can be no law in the sense of universal rules of conduct', argued Hayek, 'which does not determine boundaries of the domains of freedom by laying down rules that enable each to ascertain where he is free to act' (2013, p. 102).

Following Hayek's ideas it is important to understand the relevance of Equity as a mode of *private* and *property* law in order to further develop the connection between Equity, self-interest (what is arguably Hayek's notion of freedom to act), and capitalism. In his reading of Marx's Capital, Étienne Balibar makes a similar distinction, although he does not proceed further than questioning the distinction between property law and the concept that informs it, namely property. 'Distinguishing sharply between the connexion that we have called 'property' and the *law of prop-erty*', Balibar maintains, 'is of fundamental importance in characterizing the degree of relative autonomy of the economic structure with respect to the equally "regional" structure of the "legal and political forms", i.e., in initiating an analysis of the articulation of regional structures or instances within the social formation' (Althusser and Balibar 2009, p. 254). As an administrator of private property law, Equity contributes significantly to articulations of the regional structures that Balibar highlights. To echo Arendt, Equity's private law status prefigures juridical conditions that resist on behalf of stakeholders the widest publicity. Roger Cotterrell has argued that the 'ideological significance of the distinction between private and public law is to affirm the existence of a private sphere (civil society) distinct from the state and unaffected by the public law which structures the state; a private sphere in which individuals deal with each other as equal subjects and in which the existence of private power is legally unrecognised', and the prerequisite of a substantial claim that we find deepens the ideological significance referred to by Cotterrell (1987, p. 83). We will return to Equity's particular contributions to property law shortly.

The Property Concept

'Property' is a notoriously difficult concept to define, not least because many aspects and characteristics of property are emphasized in different ways by the various disciplines that seek to contextualize and explain it. The classic legal idea of private property is that it is not a relationship between a person and a thing, but a collection or bundle of rights. These rights underscore duties and obligations that individuals hold regarding one another. But, importantly, they also extend control over property from mere possession to ownership, unleashing a range of further actions (or inactions) and interests the owner has rights over. These include rights to *use* the thing as the owner sees fit, and the right to *exclude* the world from it. Of all property rights, exclusion appears the most effective in explaining not the concept of property but the particular jealous nature of ownership that demands privacy. Exclusion, notionally a right held against the entire world, is an excellent way of both withdrawing and concealing property from public interference. Whether property exists in a physical or tangible form, for example, land or chattels, or in an intangible form such as debts, securities or future interests, what remains consistent is the control that factors such as exclusion allow. Exclusion with use, which, importantly, includes rights of alienability and transferability for value, are central to explaining the augmentation of rights and benefits that Equity brings to the general scheme of property law beyond basic legal ownership, and the basis of Equity's remedial action. Sarah Worthington argues that trading property is key because it gives it commercial value (2006, p. 52). 'Law must also define possession by detailing those whom the possessor can exclude and under what circumstances she can exclude them', maintains Jeanne Schroeder, concluding that in a world 'in which third parties or dynamite exists, any limitation of a possessory right is equivalent to imposing n intersubjective valuation on the possessor. Property remedies inevitably merge into liability remedies, and liability regimes presuppose a property regime' (2004, p. 183).

In the introduction to this book I claimed that private property (as the focus here) is contingent on notions of resource *scarcity* that give form to social relations (and market relations in a neoliberal capitalist schema) through bundles of legal, moral and customary rights, concepts and practices including those of use, possession, ownership, enjoyment and exclusion. In the private property context, these mechanisms can assume a particular quality as *safeguarding* functions that guarantee full assignment of separate objects (things) to individuals. As Thomas C. Grey maintains: 'Most people, including most specialists in their unprofessional moments, conceive of property as *things* that *are owned by persons.* To own property is to have exclusive control of something - to be able to use it as one wishes, to sell it, give it away, leave it idle, or destroy it' (1980, p. 69). And Grey sums up the perception of ownership as a safeguarding mechanism over private property maintaining that, 'legal restraints on the free use of one's property are conceived as departures from an ideal conception of full ownership' (1980, p. 69). Similarly, Michael A. Heller argues that private property requires that 'one owner has full decision-making [*sic*] authority over an object, subject to some common law and regulatory limits' (1998, p. 662). Freed from these restraints, the perception continues that rights to private property ought to create or generate value, which when maximized and exploited contributes to the wealth of an individual or corporate stakeholder.

'The bedrock of the theory of the market economy is the assumption of private property rights', argues Samuel Bostaph, and without 'the command of property assured to the individual by his or her property rights, there can be no regularity and stability in the exchange of things. Without stability in exchange, there will prices set in markets that reflect market conditions of demand and supply, themselves reflective of relative resource abundance. Without such market prices, there is no basis for rational individual planning in consumption or production activities' (2006, p. 196). In his list of eleven bases of private property, Honoré notes, in particular, the 'right to the capital value' of one's private property, including 'alienation, consumption, waste, or destruction' (2013, p. 568). Although as Richard Posner points out, the generation of wealth in this way—through freely transferable rights to property for value— must also account for the costs of the property rights system in both obvious and subtle ways (1986, p. 32). Following Posner here we can see that as a result, and especially when considered with questions of justice, property means something different to the lawyer than to the economist: the former focuses on rights and practice as the basis of the property concept, the latter on the value of private ownership and the relative merits of modes of distribution.[2] For the benefit of wider contextual considerations of the property concept within neoliberal capitalism, I consider it necessary to include legal and economic views on property. Further, as already implied, it is worth looking closely at how property the conjoined fields of law and economics define property, and in particular in the work of Richard Posner. Posner's juridical reasoning bridges several aspects covered by this book: the utilitarianism of Jeremy Bentham, the liberalism of nineteenth-century reformists and classical economists, and the neoliberalism of Frederick Hayek. We will examine Posner's idea of property shortly.

Kevin and Susan Francis Gray begin their definition of 'the elusive concept of property',

> We commonly speak of property as if its meaning were entirely clear and logical, but property is a conceptual mirage which slips tantalisingly from view just when it seems most solidly attainable. Amongst the misperceptions which dominate the conventional analysis of both lay persons and lawyers is the lazy myth that property is a 'monolithic notion of standard content and invariable intensity'. Our daily references to property, therefore, tend to comprise a mutual conspiracy of unsophisticated semantic allusions and confusions, which we tolerate – frequently, indeed, do not notice – largely because our linguistic shorthand commands a certain low-level communicative efficiency. (2009, p. 86)

As later discussions unpacking Equity fetishism in more detail will show, semantic allusions, the language (of Equity) that Gray and Gray highlight above, play a crucial role in structuring the fantasy of private property law within capitalism. Therefore, whilst Gray and Gray consider their task 'to jolt ourselves out of our traditional, reassuringly three-dimensional, imagery about property' by attacking 'limitations of the property reference' and the 'mistaken reification of property', this book will show why these features of the stakeholder relationship to property are in actuality critical to sustain the private property regime within capitalism (2009, pp. 86–87). And this latter point, as a political consideration, is one not

---

[2] For example: Posner (1986) (law and economics); J.E. Penner (1997) (the lawyer); John E. Roemer (1996) (the economist).

overlooked by Gray and Gray, but seized upon by them as the ultimate definition of property,

> Deep at the heart of the phenomenon of property is the semantic reality that 'property' is not a thing, but rather the condition of being 'proper' to a particular person (e.g. 'That book/car/house is *proper* to me'). For serious students of property, the beginning of truth is the recognition that property is not a thing but a *power relationship* – a relationship of social and legal legitimacy existing between a person and a valued resource (whether tangible or intangible). To claim 'property' in a resource is, in effect, to assert a significant degree of control over the resource. *'Property' ultimately articulates a political relationship between persons* [emphasis added]. (2009, pp. 87–88)

The institutions and systems of civil justice have over time shaped the broad nature of the property concept as defined variously above and, therefore, also the social and political relationships that according to Gray and Gray make up property. In their insistence on the relational basis of property, Gray and Gray are echoing the ideas of Evgeny Pashukanis. Within capitalism Pashukanis recognized the significance of a wide and integral set of legal relations,

> In as much as the wealth of capitalist society appears as 'an immense collection of commodities', so this society itself appears as an endless chain of legal relations. Commodity exchange presupposes an atomised economy. The link between isolated private economic units is maintained in each case by successfully concluded business deals. The legal relation between subjects is simply the reverse side of the relation between products of labour which have become commodities. (1989, p. 85)

The extent to which law and civil justice have defined the property concept deliberately or consciously for the widest benefit, beyond the needs and desires of privileged networks of capitalist power within societies, is challenged by several critical theories, including feminist and queer theories of property, and Equity and trusts (Bottomley [ed.] 1996; Davies 1999, pp. 327–352; Probert 2001, pp. 275–286; Auchmuty 2012, pp. 71–87). Margaret Davis, for instance, has shown how the nature of social relations in property are pertinent from the point of view of a queer critique of property law, which echoes Gray and Gray's claims that property 'has an unavoidably intersubjective element, meaning that although it may attach to a concrete or abstract object, "property" is primarily a relation between legal subjects which has things as its focus' (1999, p. 328). For Davies the role of property law is to determine the quality 'mine', and that property is 'also characterised by an immensely strong symbolic power and is both expressive and constitutive of the person' (1999, p. 328). This notion of property and legal relationships in Davies' particular reading reflects certain social hierarchies 'organised around sex and sexuality' (1999, p. 329). This book follows a very similar notion of property to Davies', albeit one in which the meta-psychology of sexual desire manifests in the stakeholder's concealment of castration as fundamental basis of subjectivity and being in the world, a form of sexual desire projected onto and mediated by a conjunction of law (Equity and institutions of civil justice for example) and economics (capitalism and capitalist logic of efficiency, competition, and so on) that finds form, so to speak, in ECJ and Equity fetishism.

Administration of the private property order in line with the notion of complete justice *qua* civil procedural and substantive merits-based justice cuts across legal and economic definitions of property and the administration, protection, transaction and distribution of property. Key to civil justice administration is supporting a regime of private property ownership that enfolds the means of wealth extraction from property—Honoré's 'right to capital' (2013, p. 568). Creative civil justice approaches to property rights and ownership are symptomatic of Equity's 'flexible' contributions to private, personal and corporate wealth generation. As Lord Neuberger maintains: 'Like any organic entity, equity has always developed as a result of both the internal influences from its genes received from its forebears and the external influences which permeate its environment. Its parental genes are fairness and flexibility, as equity was developed to mitigate the rigours and technicalities of the common law. Its environmental influences are multifarious, but they include the need for consistency and certainty, without which any legal code risks falling into disrepute' (2014, at 7). Principle examples of Equity's influence on the legal landscape include the trust, which in spite of assuming a variety of forms seen as socially progressive, including as charitable, is notable for offshore tax avoidance and 'aggressive financial management' (Harrington 2016, p. 131). This opportunistic and morally questionable, albeit entirely legal use of trusts to reduce stakeholder tax liabilities in ways that the *Tax Justice Network* argues, impoverish the national tax base and offend public interest, presumably counts as one of Neuberger's 'environmental influences'. We can see in Neuberger's euphemism, therefore, a reluctance to name capitalism (let alone neoliberal capitalism), as that which commands law and is the one that ultimately has the power to bring it into 'disrepute'. In later chapters, however, we see that Lord Neuberger has not always been so veiled as to the realities of the role of law in contemporary capitalist society.

Contra Neuberger's reluctance to name the *disreputee qua* capitalist stakeholder, I claim that trusts, which will discussed further later in this chapter, signal a proliferation of wealth generating opportunities suited to stakeholders, who, under capitalist ideology are keen to show not so much that 'a society that safeguards property is wealthier than one that does not', but that the *private* stakeholder who does will be wealthier than the one who does not (Worthington 2006, p. 53). Trusts and the property that makes up them are, as Gray and Gray contend, vehicles for ideology (2009, p. 88). 'This emphasis on the creation of exchange value as the basis of property is', Wood argues, 'a critical move in the theorization of capitalist property' (2017, p. 111). Beyond the notion of property as an 'epithet used to identify that which people most greatly value', I argue private property within capitalism exists on an even more abstract level, that of wealth creation, to which desires more easily attached and around which fantasies more easily gather (Gray and Gray 2009, p. 88). As Freud maintained, 'the mutual relations of men are profoundly influenced by the amount of instinctual satisfaction which the existing wealth makes possible' (2001, p. 6). Further, Penner maintains in his discussion of Hannah Arendt's theories of public and private that circulate her interpretation of the private property concept as 'a kind of necessary contrast to, and base from which a person could enter the public realm. This is all to be sharply contrasted with wealth. Wealth is merely economic power, undifferentiated and unrealized. Wealth is necessary to sustain property and thus the private realm, but it is not to be exalted for its own sake' (1997, p. 216). The crucial point that Penner touches on is that private property signals ontological privilege and above all else power. This makes private property something stakeholders desire and can be satisfied by if they can assert their proprietary interest.

Reflexively property as power can also be and is used to constrain and delimit the possibilities of those persons unable to assert such interests, including where they lack economic, social or political power. To make a bargain and negotiation between desire and satisfaction, therefore, requires mediating institutions and systems, hence the role of civil justice within capitalism. Including the particular contributions of Equity *qua* ECJ to construct and maintain fantasies around property. 'The fascination of property', argues Margaret Davies, is the ways 'in which the various dimensions of the property as social myth and legal category interact in a multitude of inexpressibly complex ways' (1999, p. 330). Davies concludes, with an explanation worthy of a description of the role of Equity fetishism, 'because the central social symbolism of property is of something fixed, certain, delimited and absolute, this symbolic and material mobility is forgotten or even repressed in a gesture which reinforces the ideology of centralised power and masks the underlying circulation of meanings' (1999, p. 330).

Law and Economics

The economics of property, wealth and power leads us to a consideration of the property theory devised by the conjoined field of law and economics, and in particular by American jurist and Judge Richard Posner, whose major influence the wide-ranging literature on the subject that has developed since the 1970s acknowledges (Campbell 2012, pp. 2233–2274). Economics has been pervasive in legal practice and scholarship for decades and is a product of shifts in legal reasoning developed by the likes of the Chicago school. Steve Hedley argues that 'at root economics is not a theory aimed at explaining or justifying law', instead it provides 'an external – economic efficiency – by which to evaluate legal outcomes', thus economics 'is a theory about costs and benefits, how they are distributed and they influence behaviour' (2011, p. 99). Roger Cotterrell writing in the closing decades of the twentieth century remarked that the economic analysis of law is a 'form of legal scholarship now widely established and recognised in American law schools and of increasing significance in the British academic legal world' (1989, p. 208). The aim of applying economics to law was for its proponents, as Cotterrell maintains, to fill a lack of rationality in legal reason within the Common Law, to 'promote an efficient allocation of resources in society', a competitive free-market influenced 'invisible hand' theory where it claims that, whether the judges knew what they were doing in terms of economic rationality in developing common law rules, 'the case-by-case evolution of common law has in fact led to outcomes with a high degree of allocative efficiency' (1989, p. 209). And it is on this latter point that Cotterrell cites the work of Richard Posner.

For William Davies, Posner is key to understanding the major shift in legal reasoning that occurred in the latter half of the twentieth century, whereby the disciplinary line that separated law from neoclassical economics (lawyers from economists) blurred and arguably even vanished, paving the way for the comprehensive economization of law (2017, p. 76). Echoing the unification and resultant complete justice of Equity and Common Law after Judicature, Davies makes a case for the fusion of law and economics with Posner as a central actor (2017, pp. 79–91). The fusion of law and economics meant neoclassical economics gained a 'liberal spirit' and economists emerged as '*quasi-judicial* in their authority', which included ensuring 'all combatants [claimants and defendants, creditors and debtors, and so on] are equal before the measure of efficiency, in the same way that judges ensure that all citizens are equal before the law' (Davies 2017, p. 77). The economic empiricism applied to legal situations by the likes of Posner revealed a 'purported fairness and blindness' that was central to neoliberal juridical thinking.

Duncan Kennedy, too, is sceptical of the mix of law and economics espoused by the likes of Posner, not least because, as Cotterrell claims, it leads to over-rationalization (1989, p. 209). Kennedy's scepticism parallels Yip and Lee's concerns, at the level of Equity doctrine, of the effect of 'commercial pragmatism' (2017, p. 648). An effect, I argue, symptomatic not of a failure or flaw in the internal logic and reason of law but of the dominion of economic over legal reason that punctures the carapace of doctrinal reasoning to inject economic rationalities and market solutions. For Kennedy classical economics 'needed a theory of law if they were to make good their basic claims about the nature of economic life' and were content 'with frequent allusions to the "sacredness" of property and to the disastrous consequences of "government interference with contracts"' (1985, p. 950). Further, and here we can see the attractiveness of Equity to economic thought, Kennedy claims that proof 'of the validity of economic laws relied crucially on concepts like freedom and justice. They [classical economists] spent much of their time trying to persuade their readers not of the existence of particular facts but of the "naturalness", "fairness", or "optimality" of those facts' (1985, p. 949).

Posner's description of the property concept begins in the Common Law 'applied by the royal law courts of England in the eighteenth century' divided across three domains: the law of property, the law of contracts, and the law of torts (1986, p. 29). For present purposes, it is the first two, the laws of property and contract, which are of interest, and especially the influence of Equity jurisprudence (what Posner refers to as a specialized subcategory) on them (1986, p. 29). We ought to, I suggest, read Posner's reference to the historical roots of the property concept and thus his description of property considering the conjunction of the socio-psychological with the economic that draws him to a fundamental relationship between property, efficiency, rationality and self-interest. For Posner, economics must explore the implications of 'assuming man is a rational maximizer of his ends in life, his satisfactions – what we shall call his "self-interest"' (1986, p. 3). Posner's analysis of property is remarkably similar to the one undertaken by this book. The crucial difference being the political motivations and justifications Posner relies on, perhaps most notably regarding justice, which Posner allies with a robust and definitive ownership of private property in his private law examples (he also relies on public and criminal law examples in his account of law and economics which account for different ideals of justice), and over which he claims, 'economics can provide value clarification by showing the society what it must give up to achieve a noneconomic ideal of justice' (1986, p. 26). Posner's logic here is both fascinating and somewhat contradictory, not least because he insists on economics for evaluating justice to, so it seems, justify how to define justice *without* economics, a point he justifies by suggesting that the 'demand for justice is not independent of price' (1986, p. 26).

Substantively Posner's approach to property turns on the legal protection of transferable property rights in order to 'create incentives to use resources efficiently' (1986, pp. 30–31). 'The proper incentives are created by parcelling out mutually exclusive rights to the use of particular resources among the members of society', claims Posner, and whilst his initial example chooses land as the property in question, he is quick to acknowledge that the same principle 'applies to all valuable resources' (1986, p. 30). Posner's ideas here do not depart from conventional notions of the property concept outlined above. But the centrality of the logic of competition and efficiency to his idea of property shows the univocal economic potentialities Posner considers all forms of property to possess. Like buried treasure or a seam of coal, the wealth-giving properties of private property are, on Posner's account, awaiting discovery by the one who *owns*. And in this determination, he is arguably more honest in his definition of property than many others who are reluctant to admit the indisputable nature of property's ideological role within capitalism, rather than property being inherently defined as a product of legal determinacy. Also, Posner's notion of precedent as a product of legal rule-making as 'capital stock' is another way he reveals the grasp capitalism has on law, albeit one he supports rather than contests (1986, p. 509 and p. 517).

Importantly, Posner considers this approach a viable route for lawmakers and governments. 'The economist can assist the policymaker not only by explaining the effects of a policy on the efficiency with which resources are used', claims Posner, 'but also by tracing its effects on the distribution of income and wealth' (1986, p. 71). With property law, Posner also considers the role of contract in shaping his definition of the property concept. As a precursor to a closer look at Equity's interventions in the private property regime, therefore, we will look at aspects of contract law within Posner's property theory. And also consider how the influence of contract law extends because of intervention of law and economics. Citing US valorization of freedom of contract as 'necessary to preserve, or simulate the results of, free markets' during the nineteenth century and continuing through the latter part of the twentieth century (Posner was initially talking about the 1970s, although the text referenced here is an edition from the 1980s), Posner traces the commercial influence of contract on the transformation of US law and judicial reasoning, through the revival of thinking, since the 1930s, turned against contract as a 'grotesque distortion' of constitutional principle (1986, p. 589). As the preferred legal mechanism of classical economics and thus central to 'maximisation of wealth', what Jeanne Schroeder's calls the proposition most closely associated with Posner, the revival of contract also elevated the status of economics in law, which elevated the status of economic rights and liberties that, through the medium of contract, reflected 'dominant public opinion' (2004, pp. 208–229). Thus what the public desired, claims Posner, was to be freely contracting economic citizens, and it was wrong for judges to deny this fact, or for the law to countermand it, both of which signalled a justice system that was 'out of step' (1986, p. 590).

Posner does not make the case for freedom of contract as an economic right or liberty exercisable at a constitutional level, however, instead he locates contract as fundamental to intersubjective bargaining, and thus implies factors of shame and contentiousness as structuring all forms of transaction. 'Someone who is known not to perform his side of bargains will find it difficult to find anyone willing to make exchanges with him in the future', claims Posner, 'which is a costly penalty for taking advantage of the vulnerability of the other party to a contract, the vulnerability that is due to the sequential character of performance' (1986, p. 81). And following Hobbes's conception of the social contract, Posner defines the rationale for contract being, 'to deter people from behaving opportunistically toward their contracting parties, in order to encourage the optimal timing of economic activity and make costly self-protective measures unnecessary' (1986, p. 81). The 'familiar' and desirable role of contract is, therefore, economizing transaction costs, and whilst this may begin or relate directly to an *actual* commodity of financial transaction, the efficiency gains ought, by Posner's reasoning, to extend to the behaviour of contracting parties (1986, p. 100). Further, Posner's view of contract regulating party behaviour perhaps explains why he places less emphasis on the role of fiduciary obligations to achieve that end. This in contrast, for example, with his contemporary Tamar Frankel who suggests the primary focus of fiduciary law is 'the *relative power relationship among parties*' (2014, p. 247).

For Posner, the fiduciary principle is 'law's answer to the problem of unequal costs of information' but concludes that most 'consumers' are intelligent enough to protect themselves, presumably by contract, without needing to rely on fiduciary law (1986, p. 101). A position contested by Daniel Markovits, who views fiduciary duties as 'natural response to the structural problems out of which fiduciary relations generally arise' and which cannot be construed by the contract (2014, p. 215). Fiduciary obligations, therefore, substitute 'for the specification of contract duties and the verification of importance' (Markovits 2014, p. 215). We can also see this as a so-called 'agency problem' that arises from incomplete contracting and sets into action an expansive application of core fiduciary duties of loyalty and care (Sitkoff 2011, p. 1044). Posner's treatment of the fiduciary principle may appear cursory and a second-order mechanism compared to contract, but I conclude with it here to move on to look in more detail at Equity's peculiar contributions to private law, including fiduciary doctrine.

Fiduciaries

We have reviewed key areas of the property concept and property rights, including Posner's particular interpretation through the lens of law and economics. Further to the definitions above and to understand the connection between Equity jurisprudence, property, and stakeholder desires under capitalism, it is necessary to look in more depth at Equity's administration of property and the nature of property defined through private civil law obligations and practices. As a branch of private law Equity has a variety of objectives including coercion, compensation, disgorgement, restitution, and vindication of the personal and proprietary rights that underpin private ownership; ensuring performance of contracts; and maintaining and regulating definitions of duties and obligations within fiduciary law, including those of trustees (Burn and Virgo 2008, pp. 5–6; Bryan and Vann 2012, pp. 26–31; Virgo 2012, pp. 19–22).

'In general', maintains James Penner, 'equity worked to amend or supplement rules of law over the breadth of private common law' (1997, p. 133). Equity's responsibility on behalf of stakeholders to uphold private interests in property extends to obligations and duties, material forms of property, and property rights. Equity creates, maintains, and enforces particular relationships under the heading of 'fiduciaries' to enable individuals to work on behalf of each other selflessly, and, it is argued, in contradistinction with contractarian relational objectives that are self-promoting (Samet 2018). As Samet argues, 'like all contractual promises and promisors, these parties keep the self-promoting move as a viable option, one that is always on the table and always in competition with the selfless alternative. And it is this foundational element of contracts that Equity sets out to remove in the context of fiduciary relationship' (2018, p. 125). Fiduciary relationships are not politically neutral, however, and here Samet and I disagree on the victory over self-interest that fiduciary law purports to represent, what Samet refers to as 'an island of other-regarding attitude in a rough sea of self-interest pursuit' (2018, p. 126). Rather, I argue, the jurisprudence and forms of procedure developed over time work with and not against selfishness and self-interest by ensuring a private property rights regime that corresponds with capitalist and commercial logic. 'The widespread notion that persons have some sort of natural right to own property draws upon the idea that human personhood necessarily contains with it an ability and need to control external resources', claims Margaret Davies, ideologically 'property defines an area of privacy, of personal autonomy and personal sovereignty so that the owner has a much greater sphere of protected rights than the non-owner' (1999, p. 335). Equity's contribution to and shaping of fiduciary law, introduced above, is a good example of both Penner's and Davies' claims and will, therefore, be the focus of this section.

Millett LJ described some essential characteristics of the fiduciary in *Bristol and West Building Society v Mothew* [1998] Ch 1,

> A fiduciary is someone who has undertaken to act for on behalf of another in a particular matter in circumstances which give rise to a relationship of trust and confidence. The distinguishing obligation of the fiduciary is the obligation of loyalty. The principal is entitled to the single-minded loyalty of his fiduciary. This core liability has several facets. A fiduciary must act in good faith; he must not make a profit out of his trust; he must not place himself in a position where his duty and his interest may conflict; he may not act for his own benefit or the benefit of a third person without the informed consent of his principal. This is not intended as an exhaustive list, but is sufficient to indicate the nature of fiduciary obligations. (at 18)

The fiduciary relationship has, as Anthony Mason suggests, 'been the spearhead of equity's incursions into the area of commerce', and it is vital to several commercial relationships, which shows its significance to stakeholders (1994, p. 245). But also, as Joseph F. Johnson Jr has highlighted in terms of modern corporate business practices, shareholders. 'Shareholders, as the residual risk takers, have entrusted their funds to the corporation for the purposes of gaining profit', argues Johnson, and this creates 'a relationship of trust that, in law and equity, takes precedence over the inclination of managers to be charitable with other people's money. It is entirely justifiable' he concludes, 'that corporate managers should consider the legitimate interests of employees, customers, suppliers, and other constituencies, including the community, *but only so long as there is a rational and perceptible nexus between actions favouring other constituencies and long-term shareholder benefit*' [emphasis added] (2005, p. 44). This last passage is provocative, not least because it highlights the necessity of economic and self-interested benefit as transcendent of the key features of fiduciaries often foregrounded in normative legal thinking and statements, including notions of good faith and fealty that the fiduciary must represent. Johnson's honest appraisal of the brute economics that lie at the heart of fiduciary law is an interesting counterpoint to Henry Smith's interpretation. For Smith, the fiduciary comes with a risk of opportunism that he considers Equity well-suited to mitigate, as a means of anti-opportunism within the private law context (2014, p. 281). Fiduciary law is, for Smith, an 'outgrowth' of Equity and thus prompts innovation of a 'high moral standard' (2014, p. 272).

Within the context of modern corporate practices, the promotion of fair dealing practices in commercial settings and across markets, the fiduciary has parried with contract (Gautreau 1989, pp. 14–18). As a complete justice solution within the Common Law traditions of Western capitalism (the US especially, but also the UK, Canada and Australia) the laws of contract and fiduciary law have, together, provided the structure that business relies on (*Tracy v Atkins* (1977) 83 DLR (3d) 47 (BCSC); Gautreau 1989, p. 29). Justice Cardoza offered a powerful statement on the significance of fiduciary law,

> Joint adventurers, like copartners, owe to one another, while the enterprise continues, the duty of the finest loyalty. Many forms of conduct permissible in a workaday world for those acting at arm's length, are forbidden to those bound by fiduciary ties. A trustee is held to something stricter than the morals of the market place. Not honesty alone, but the punctilio of an honor the most sensitive, is then the standard of behavior. As to this there has developed a tradition that is unbending and inveterate. Uncompromising rigidity has been the attitude of courts of equity when petitioned to undermine the rule of undivided loyalty by the "disintegrating erosion" of particular exceptions (*Wendt v. Fischer*, 243 N. Y. 439, 444). Only thus has the level of conduct for fiduciaries been kept at a level higher than that trodden by the crowd. It will not consciously be lowered by any judgment of this court. (at 463 and 464)

Justice Cardozo's deliberate reference to the market as a place in which honour ought to prevail is telling. Not least, if we are to believe Posner, because this judgement was on the cusp of the re-emergence of contract (after the 1930s) as a mechanism of commercial good faith that did not require the nebulous presentiments of altruism and honour that non-contractualism involved but of which Cardoza was in favour (Markovits 2014, p. 214). As Michele Graziadei contends: 'Looking at the history of fiduciary relationships from a contemporary perspective one notices a tension between the increasing tendency to view contracts from a market-orientated and utilitarian perspective and the ideals of liberality and honorary service' (2014, p. 291). The legal economists contractarian view of fiduciary law and its view of loyalty as a keystone structuring fiduciary relationships in particular is, for Irit Samet, based on a neglect of 'the role of *internal* incentives in the battle against fiduciary disloyalty' and a failure to recognize ethical implications at the heart of fiduciary law (2018, pp. 138–139). 'To the fight against disloyalty we must also enlist the fiduciary's moral sensitivities, viz. her sense of guilt and shame which can strengthen her ability to resist the temptation inherent in her position', argues Samet, continuing,

> And this is exactly what Equity is doing when it uses the ethically loaded terminology of 'loyalty' to describe the fiduciary duty. By casting the basic legal duty of the fiduciary in terms of 'loyalty', Equity aims to recalibrate the fiduciary's inner compass in a direction that is very different form the standard of other-regarding behaviour which is normally expected din private law. (2018, p. 139)

The equitable fiduciary construct aims to countermand, as Smith suggests, opportunistic actors, and here we need to understand that in relation to corporate, capitalist, and commercial practices in particular. We have earlier discussed the inference of self-interest in the practices of capitalism, and the role of conscience historically in marking Equity as a moral and just jurisprudence for counterbalancing the tendencies of self-interest. For Graziadei the rejection by English law of the notion of fiduciary obligations as contractual stems from 'the fundamental idea that under English law contracts are self-regarding acts in which each party to the transaction must be presumed to be pursuing his or her own interests' (2014, p. 291). This means that contract has always served 'one purpose and fiduciary obligations another, and both are conceptually distinct even where obligations generated by the two work to the same purpose' (2014, p. 291). As we saw above, a key to the fiduciary role is completing incomplete contracts by initiating core fiduciary duties and obligations, notably that of loyalty. But such duties are problematic because they are uncertain and potentially inconsistent with the 'common sense' of contemporary commercial practices (Cooter and Freedman 1991, p. 1074). We might assume that loyalty ought to remain distinct from contract, at least conceptually, in order not to risk sullying the relative certainty of the contractual ideal. Economic analysis of the interrelationship between fiduciary and contract law disagree, however. Robert Cooter and Bradley J. Freedman argue that 'the duty of loyalty, far from violating the postulate of self-interested behaviour, is based upon it. The duty of loyalty must be understood as the law's attempt to create an incentive structure in which the fiduciary's self-interest directs her to act in the best interest of the beneficiary' (1991, p. 1074). Samet vigorously disagrees but maintains that the commercial landscape (undergirded by capitalism) that fiduciaries operate in is one in which the cultural propensities of contract towards self-interest are a constant strain on fiduciary loyalty to their principal.

> The pursuit of self-interest is nowadays so widely legitimised (and often praised as 'individualism') that selflessness has become a rare and fragile virtue, one that hardly features in any other field of law. It is easy therefore, almost natural, for fiduciaries to slide back into a default state of mind of self-regard; especially so if in their social circle, or industry, fiduciary disloyalty is not considered as particularly shameful (not any worse than breaching a contract). (Samet 2018, p. 130)

Of course, the pressures created by capitalism on fiduciaries that Samet describes are not limited to this aspect of the law but reflect a general trend that leads, as I argue, law (and Equity) into complicity with the aims of capital. As Paddy Ireland contends, echoing parts of Samet's analysis, that under capitalism 'outdoing and eliminating your rivals is not only legitimate but admirable', and so, he concludes, 'entrepreneurially and inventively twisting (or avoiding) rules to one's advantage is often seen – sometimes openly and publicly, sometimes more covertly – as something to be admired ('smart'), rather than as something to be condemned' (2018, p. 8). Amid shifting emphases in the fiduciary's nature within economic and legal terms, and wrangles between fiduciary and contract law, the fiduciary, and in particular the loyal one, both mediates and reconfigures the notion of 'mine' that Margaret Davies attributed to the basic role of law in defining private property (1999, p. 328). At the fundamental level of the property concept, instead of realizing direct attribution of the *thing* to me and what we call, at Common Law or in Equity, 'mine' through ownership and possession, the fiduciary interposes a managerial role. This does not negate or defeat what is 'mine' but releases me from the onerous need to patrol the boundaries of what is mine to exclude others and finds imaginative ways to use and exploit it for economic advantage and gain.

Trusts, Securities and the Fantasy of Finding the Lost Object

Equity's long and notable jurisdiction over what Maitland calls the 'fruitful field' of the trust arguably provides one of the most enduring pieces of evidence of Equity's commitment to ensuring reproduction of the ideology of capitalism, and that capitalist class power is further entrenched (1969, p. 7). Behind the technicalities of trusts law lies the incontrovertible role that trusts play within capitalist societies: to facilitate on behalf of trust beneficiaries a greater and more absolute enjoyment of capital (Herian 2016, p. 99). The trust as a rudimentary yet innovative legal mechanism predates the rise of capitalism. It brings to light that fiduciary obligations and duties, located here in the trustee, are equally long-standing principles only latterly shaped by capitalism. 'The survival of the Anglo-Saxon word "trust" is evidence enough that a connection has been maintained with an Anglo-Saxon original', argues Gary Watt, 'despite the subsequent overlaying of the Latinate language of "use", "conscience" and "fiduciary duty"' (2012, p. 121).

But an unmistakable shift in trusts law practices occurred once exposed to the forces of capitalist ideology, however, and in particular the demands of commercialism, leading to a significant growth in trusts and an industry to support them for 'valid and legitimate reasons', but equally 'abusive ones' (Christensen 2015, p. 141). Remarking on the evolution of trusteeship during the nineteenth century, Chantal Stebbings maintains that the 'new commercialisation of the English society and economy, begun in the late eighteenth century and reached its zenith in the Victorian period, changed the character of the office of trustee [...] the Victorian period saw the transformation of the trustee from amateur to professional, from layman to businessman' (2002, pp. 129–130). This exposure to commercialism within capitalism also affected beneficiaries as it shaped both their demands and entitlements (Stebbings 2002, p. 128). These factors made and continue to make the trust a pervasive example of the use by capitalist class power of legal mechanisms to further disseminate ideology through exploitation of permissive and flexible laws (Christensen 2015, p. 137). As Roger Cotterrell maintains, via trusts (and thus also via the assets held on trust) Equity channels capitalist class power 'rather than obscuring or disguising of it' (1987, p. 87). And Alastair Hudson maintains that a 'politics of trusts law would have to account, ironically, for the way in which structures which are built on conscience are used to facilitate crime and to avoid taxation' (2017, p. 66).

Like Equity, the trust offers stakeholders a fetish where it enables the stakeholder to believe in the promise made by capitalism for unencumbered wealth creation that will satisfy their unmet desires. Unencumbered in this context could relate, for example, to the use of trusts to avoid or diminish certain tax obligations and thus help increase the net worth of the stakeholder. The use of trusts by individuals and corporations to aggressively manage tax affairs is one of the most significant uses under contemporary capitalism (Shaxson 2011; Harrington 2016). Trusts, under the fantasies promulgated by capitalism to maintain stakeholder investment and engagement, depends 'on the idea of obtaining the object' (McGowan 2013, p. 60). And fetishization is, therefore, perhaps the most effective explanation of the ability of stakeholders to use trusts for morally questionable ends without being comprehensively morally comprised at the political and social level. Trusts assume a wide variety of forms, especially in contemporary use within commercial capitalist settings. As Lord Browne-Wilkinson maintains in *Target Holdings Ltd v Redferns* [1996] AC 421: 'In the modern world the trust has become a valuable device in commercial and financial dealings', and, indeed, this led his reasoning to demand that the nuances of commercial trusts be recognized and differentiated from that of so-called 'traditional trusts' (at 435). At a fundamental level, a trust offers a 'unique way of owning property under which assets are held by a trustee for the benefit of another person, or for certain purposes, in accordance with special equitable obligations' (Watt 2014, p. 18). Importantly, however, trusts offer 'versatility' to the domain of private property that other legal mechanisms do not, and this applies in commercial and non-commercial contexts, as Jonathan Garton explains,

> The secret of the trust's success is to be found in three things. First, in establishing a trust, a founder (or a court, in the case of 'imputed trusts') can play a whole range of 'tricks' with three particular aspects of property ownership: nominal title, benefit and control. The founder (or the court) can juggle these around in a variety of ways. Second, the rights and obligations expressly created in a trust are fortified by effective remedies and supplemented, so far as is necessary, by a substratum of detailed legal rules. Third, in the areas where it is predominately used, the trust performs its 'tricks' with property better, and has stronger legal reinforcement, than other competing legal institutions. (2015, p. 5)

It is no mystery, I suggest, that trusts are a crucial weapon in the capitalist stakeholder arsenal because of their ability, not least via the 'tricks' Garton talks of, to increase private power through secreted wealth and capital holdings. In a robust argument regarding trusts and capitalism, Mitchell

Franklin, in his reference during the 1930s to the Anglo-American capitalist deployment of trusts, asked,

> What is the significance of the dominant role of the trust in Anglo-American juridical theory? Why is it that the jurists, who have jeered at the spectacle of parallel systems of law, in which "equity" is expected to contradict "law", and in which there is a hierarchy of courts with the "equity" courts holding rank of the first class and the "law" courts holding rank of the second class (though the same judge may now play both roles at once), have refrained from liquidating the trust? Why has the trust survived repeated legislative assault except when the fisc [*sic*] is harassed? The answers come when the role of trusts under the regime of liberal capitalism is understood. The trust is an effort to escape from the ever-deepening and ever-recurrent crises in capitalism. (1934, p. 475)

The global significance and popularity of trusts within capitalism as Franklin described them has not disappeared in the years since he was writing. Instead, they have become more pervasive because, I argue, at a fundamental psychical level they offer a reassuring promise to stakeholders of obtaining *their* object of desire. But as psychoanalysis routinely tells us, we can never get the object, and the fantasies and illusions of fetishism are testaments to how stakeholders (subjects) manage this reality. Far from discouraging the stakeholder, the fantasy acts as a primary motivation for unleashing myriad ways in which they believe they might get the object. This notion returns us to the fundamental 'creativity' attributed to Equity mentioned earlier, whereby approaches to rights and ownership that have allowed private property to remain vital to wealth generation are symptomatic of Equity's contribution to the governance and administration of the private property order. 'Equity', Sarah Worthington explains, 'took a "bundle of rights" already regarded by Common Law as "proprietary" and divided the bundle between two or more people so that the interests of each were still significant enough to be regarded as proprietary' (Worthington 2006, p. 63). To echo Franklin, 'professional trustees, the habitual managers of capital, especially as they have been used in the states where the middle class is most class conscious, enjoy a role of the highest importance under capitalism: they are the *Fuehrers* of liberal capitalism' (1934, p. 475). Trusts provide an attractive proposition for stakeholders in search of proprietary and personal rights, to secure assets, and to generate wealth—a conjunction and causality of factors underscored by the desire for the lost object. In order to further describe how Equity manipulates the property concept to these ends, security interests and charges offer instructive examples besides trusts.

Charges are forms of security that only take effect in Equity and grant the 'secured party some right by virtue of the parties' contract to sell the assets provided by way of a security, whether that property is held at the time of the creation of charge or whether it is only capable of first coming into existence once the specific property comes into the hands of the chargor' (*Re Coslett Contractors Ltd* [1998] Ch 495; Hudson 2013, pp. 653–654). Equity creates a new form of proprietary interest 'that is quite distinct from ownership or possession', by demarcating certain rights for secondary parties over property legally owned by another (Worthington 2006, p. 78). Equity 'took a personal obligation that related to property', such as a contractual obligation to discharge a debt, 'insisted it was specifically enforceable, and then protected the right against interference by strangers', namely other secured (and unsecured) creditors (Worthington 2006, p. 78). A key and 'outstanding' feature of Equity's intervention is therefore temporal, as it creates proprietary rights in *future* interests where the Common Law does not (Beale et al. 2012, p. 8). In Equity, as Beale et al. state, a debtor can 'raise finance on the basis of an ever-changing asset base such as present and future book debts' (2012, p. 8). Equity has fostered a crucial role for itself in modern finance and commerce by making charges and associated future interests in intangible assets highly prized commercial entities that circulate via special purpose vehicles ("SPVs"). In contemporary fiscally liberal, financialized, and commercialized societies where a vast majority of activity, whether domestic or multinational, involves a constant tension between debt and credit, demands for safeguards to prevent financial loss and mitigate unjust claims are commonplace. Also, the ability of one party to transfer property and the bundle of rights over it to another party on credit, thus replacing the immediate discharge of a debt in favour of an obligation to do so at a later date is, arguably, and at least on a par with trusts as an engine of wealth and desire.

By 'hiving off' certain rights from property's overall bundle, Equity not only introduces flexibility into property law but also reveals how a veritable matryoshka doll of different interests (of property within property within property) emerges. And these interests generate wealth, often many times over the initial value of any single asset. This form of pure use (trade, transfer and profiteering) is fundamental to understanding stakeholder reliance on private property in contemporary capitalist society. The

right of exclusion is only really a concern for a chargor in so far as it
facilitates and guarantees further profitable use—onward transferability of
assets, for example, as in forcing the sale of property subject to a charge
and where the debt has failed to be discharged. Penner argues that, 'the
law of property is driven by an analysis which takes the perspective of
exclusion, rather than one which elaborates a right to use. In other words,
in order to understand property, we must look to the way that the law
contours the duties it imposes on people to exclude themselves from the
property of others, rather than regarding the law as instituting a series of
positive liberties or powers to use particular things' (1997, p. 71). The
argument made here is that the forms of property created by Equity, that
service wealth creation, in contrast to Penner's claim, are absolutely the
preserve of positive liberties to use the property of or in another, especially where this guarantees a profit. Whilst rules and regulation exist that
prevents arbitrary interference with the property of another where that
property is subject to a charge, including those covered under the *Law of
Property Act* 1925, thus mitigating unencumbered profiteering to some
extent, this still does not amount to exclusion overriding use as the way
to understand property, at least not in today's society.

Conclusion

Over the course of the last two hundred years, capitalism and a growth in
competitive free markets has sped up exclusion, exclusivity and demands
for private property. Alongside this we find the self-interest of economic
and legal subjects defined by portfolios of property holdings and the
wealth and capital gains they produce. This socioeconomic development
has placed a significant onus on Equity to preside over ever more indi-
vidualized private domains that are both domestic and commercial and
manage *abstract value*, increasingly divorced from tangible or material
counterparts, to ensure the fruitfulness of those private domains. 'In
crafting the fiduciary duty as a specialised regime', argues Samet, 'Equity
creates a social context in which players understand themselves as partic-
ipating in a collaboration, rather than a contest' (2018, p. 131). Yet, the
solution of fiduciary law to the ills of self-regarding legal economism and
contractarianism are, arguably, overstated. Instead we find, for example,
"collaboration" between interests in aggressive forms of wealth and
financial management, facilitated by trusts as major strategic growth
engines.

The profound influence vouchsafed by capitalism to Equity's various mechanisms such as trusts and securities forces a shift in emphasis from a particular material asset held at any time, feudal land for example, to the abstract value of what is owned. Freed from constraints of material holdings and of the responsibilities, obligations and duties that accompany property stewardship and management, trusts and securities have been effective in providing far-reaching benefits and gains for stakeholders. This leaves only concerns for the most efficient maintenance of the 'value which presently held trust assets represent', whilst stakeholders unconsciously enjoy greater levels of property as an escape form the traumatic truth of castrated subjectivity (Cotterrell 1987, p. 85).

REFERENCES

BOOKS & ARTICLES

Althusser, L., Balibar, E. *Reading Capital.* Translated by Ben Brewster. 2009. London: Verso.

Arendt, H. *The Portable Hannah Arendt.* Edited by Peter Baehr. 2000. London: Penguin Books.

Atkinson, A.B. *Inequality: What Can Be Done?* 2015. Cambridge: Harvard University Press.

Auchmuty, R. Law and the Power of Feminism: How Marriage Lost Its Power to Oppress Women. *Feminist Legal Studies*, Vol. 20, No. 2 (August 2012), pp. 71–87.

Beale, H., Bridge, M., Gullifer, L., Lomnicka, E. *The Law of Security and Title Based Financing.* 2nd Edition. 2012. Oxford: Oxford University Press.

Birks, P. Equity in the Modern Law: An Exercise in Taxonomy. *Western Australian Law Review*, Vol. 26, No. 1 (July 1996), pp. 1–99.

Bostaph, S. Utopia from and Economist's Perspective. *Thomas More Studies 1: Utopia* (2006), pp. 196–198.

Bottomley, A. (ed.). *Feminist Perspectives on the Foundational Subjects of Law.* 1996. London: Cavendish Publishing.

Bryan, M.W., Vann, V.J. *Equity & Trusts in Australia.* 2012. Cambridge: Cambridge University Press.

Burn, E.H., Virgo, G.J. *Maudsley & Burn's Trusts & Trustees, Cases & Materials.* 7th Edition. 2008. Oxford: Oxford University Press.

Campbell, D. Welfare Economics for Capitalists: The Economic Consequences of Judge Posner. *Cardoza Law Review*, Vol. 33, No. 6 (August 2012), pp. 2233–2274.

Chiesa, L., Toscano, A. Agape and the Anonymous Religion of Atheism. *Angelaki Journal of Theoretical Humanities*, Vol. 12, No. 1 (April 2007), pp. 113–126.

Christensen, J. In Trusts We Trust. *The Greatest Invention: Tax and the Campaign for a Just Society*. 2015. Margate: Commonwealth Publishing, pp. 130–145.

Cooter, R., Freedman, B.J. The Fiduciary Relationship: Its Economic Character and Legal Consequences. *New York University Law Review*, Vol. 66 (October 1991), pp. 1045–1075.

Cotterrell, R. Power, Property and the Law of Trusts: A Partial Agenda for Critical Legal Scholarship. *Journal of Law and Society*, Vol. 14, No. 1 (Spring 1987), pp. 77–90.

Cotterrell, R. *The Politics of Jurisprudence: A Critical Introduction to Legal Philosophy*. 1989. London: Butterworths.

Davies, M. Queer Property, Queer Persons: Self-Ownership and Beyond. *Social & Legal Studies*, Vol. 8, No. 3 (September 1999), pp. 327–352.

Davies, W. *The Limits of Neoliberalism: Authority, Sovereignty and the Logic of Competition*. 2017. London: Sage.

Dean, J. *The Communist Horizon*. 2012. London: Verso.

Fortier, M. *The Culture of Equity in Early Modern England*. 2005. Farnham: Ashgate.

Frankel, T. Watering Down Fiduciary Duties. *Philosophical Foundations of Fiduciary Law*. Edited by Andrew S. Gold and Paul B. Miller. 2014. Oxford: Oxford University Press, pp. 242–260.

Franklin, M. Book Reviews. *Tulane Law Review*, Vol. 8, No. 3 (April 1934), pp. 473–476.

Freud, S. *The Future of an Illusion, Civilization and Its Discontents and Other Works: The Standard Edition Volume XXI (1927–1931)*. Translated and Edited by James Strachey. 2001. London: Vintage.

Galsworthy, J. *Forsyte Saga, Volume 1: The Man of Property, in Chancery, and To Let*. 2001. London Penguin Classics.

Garton, J. *Moffat's Trusts Law, Text and Materials*. 6th Edition. 2015. Cambridge: Cambridge University Press.

Gautreau, J.R.M. Demystifying the Fiduciary Mystique. *The Canadian Bar Review*, Vol. 68, No. 1 (March 1989), pp. 14–18.

Gramsci, A. *Selections from the Prison Notebook*. Edited and Translated by Quintin Hoare and Geoffrey Nowell Smith. 1971. London: Lawrence & Wishart.

Gray, K., Gray, S.F. *Elements of Land Law*. 5th Edition. 2009. Oxford: Oxford University Press.

Graziadei, M. Virtue and Utility. *Philosophical Foundations of Fiduciary Law*. Edited by Andrew S. Gold and Paul B. Miller. 2014. Oxford: Oxford University Press, pp. 287–301.

Grey, T.C. The Disintegration of Property. *Nomos*, Vol. 22, Property, 1980, pp. 69–85.

Harrington, B. *Capital Without Borders: Wealth Managers and the One Percent.* 2016. Cambridge: Harvard University Press.

Hayek, F.A. *Law, Legislation and Liberty.* 2013. London: Routledge Classics.

Hedley, S. Is Private Law Meaningless? *Current Legal Problems*, Vol. 64 (2011), pp. 89–116.

Heller, M.A. The Tragedy of the Anticommons: Property in the Transition from Marx to Markets. *Harvard Law Review*, Vol. 111, No. 3 (January 1998), pp. 622–688.

Herian, R. The Castrated Trustee: Jouissance and Breach of Trust. *Pólemos*, Vol. 10, No. 2 (September 2016), pp. 97–115.

Holdsworth, W.S. *Sources and Literature of English Law.* 1925. Oxford: Clarendon Press.

Honoré, A.M. Ownership. *Readings in the Philosophy of Law.* Edited by Jules L. Coleman. 2013. New York: Routledge, pp. 563–574.

Hudson, A. *The Law of Finance.* 2nd Edition. 2013. London: Sweet & Maxwell.

Hudson, A. *Equity and Trusts.* 9th Edition. 2017. London: Routledge.

Ireland, P. From Lonrho to BHS; The Changing Character of Corporate Governance in Contemporary Capitalism. *King's Law Journal*, Vol. 29, No. 1 (2018), pp. 3–35.

Johnson Jr, J.F. Natural Law and the Fiduciary Duties of Business Managers. *Journal of Markets and Morality*, Vol. 8, No. 1 (Spring 2005), pp. 27–51.

Jolowicz, J.A. General Ideas and the Reform of Civil Procedure. *Legal Studies*, Vol. 3, No. 3 (November 1983), pp. 295–314.

Kennedy, D. The Role of Law in Economic Thought: Essays on the Fetishism of Commodities. *The American University Law Review*, Vol. 34, No. 4 (Summer 1985), pp. 939–1001.

Lobban, M. Preparing for Fusion: Reforming the Nineteenth-Century Court of Chancery, Part II. *Law and History Review*, Vol. 22, No. 3 (Fall 2004), pp. 565–599.

Maitland, F.W. *Equity: A Course of Lectures.* 1969. Cambridge: Cambridge University Press.

Marx, K., Engels, F. *Collected Works, Volume 3 1843–1844.* 1975. London: Lawrence & Wishart.

Markovits, D. Sharing Ex Ante and Sharing Ex Post. *Philosophical Foundations of Fiduciary Law.* Edited by Andrew S. Gold and Paul B. Miller. 2014. Oxford: Oxford University Press, pp. 209–224.

Mason, A. The Place of Equity and Equitable Remedies in the Contemporary Common Law World. *Law Quarterly Review*, Vol. 110 (April 1994), pp. 238–259.

McGowan, T. *Enjoying What We Don't Have: The Political Project of Psychoanalysis*. 2013. Lincoln: University of Nebraska Press.

McGowan, T. *Capitalism and Desire: The Psychic Cost of Free* Markets. 2016. New York: Columbia University Press.

Neuberger, L. *Equity—The Soul and Spirit of All Law or a Roguish Thing?* Lehane Lecture 2014, Supreme Court of New South Wales, Sydney. 4 August 2014. https://www.supremecourt.uk/docs/speech-140804.pdf.

Pashukanis, E.B. *Law & Marxism: A General Theory Towards a Critique of the Fundamental Juridical Concepts*. Translated by Barbara Einhorn. Edited by Chris Arthur. 1989. London: Pluto Press.

Pawlowski, M. Unconscionability as a Unifying Concept in Equity. *The Denning Law Journal*, Vol. 16 (2001), pp. 79–96.

Penner, J.E. *The Idea of Property in Law*. 1997. Oxford: Oxford University Press.

Polanyi, K. *Great Transformation: The Political and Economic Origins of Our Time*. 2001. Boston: Beacon Press.

Posner, Richard A. *Economic Analysis of Law*. 3rd Edition. 1986. Boston: Little, Brown and Company.

Probert, R. Trusts and the Modern Woman—Establishing an Interest in the Family Home. *Child and Family Law Quarterly*, Vol. 13, No. 3 (2001), pp. 275–286.

Roemer, J.E. *Theories of Distributive Justice*. 1996. Cambridge: Harvard University Press.

Samet, I. *Equity: Conscience Goes to Market*. 2018. Oxford: Oxford University Press.

Schroeder, J.L. *The Triumph of Venus: The Erotics of the Market*. 2004. Berkeley: University of California Press.

Shaxson, N. *Treasure Islands: Tax Havens and the Men Who Stole the World*. 2011. London: Vintage.

Sitkoff, R. The Economic Structure of Fiduciary Law. *Boston University Law Review*, Vol. 91 (2011), pp. 1039–1049.

Smith, H. Why Fiduciary Law is Equitable. *Philosophical Foundations of Fiduciary Law*. Edited by Andrew S. Gold and Paul B. Miller. 2014. Oxford: Oxford University Press, pp. 261–284.

Stebbings, C. *The Private Trustee in Victorian England*. 2002. Cambridge: Cambridge University Press.

Virgo, G. *The Principles of Equity & Trusts*. 2012. Oxford: Oxford University Press.

Watt, G. *Equity Stirring: The Story of Justice Beyond Law*. 2012. Oxford: Hart Publishing.

Watt, G. *Trusts & Equity*. 6th Edition. 2014. Oxford: Oxford University Press.

Williams, R. *Keywords: A Vocabulary of Culture and Society*. 1988. London: Fontana Press.

Wood, E.M. *The Origins of Capitalism: A Longer View.* 2017. London: Verso.
Worthington, S. *Equity.* 2nd Edition. 2006. Oxford: Oxford University Press.
Yip, M., Lee, J. The Commercialisation of Equity. *Legal Studies*, Vol. 37, No. 4 (2017), pp. 647–671.

MISCELLANEOUS ONLINE RESOURCES

Ministry of Justice. *Civil Justice Statistics Quarterly, England and Wales (Incorporating The Royal Courts of Justice 2015).* 2016. https://www.gov.uk/gov ernment/uploads/system/uploads/attachment_data/file/527018/civil-jus tice-statistics-january-march-2016.pdf.

CASE-LAW & LEGISLATION

Law of Property Act 1925 (c.20).
Re Coslett Contractors Ltd [1998] Ch 495.
Tracy v Atkins (1977) 83 DLR (3d) 47 (BCSC).

CHAPTER 6

A Different Theory of Civil Justice

An Introduction to Equity Fetishism

'Equity in Law, is the same that the Spirit is in Religion, what everyone pleases to make of it' said John Selden in his *Table Talk* published in the sixteenth century (1856, p. 49). Selden's description points to a certain truth that concerns the slipperiness of Equity. The heterogeneity of legal contexts that Equity works with makes it disorientating and hard to define, hence, 'Equity can be described but not defined' (Meagher et al. 1992, p. 3). It is, by turns, considered fixed and flexible, wide and narrow, objective and subjective (Martin 2012, p. 3). Equity's impact upon the many legal domains on to which we project it occurs through an incorporation and subsequent radiation of meanings and powers ascribed to it, whereby it is said to extend the general Law by a 'process of deduction from existing principle' (Halliwell 2004, p. 150). As we have seen, a variety of legal contexts apply Equity flexibly and reflexively to address conceptual, systemic, or experiential inequities and inequalities that stem from formal rule compliance construed as overly harsh. This involves, for instance, proceedings applying Equity's jurisprudence based on questions of what is just and fair. Central to this view of Equity is what Simon Chesterman has called, 'the recurrent theme of unconscionability', which has long helped to shape the nature of Equity's intellectual development and application in practice (1997, p. 351).

© The Author(s), under exclusive license to Springer Nature
Switzerland AG 2021
R. Herian, *Capitalism and the Equity Fetish*,
https://doi.org/10.1007/978-3-030-66523-4_6

From the point of view of civil justice, unconscionability assumes something of a universal and unifying form (see, for example, Lord Walker in *Cobbe v Yeoman's Row Management Ltd and another* [2008] 1 WLR 1752 at 92). It does so in dialogue with a 'problematic of judicial decision-making (the necessarily impossible demand to *do justice*)' that occurs within the interrelated domains of *private* and *property* law (Chesterman 1997, p. 358). This is a condition underscored by Equity's liberalization of legal principles and maxims, rules and doctrines that operate in the main to support the private property order (Virgo 2012, pp. 26–39). I argue, a socioeconomic order predicated on the vindication of property rights as a basis for ownership and certainty of title that not only relates to the interest of individual and corporate stakeholders but is crucial for the survival of capitalist ideology and capitalism as a mode of social organization. Marx claimed that capitalism 'begins by seeming to acknowledge man (his independence, spontaneity, etc.); then, locating private property in man's own being, it can no longer be conditioned by the local, national or other *characteristics of private property* as of *something existing outside itself*. This political economy, consequently, displays a *cosmopolitan*, universal energy which overthrows every restriction and bond so as to establish itself instead as the *sole* politics, the sole universality, the sole limit, the sole bond' (Marx and Engels 1975, p. 291). As a concurrent body of law alongside the Common Law and a keystone of civil justice regarding property, Equity is demonstrably political on Marx's terms, and thus forms a significant part of what Louis Althusser calls the 'legal ISA' (ideological state apparatus) (2008, p. 17).

Whilst the civil justice of which Equity forms a part is definitively an entity of the State (and part of a political unity in public services at any one given moment in time, normatively a term of government), the private actors whose influence on the system is transformative points less to State ideology than the ideology of powerful private economic interests. This is perhaps unsurprising given the trend in State ideology since at least the nineteenth century in supporting economic growth, reason and expedience in ways that do not diverge from capitalist ideology as it exists in the private domain but shadow it. The civil justice system, like all or many other State entities, is a logic of production and economy characterized, as André Gorz has argued, 'by the desire to *economize*' and 'use the factors of production as efficiently as possible' (1989, pp. 2–3). State ideology is always already the ideology of private interests. Fetishism qua ECJ is complex and variegated because it involves real-world effects that manifest through practices of economic reason and capitalist ideology in civil justice, thus making it a mode of production. This is a point of view that Gary Watt acknowledges when he says that 'it is true that economic language has embraced the idea of equity almost to the point of suffocating it' (2012, p. 37). Although Watt remains optimistic that, 'it is within our power to loosen its grip' (2012, p. 37).

At heart, Equity fetishism is, as the earlier discussion on Bentham also implied, a product of psychological affect and a mode of subjection 'concerned with the relation between practices and a symbolic order constituted within history' (Balibar 2017, p. 72). This makes it a psychological mechanism through which economic subjects sustain belief in the certainty and completeness, an uncastrated and un-lacking nature, of civil justice *within* the confines of the capitalist superstructure. This belief from within the ambit of capitalist ideology insists that 'without Equity, the common law would be an incomplete means to achieve justice' (Neuberger 2010, p. 1). The obvious influence of political economy and economic reason prompts the need to consider a particular formulation of fetishism able to account for that influence. With roots in the property basis of civil justice, Equity fetishism brings together the political and economic considerations of commodity fetishism under capitalism, and the fetishism related to the fantasies and desires for complete justice also promulgated under capitalism. To reconcile these two positions requires, I claim, a discussion of the relationship between Marx and Freud's theories of fetishism, a discussion that will follow later in this chapter.

In the fantasy life of stakeholders, Equity fetishism does not exist magically or transcendentally so much as institutionally, systemically, bureaucratically, and thus somewhat prosaically. Equity is rarely if ever spectacular in the sense that it encourages any radical or serious refinement of the law, where the ramifications of such refinements upset the economic base or the very heart of capitalist ideology. Neither is Equity uncertain by any normative economic definition of the term. Rather, Equity's jurisprudence and its status to complete justice rely on inflexions of conscience and a syntax of fairness that contributes to a particular distribution of economic power that benefits those able 'to shape the rule of law to provide a framework within which they can exploit others' (Stiglitz 2013, p. 238).

Instrumental to the implementation and practice of economic reason, we can understand Equity in terms of a legacy of practical reason traceable to the pre-capitalist notion of synderesis, that Piyel Haldar maintains in its early modern form 'was elaborated both by theologians and by jurists […] the spark of conscience (*scintilla conscientiae*) given to and shared by each individual rational creature' (2016, p. 313). Yet, the net effect of capitalist ideology and economic reason has not been to celebrate or promote this legacy of Equity in law. Nor use it as an effective way of addressing distortions in the economy fostered by advocates of legal frameworks who claim to be promoting an efficient economy (Stiglitz 2013, p. 235). Instead, capitalism has reconfigured the uncertainty engendered by Equity, crystallized in the notion and practice of conscience, to mask and conceal a reality of social relations. Including masking the power relations, as a core of the property form, that articulate political relations between people. Instead where capitalism insists *ex cathedra* on the illusion of property as mere cold dead *things* (Gray and Gray 2009, p. 88)

THE LANGUAGE OF EQUITY

In his mission to classify the whole of the law for greater certainty, Peter Birks focused intently on the failure of language to describe what it was the law was doing or expected to do. Central to his critique was Equity and the vocabulary and language associated with it, including fairness, justice, and what he construed as definitive elements of fiduciary law (Birks 1996, pp. 16–17). Like Bentham's view of natural law, for Birks this language is, on the whole, 'so unspecific' it conceals 'a private and intuitive evaluation', and the difficulty with fiduciary law 'is that its meaning has been allowed to become completely uncertain' (1996, p. 17). Yet, as a discrete jurisprudence, and a mode of practice and reasoning, historical portraits of Equity paint it as a site for the reconciliation of antagonistic concepts found at the intersection of the objective and subjective struggle over justice, and achieving this relies on the language Birks dislikes. This is, in part, the view Aristotle expressed on Equity, claiming Equity to be 'a correction of law where it is defective owing to its universality' (Aristotle 2009, p. 99). To fully understand what capitalism expects Equity to achieve in the civil justice system, it is necessary to unpack what it means for the justice that Equity represents to be *complete*. To do this requires an analysis of the function of Equity's language and how it is used to construct the notion of complete justice in, for example, case-law judgements, and in the form of individual principles, doctrines, and rules of practice and procedure.

There is no material form of Equity able to perform the role of ritual object, talisman, or amulet *qua* fetish. But language can serve this purpose by providing an anchor of meaning for the subject, whether subtle or specific, which can motivate demand and desire. For instance, at the level of interpellated economic subjects and their relationship with property, Equity promises to provide a solution to the stakeholder's problem of what is *fair* (albeit a response which may not be a fair one) or *just* regarding the means of and necessity to create proprietary and personal rights from what Virgo calls 'particular events' (2012, p. 19). Unconscionability, the long-standing doctrine at the heart of the notion of Equity is especially important in shaping narratives surrounding ECJ and thus to establishing it as a fetish. In the framework of Equity fetishism, unconscionability creates an important veil of belief in which the subject confidently conceals the fallacy of complete justice in particular and the fact that 'no object is whole or fulfilling for the subject' (McGowan 2016, p. 24). Or, as Birks argues, to conceal the presence, prevalence, and problematic of 'private and intuitive evaluation' (1996, p. 17). We may encounter Equity through particular and sometimes visceral juridical gestures (the constraint of an agent subject to a fiduciary obligation, for example), or through decorum or manners as Haldar has suggested. It is both as applied juridical texts and an object of desire in adjudication, identified and named in and through other juridical texts, that establish the specific form that Equity fetishism takes.

That the language of Equity (or any language) does not amount to all it promises emerges in Freud's belief that 'unconscious mental disturbances produced symptomatic linguistic *formations or deformations*' [my emphasis] (Harpham 2002, p. 175). And using language in a situation involves a degree of 'turbulence, disorder, or misalignment' (Harpham 2002, p. 175). 'Equity', therefore, is never just Equity but always already unsatisfactorily defined by a growing series or chain of other signs that betray 'the subsurface burbling of psychic disturbances' (Harpham 2002, p. 175). Language always confronts the subject who comes to the civil justice system as a precursor to action (a judgement or order, for instance); language that is 'caught in a system of assemblage and separation, in a code' (Baudrillard 1981, p. 95). But, Baudrillard concludes, 'circumscribed in this way, they [the fetish] become the possible objects of security giving worship' (1981, p. 95). What first appears as the apparent disorder of a resolutely indefinable 'Equity' (a series of signs to nowhere) therefore, is, in fact, a crucial element of Equity fetishism, because language is necessary to create the gap-filling, fetishized object validated and legitimized at the moment of enunciation and adjudication of civil justice. The divergent language basis to Equity fetishism is noteworthy in portraits that paint Equity as a spectacular, rarefied, or an extraordinary mode of justice, morality, or conscience capable of transcending the harsh if somewhat banal and normative functions of Law (as justice *beyond* the law). This fetishization belongs to the subject knowing that Equity as 'the word' on justice is not 'the thing itself', yet persisting in 'ignoring this knowledge' and doing so through recourse to a litany of other words, fairness, equality, and so on, which appear to represent Equity but are in fact chains of signs that lead nowhere (Aristodemou 2014, pp. 23–24). Jacques Lacan's assertion of 'a locus in which language questions us as to its very nature' is thus instructive on the matter of what I referred to previously as Equity's *slipperiness* (2001, p. 166).

'No signification can be sustained other than by reference to another signification', claims Lacan, and 'in its extreme form this amounts to the proposition that there is no language (*langue*) in existence for which there is any question of its inability to cover the whole field of the signified' (2001, p. 165). Further, 'if we try to grasp in language the constitution of the object [the *thing*], we cannot fail to notice that this constitution is to be found only at the level of concept' [my addition] (Lacan 2001, p. 165). This last point applies to understanding Equity fetishism because it points to an interpretation of the slipperiness of Equity that, I argue, supports rather than undermines fetishization. Considering fiduciaries, Birks, for example, insists that 'we ought to recognise that the language of fiduciary relationships and obligations is wholly unsatisfactory', but he errs on Lacan's account by further insisting that is essential 'to find other words to *denote with precision* the different things which in different contexts the overworked fiduciary language has been trying to denote' [emphasis added] (1996, p. 18). In attempting to 'grasp' Equity or its associated mechanisms as Birks suggests, via fiduciaries as a particular *thing*, for example, inevitably leads to the thing breaking up into myriad other signs, which inevitably result in vagueness—as fairness, equality, justice, and so on. *Contra* Birks' insistence that we can solve law's failed attempts to counteract the vagueness of terms such just, and fair, Lacan argues that language is always indeterminate in signifying and representing the subject or object—it is not possible, for instance, for us to complete justice *in* or *through* language. More or different language, as Birks argues, cannot change this. More or different language instead provides new openings for the stakeholder to exercise lack of satisfaction in the *thing* offered to them, and an opportunity to (continue to) demand and desire when satisfaction does not materialize or come.

Instead of language signalling an end to Equity as a fetish because of a lack of linguistic coherence, however, two forms of fetishism occur in order for the subject to sustain belief in the authority and legitimacy of ECJ. First, there is a fetishism of the very lack of coherence itself, in the form of new constitutions of language that recycle the defiance of incoherence and uncertainty. We can see this fetishism, for example, in Gary Watt's claim that, 'it is in some respects easier to know what equity is not, than to know what equity is' (2012, p. 39). Second, although related to the first, is fetishism indexed to an initial neurotic vindication of ECJ by the legal community as purveyors of expertise, knowledge, and meaning (judges, lawyers, legal academics, and so on). This neuroticism, born of the need to stave off the frustrations of uncertainty within capitalist civilization by defining limits and constraints in law on forms of economic existence, Birks displays in his project of taxonomy, Bentham in his *pannomion*, and Posner in his reduction of the law to the calculable logic of economics. All these work hand-in-hand, I suggest, with the perverse insistence of stakeholders in the lost object-locating potentialities of civil justice within capitalism. 'It was discovered that a person becomes neurotic', claims Freud, 'because he cannot tolerate the amount of frustration which society imposes on him in the service of it cultural ideals, and it was inferred from this that the abolition or reduction of those demands would result in a return to possibilities of happiness' (2001, p. 87)

At its most basic this form of fetishism turns on Lacan's notion as highlighted above that, faced with the failure of language to grasp the object, the constitution of the *thing* can only live at the level of concept. There is, therefore, a professional process of *conceptualisation* which produces and vindicates a particular concept *qua* fetish. Hence the notion of complete justice relies on an initial neurotic conceptualization by the legal community prior to stakeholder inference in order not only to produce but also legitimize and vindicate the fetish. As I claimed a moment ago, Birks offered a particular example of this neurotic conceptualization with his project of legal taxonomy 1996, 2005). 'One advantage of a good classification is that it keeps all relevant possibilities in view and reduces the risk that one might be overlooked', claimed Birks, moreover that 'it militates against the tricks that complex language can play in concealing similarities and unnecessarily proliferating entities' (1996, p. 16). This strict observance of the proper place and definition of law was not for everyone Birks claims, however, it can do nothing 'for an observer who lacks the exacting taxonomic mentality' and that, for example, the 'lawyer who deals with "unconscionable behaviour" is rather like the ornithologist content with a "small brown bird"' (1996, p. 16).

As neurotics the legal community aims to justify and defend legal expertise though language and knowledge that possesses discrete value and, following Birks, levels of categorical accuracy befitting internal and external (economic) demands for certainty, especially demands that have commercial consequences. As Millett robustly maintained, 'Businessmen need speed and certainty; these do not permit a detailed and leisurely examination of the parties' conduct. Commerce needs the kind of bright-line rules which the common law provides and which equity abhors' (1998, p. 214). Graham Virgo's insistence on the role fiduciaries play in, what he calls, the cynicism of Equity, is yet another example. 'Equity requires the highest standards of fiduciaries because of fears that people occupying such positions of trust and confidence may be tempted to prefer their own interests over those of their principals', states Virgo, 'It is for this reason that a fiduciary who makes any profit from their relationship will be liable to disgorge it to the principal, even if this was part of a transaction that was for the benefit of the principal' (2012, p. 35).

It would be wrong to say that the concepts discussed above, despite their lack of concreteness in language, do not have real-world effects. A wide community of stakeholders appropriate the language (if not precisely the knowledge) of Equity at the superficial yet potent level of the concept, a community for whom the language underscores economic events and commercial opportunities. Perhaps the 'concept' in question here is not ethereal, nor has it ever been, even during the earlier periods of Equity's history. Narratives on Equity by the likes of Sir Henry Maine and F. W. Maitland highlight the influence of ecclesiastical (Roman Catholic) thought and practice on Equity jurisprudence that returns though concepts relating to a language of conscience, most notably in the doctrine of unconscionability. Where these concepts and language feature as a basis for judicial reason and thus inform the implementation of complete justice, and, for example, the application of remedies that have real-world effects, it is hard to see them entirely lacking material constitution. We have evidence of the apparent conceptual concreteness of unconscionability in many judgements that have applied the doctrine (despite Birks' fervent dislike of the term and the problematic of intuition it encapsulates) and produced material effects at some discernible level in the world—the reversal of an unjust enrichment for instance, and its impact on parties to a commercial transaction (see, for example, Lord Scarman in the Privy Council case, *Pao On v Lau Yiu Long* [1980] AC 614). This suggests the production of an object or *thing* that can be more readily fetishized than reference to a concept alone.

'Without good taxonomy and a vigorous taxonomic debate', argues Birks, 'the law loses its rational integrity' (1996, p. 22). And in order for rationality to prevail expertise within the law, of the lawyer, the judge, the academic, must seize language and direct it to the thing they must consent Birks's claims 'to be prisoners of their own expertise' (1996, p. 22). Further, it is 'essential to come to the law armed with a belief in the fallibility of intuition and a consequent aversion to all forms of thought and expression which are no more than vehicles of the gut reaction' and that 'a sophisticated modern legal system should in general regard direct appeals to "justice and good conscience" and "large principles of equity" with deep suspicion' (Birks 1996, pp. 22–23). I argue, however, that Birks' proposal cannot solve the problem he names, but drives the neuroticism within legal thinking focused on, at least regarding Equity, a strange conjunction of flexibility and certainty articulated through language.

Gabel and Feinman, in their assessment of an analogous relationship between contract and ideology, state that 'most of the time the socioeconomic system operates without any need for law as such because people at every level have been imbued with its inevitability and necessity. When the system breaks down and conflicts arise, a legal case comes into being. This is the "moment" of legal ideology, the moment at which lawyers and judges, in *their* narrow, functional roles seek to justify the normal functioning of the system by resolving the conflict through an idealized way of thinking about it' (1998, p. 508). Yet actual closure or resolution of the problem presented to law in and with language is not possible. Instead fantasies redirect language around the constant (re)conceptualizing of legal expertise, which, I claim, occurs within capitalism on behalf of stakeholders as part of the broader perfectibility demanded by economic reason. Law aids economic reason in constructing and maintaining fetishized frameworks of civil justice.

FREUD WITH MARX

'To this enlightened political economy, which has discovered – within private property – the *subjective essence* of wealth', claims Marx, 'the adherents of the monetary and mercantile system, who look upon private property *only as an objective* substance confronting men, seem therefore to be *fetishists*' (Marx and Engels 1975, p. 290). Equity makes up a stakeholder fetishism that, I have argued, begins in the private property order. Equity fetishism is not commodity fetishism per se, but a perverse compliment to it. It is fetishism that always returns to a specific unconscious desire for complete justice to avoid castration, which reflects the structure and meaning of the various rules, doctrines, and principles that comprise Equity's jurisprudence and its contribution to civil justice. Neither Marx nor Freud's concepts of fetishism alone are sufficient therefore, and we need both. On this point, I largely echo Evgeny Pashukanis when he says,

> We are justified in speaking of a commodity-orientated ideology, or, as Marx called it, 'commodity fetishism', and in classing this phenomenon as a psychological one. What we need to establish, therefore, is not whether general juridical concepts can be incorporated into ideological processes and ideological systems – there is no argument about this – but whether or not social reality, which is to certain extent mystified and veiled, can be discovered by means of these concepts. (1989, pp. 73–74)

Fetishism describes a psychological effect and a mode of subjection 'concerned with the relation between practices and a symbolic order constituted within history', where those practices and that symbolic order describe the conduct of civil justice within capitalism (Balibar 2017, p. 72). This definition is important because it goes a long way to reconciling the historical materialism of Marx, which views social existence as the determinant of the subject's consciousness, with Freud's notion of castration as key to the subject's place within the symbolic realm of social existence. Locating this dual definition of fetishism in Equity fetishism reveals it as a psychological mechanism through which the stakeholder sustains a belief in the certainty and completeness, the uncastrated and unlacking nature, of civil justice within capitalism. Whilst Freud tells us that a subject sustains belief because of unconscious desires, Marx's historical materialism brings to light essential details relating to belief determined by the political economy of capitalism and neoliberal capitalism.

Freud's work on fetishism from 1927 onwards forms the larger part of the fetishism I am discussing here. But, and somewhat contrary to the idea that at a theoretical level Freud prefigures Marx, I will drawn on his concept of fetishism from Marx's earlier use of the concept in relation to commodities. To be clear, therefore, I claim that Equity fetishism brings together the political and economic considerations of commodity fetishism under capitalism, and the psychological fetishism related to the fantasies and desires for complete justice promulgated by capitalism. Freud picks up strands of Marx and develops them under the aegis of psychology, rather than a material or politico-economic understanding of social relations. Slavoj Žižek maintains that 'in Marxism a fetish conceals the positive network of social relations, whereas in Freud a fetish conceals the lack ("castration") around which the symbolic network is articulated' (1989, p. 50). The two interpretations are, therefore, not irreconcilable and in Equity fetishism we find a site in which it is possible to describe how they come together in what is yet another point of *fusion*, a 'psychoanalytic process of perverse structure at the level of the process of ideological production' (Baudrillard 1981, p. 90). The notion of concealment, in particular, helps reconcile fetishism in Marx and Freud. Georg Lukács, as the following passage shows, is instructive,

> The fetishistic illusions enveloping all phenomena in capitalist society succeed in concealing reality, but more is concealed than the historical, i.e. transitory, ephemeral nature of phenomena. *This* concealment is made possible by the fact that in capitalist society man's environment, and especially the categories of economics, appear to him immediately and necessarily in forms of objectivity which conceal the fact that they are the categories of the *relations of men with each other*. Instead, they appear as things and the relations of things with each other. (1971, p. 14)

For Lukács, economics play an important role in masking the reality of social relations under capitalism. This notion is accepted by this book but not an accusation reserved for economics alone. Rather, ECJ, and the conjunction of law and economics it represents, performs a complimentary role both to extend economic reason and in the more specific terms of being a source of fantasy concerning civil justice, one that translates into a disavowal of castration. In short, ECJ acts as a mask that stakeholders rely on to perform the concealment that Lukács describes.

Just as the notion of concealment ties Marx and Freud together, so too does completeness. Capitalism relies to a large extent on the failure of the subject to perfect or complete itself. This failure drives demand and desire, and thus the constant and repetitious renewal of systems, institutions, and fantasies at the level of the capitalist superstructure able to offer opportunities for stakeholder satisfaction. It allows them to believe in a chance of finding the lost object. Capitalism thrives on lack of perfection as a general rule, whether at the level of the commodity, institution, system, or subject, whilst offering the promise to subjects that perfection is always near. For Walter Benjamin, this made capitalism 'a religion of pure cult, without dogma'. 'The nature of the religious movement which is capitalism', Benjamin claims, 'entails endurance right to the end, to the point where God, too, finally takes on the entire burden of guilt, to the point where the universe has been taken over by that despair which is actually its secret *hope*' (1996, p. 289).

Central to the notion of Equity fetishism is its ability to provide the subject, via language, with a means of enjoyment and disavowal of doubts regarding the promises that capitalism makes. Enjoyment that encompasses bureaucratic processes of civil justice that support stakeholder engagement in economic activity, competition with peers (fellow stakeholders), and the variegated risks of the market. Freud with Marx is, therefore, crucial to understanding the desires that underpin Equity and civil justice as part of a 'specific transformation of desire within and through the implementation of the capitalist worldview in social and subjective reality' (Tomšič 2015, p. 154). 'If we were to force the analogy between Freudian fetishism and Marxian fetishism' says Jean-Joseph Goux, 'we might say that the *void* that is filled and veiled by the economic fetish is the "transcendental" element of interpersonal relations, of the exchange of vital activities' (1990, p. 158). He concludes, 'But this "transcendental" aspect of exchange is precisely the location of the surplus value, which is concerned not only with the political economy but with social *power* in general' (Goux 1990, p. 158).

REFERENCES

BOOKS AND ARTICLES

Althusser, L. *On Ideology*. 2008. London: Verso.
Aristodemou, M. *Law, Psychoanalysis, Society: Taking the Unconscious Seriously*. 2014. Abingdon: Routledge.
Aristotle. *The Nicomachean Ethics*. Translated by David Ross. 2009. Oxford: Oxford World Classics.

Balibar, E. *The Philosophy of Marx*. Translated by Chris Turner. 2017. London: Verso.

Baudrillard, J. *For a Critique of the Political Economy of the Sign*. Translated by Charles Levin. 1981. St. Louis: Telos Press Ltd.

Benjamin, W. *Walter Benjamin Selected Writings, Volume 1, 1913–1926*. Edited by Marcus Bullock and Michael W. Jennings. 1996. Cambridge: The Belknap Press of Harvard University Press.

Birks, P. Equity in the Modern Law: An Exercise in Taxonomy. *Western Australian Law Review*, Vol. 26, No. 1 (July 1996), pp. 1–99.

Birks, P. *Unjust Enrichment*. 2nd Edition. 2005. Oxford: Oxford University Press.

Chesterman, S. Beyond Fusion Fallacy: The Transformation of Equity and Derrida's 'The Force of Law'. *Journal of Law and Society*, Vol. 24, No. 3 (September 1997), pp. 350–376.

Freud, S. *The Future of an Illusion, Civilization and Its Discontents and Other Works: The Standard Edition Volume XXI (1927–1931)*. Translated and Edited by James Strachey. 2001. London: Vintage.

Gabel, P., Feinman, J. Contract Law as Ideology. *The Politics of Law: A Progressive Critique*. 3rd Edition. Edited by David Kairys. 1998. New York: Basic Books, pp. 497–510.

Gorz, A. *Critique of Economic Reason*. 1989. London: Verso.

Goux, J.J. *Symbolic Economies: After Marx and Freud*. Translated by Jennifer Curtiss Gage. 1990. Ithaca: Cornell University Press.

Gray, K., Gray, S.F. *Elements of Land Law*. 5th Edition. 2009. Oxford: Oxford University Press.

Haldar, P. Equity as a Question of Decorum and Manners: Conscience as Vision. *Pólemos*, Vol. 10, No. 2 (September 2016), pp. 311–328.

Halliwell, M. *Equity and Good Conscience*. 2nd Edition. 2004. London: Old Bailey Press.

Harpham, G.G. *Language Alone: The Critical Fetish of Modernity*. 2002. London: Routledge.

Lacan, J. *Écrits: A Selection*. Translated by Alan Sheridan. 2001. London: Routledge Classics.

Lukács, G. *History and Class Consciousness: Studies in Marxist Dialectics*. Translated by Rodney Livingstone. 1971. London: Merlin Press.

Marx, K., Engels, F. *Collected Works, Volume 3 1843–1844*. 1975. London: Lawrence & Wishart.

McGowan, T. *Capitalism and Desire: The Psychic Cost of Free Markets*. 2016. New York: Columbia University Press.

Martin, J.E. *Modern Equity*. 19th Edition. 2012. London: Sweet & Maxwell.

Meagher, R.P., Gummow, W.M.C., Lehane, J.R.F. *Equity Doctrines & Remedies*. 3rd edition. 1992. Sydney: Butterworths.

Millett, P.J. Equity's Place in the Law of Commerce. *Law Quarterly Review*, Vol. 114 (April 1998), pp. 214–227.

Neuberger, L. Equity, ADR, Arbitration and the Law: Different Dimension of Justice. The Fourth Keating Lecture. 19 May 2010. http://www.civilmedi ation.org/downloads-get?id=98.

Pashukanis, E.B. *Law & Marxism: A General Theory Towards a Critique of the Fundamental Juridical Concepts*. Translated by Barbara Einhorn. Edited by Chris Arthur. 1989. London: Pluto Press.

Selden, J. Table Talk of John Selden. 1856. London: J.R. Smith. https://arc hive.org/details/tabletalkofjohns00seldiala.

Stiglitz, J.E. *The Price of Inequality*. 2013. London: Penguin Books.

Tomšič, S. *The Capitalist Unconscious: Marx and Lacan*. 2015. London: Verso.

Virgo, G. *The Principles of Equity & Trusts*. 2012. Oxford: Oxford University Press.

Watt, G. *Equity Stirring: The Story of Justice Beyond Law*. 2012. Oxford: Hart Publishing.

Žižek, S. *The Sublime Object of Ideology*. 1989. London: Verso.

CHAPTER 7

Fetishism in Action

INTRODUCTION

This chapter comprises two parts. First, a discussion on the relation-ship between fetishism and ideology that will look in more depth at the ideas raised earlier in the book. Second, given that fetishism is not a self-contained concept within Freud's work but exists in dialogue with several other formulations, to develop a theory of fetishism relevant to this book it is necessary to examine some other areas. Covered during this chapter will be Freud's formulations of perversion, castration, phallus, and narcissism.

FETISHISM AND IDEOLOGY

The characteristics of fetishism and ideology as they appear during this book overlap. They are individually significant, but so is the dialogue between them. To echo Henry Krips, I claim that a joint account of fetishism and ideology reveals 'how social structures, and specifically ideo-logical practices, shape psychic structures at the communal level' (1999, p. 73), with that formula applied to a public franchise with the civil justice system in particular. Further, the fetishism described here reflects the influence of capitalist ideology. Concomitant with the fantasies that capitalism arouses to shape society and the existence of subjects within it, by, for example, equating wealth and property ownership with subjective

R. Herian, *Capitalism and the Equity Fetish*,
https://doi.org/10.1007/978-3-030-66523-4_7

ideals of satisfaction, the subject engages in a fetishisitic disavowal that
permits knowledge and ignorance of the realities of capitalism and capitalist ideology to coexist (McGowan 2016, p. 97). The disavowal of the
fact that wealth and property ownership offer no guarantees of personal
satisfaction. And capitalism cynically prompts the subject to engage in
ongoing encounters between the loss of their object of primal desire and
a series of substitutions it encourages the subject to believe will make up
for that loss. It is the subject's search for the lost object and accumulation
of fetishes as substitutions for what they lose that brings them into contact
with socioeconomic and legal forms and institutions that promise to both
deliver the object and help facilitate the subject's search for it. From the
point of view of this book that means Equity, private property and civil
justice, which together give the stakeholder the appearance of an answer
to the question of the lack at the centre of their unconscious desires. In
short, a fantasy built around the stakeholder's search for the lost object.
And if Equity and institutions such as trusts become substitutions for the
object themselves, they are fetishized.

At the heart of Marx's definition of 'the *fetishisitic character*, which
attaches to the products of labour so soon as they are produced in the
form of commodities', is the notion that 'the commodity form and the
value relation between the labour products which finds expression in the
commodity form have nothing whatever to do with the physical properties of the commodities or with the material relations that arise out of
these physical properties' (1930, pp. 45–46). Marx situates this definition in an analogy from the 'nebulous world of religion', whereby 'the
products of the human mind become independent shapes, endowed with
lives of their own' (1930, p. 45). Hence even though Marx himself
borrowed the concept of fetishism to address purely economic questions,
as Žižek maintains: 'the dialectics of the commodity-form present us with
a pure – distilled, so to speak – version of a mechanism offering us a
key to the theoretical understanding of phenomena which, at first sight,
have nothing whatsoever to do with the field of political economy (law,
religion, and so on)' (1989, p. 9).

Where we can show Equity fetishism's roots in the private property
order, claims that Equity and political economy can have nothing in
common, as Žižek states regarding the general law, are false. The notion
that 'in the commodity-form there is definitely more at stake than the
commodity-form itself' entirely accords with the argument made here that

Equity fetishism begins with commodity fetishism, augments or channels it and thus fosters a peculiar (if not exactly new) modality rooted in the subject's belief in and devotion to the bureaucratic object(ive)s of Equity and ECJ (Žižek 1989, p. 9). This echoes Henri Lefebvre's suggestion that 'where economy and philosophy meet lies the theory of *fetishism*', and it is possible, I argue, that where economy and Equity meet, we find Equity fetishism (2014, p. 198).

Althusser's notion of interpellation explains Equity as a special signifying system *qua* fetish, via the significance of the overlap between fetishism and ideology. That 'Equity can be described but not defined' and that 'in order to understand the diversity and resultant power of equity it is vital to see it in action' shows its slipperiness and sheer instability as a sign (Meagher et al. 1992, p. 4). Equity, as we know, harbours other signs and chains of meaning: fairness, equality, 'good' conscience, and so on that allows it not only to lure subjects—a function of its fetishization; Böhme for example talks of the 'magnetic power' of the fetish, and its ability to mesmerise and entice (2014, p. 264)—but, followings Althusser's notion of interpellation, to 'hail' and thus recruit subjects and transform them into more engaged economic subjects through a system of civil justice steeped in capitalist ideology (2008, p. 48).

As I have argued, stakeholders who seek vindication of their private property rights or a remedy in the civil justice system, engages Equity and ECJ at a specific level of capitalist ideology. Étienne Balibar points to the significance of private property and the role of private law in determining the State infrastructure (the economic base) and superstructure (the politico-legal and ideological levels constructed on top of the economic base). 'The floors of the superstructure are not determinate in the last instance', says Althusser, 'they are determined by the effectivity of the base' (2008, p. 9). A notion that Balibar builds on in his consideration of the law of property when he states the importance of 'characterizing the degree of relative autonomy of the economic structure with respect to the equally "regional" structure of the "legal and political forms"' (Althusser and Balibar 2009, p. 254). Within the ambit of what Balibar calls legal forms, we can count certainty and flexibility as core intellectual and practical contributions that the conjunction of Common Law and Equity *qua* complete justice has made to the economic base of capitalist society.

Central to understanding civil justice and expectations of it on behalf of capitalist ideology to bring subjects into proximity with, what Althusser considers being, the need 'to perform their tasks conscientiously', is the range of processes and strategies shaped by ideology that ECJ facilitates and enforces (2008, p. 7). 'Law is central to capitalism', as Alastair Hudson suggests, and 'Law is the means by which capitalism gets its work done' (2018, p. 58). As we have seen, nowhere is this more apparent than the complicity of Equity in particular in the ideological processes underpinning the private property order. Under capitalism, property has unassailable significance as a potent ideological fiction of 'permanent and unstoppable progress with no foundations whatsoever in economic or political reality but which the self-proclaimed economic experts persistently substantiate with statistical data, economic mathematics and political [as well as legal] reforms throughout history' [my addition] (Tomšič 2015, pp. 162–163). Equity fetishism engenders enjoyment that relates to the ideological belief that, engagement with and in the private property order, epitomized by the use, abuse or alienation of property, enables 'a stable and full-functioning social relation' to emerge from the present social inequalities (Tomšič 2015, p. 162).

Through the practices of civil justice and the bureaucratic means set in motion by Equity's rules, doctrines and principles, capitalism sustains the fantasy of complete justice without ever being actualized or attained. Or rather, without it ever being known by the stakeholder that they can *never* attain complete justice. This point is crucial not only because it adds further to the explanation of fetishism as a function of ideology in the domain of property, but because it reveals the vital ingredient of perversion central to Freud's interpretation and understanding of fetishism. The perversion of a subject who finds enjoyment in the idea or knowledge of never locating the lost object, and, perhaps more interestingly, also in only ever mapping the coordinates of its location, namely an enjoyment in the bureaucracy of civil justice. This point recalls the earlier discussion of the significance of the neurotic legal pursuit for certainty of legal meaning in language, and its relationship to the perverse desire of the stakeholder, what I referred to previously as the two working hand-in-hand in structuring a fantasy of Equity fetishism.

Further, the fixing of enjoyment onto an object, such as a bureaucratic and juridical pursuit of certainty, other than the object of desire reflects Krips' notion of a 'chaperone', which he links with Lacan's *objet a* as 'both objects of the drive and object-cause of desire' (1999, p. 28). 'A chaperone', says Krips, 'may take on the characteristics of an *objet a*. Although not herself desired by the suitor, she is nonetheless the cause of his desire as well as the center of the evasive activities through which he produces his pleasure' (1999, p. 28). We might say that Equity chaperones the stakeholder in the private property order by creating a layer of bureaucracy that alienates and distances the subject from the notional object of desire. Baudrillard claims that fetishism attaches to a particular sign object 'eviscerated of its substance and history, and reduced to the state of marking a difference, epitomizing a whole system of differences' (1981, p. 93). To understand fetishism, therefore, we must look for a particular object that has not dissolved in the broader capitalist superstructure but completely eviscerated regarding it. The fetish is never a material or conceptual object, but a monument to castration. It at once reveals and masks a site of lack that is always already in the subject. Ideology is an additional layer, a fictive cloak which further conceals what the fetish already masks. Or, rather, there is a dialogue between fetishism and ideology that involves a doubling of concealment. Sometimes ideology precedes fetishism, in others the reverse is true.

Concepts in Relation to Fetishism

Fetishism, as succinctly put by Jean Baudrillard, is a 'psychoanalytic process of perverse structure' (1981, p. 90). This formulation of fetishism refers, as Christopher Gemerchak has claimed, to Freud's 'mature' conceptualization found in his 1927 article *Fetishism*, and in his 1938 article *The Splitting of the Ego in Defence Processes*, and finally in his 1938–1940 discussion of 'The External World' in *An Outline of Psycho-Analysis* (2004b, p. 263). All three sources build upon but differ from Freud's earlier work on fetishism stemming from his *Three Essays on Sexuality* in 1905 (2001a).

Across this body of work, we see Freud's thinking on fetishism develop from the fetish as a replacement for the 'normal sexual object [...] by another which bears some relation to it, but is entirely unsuited to serve the normal sexual aim', to the idea that the fetish replaces 'a specific and very special' object, namely the mother's phallus (2001a, p. 153; 2006, p. 90). Freud's earlier work on fetishism was also further developed in an unpublished paper, 'On the Genesis of Fetishism', presented to the Vienna Psycho-Analytical Society on 24 February 1909 (2001c, pp. 149–150). The timing of this unpublished article is notable because it immediately followed Freud's introduction of the *castration complex* in 1908 in an article 'On the Sexual Theories of Children', and immediately preceded Freud's introduction of the *Oedipus complex* in his 1910

article, 'A Special Type of Choice of Object Made by Men', both of which
would eventually come to underpin his mature theories on fetishism.
Chapter 8 will deal specifically with Equity fetishism and three of the
primary features that structure fetishism based on Freud's mature conceptualization, namely, belief, disavowal (*Verleugnung*) and memorialization.
To prepare for that later discussion, the rest of this chapter will focus
on four Freudian concepts important to understanding and explaining
fetishism in terms of the subject of this book but are themselves not
limited to fetishism. The four concepts are perversion, castration, phallus,
and narcissism.

Perversion

In the *Three Essays on Sexuality*, Freud describes perversion under the
heading 'deviations in respect of the sexual aim' (2001a, p. 149). 'The
normal sexual aim is regarded as being the union of the genitals in the
act known as copulation', says Freud, 'which leads to a release of the
sexual tension and a temporary extinction of the sexual instinct – a satisfaction analogous to the sating of hunger' (2001a, p. 149). For Freud,
there is a baseline instinct because of the subject's sexual aim which,
once met, is extinguished. Importantly this A to B undertaking by the
subject in attempting to satisfy the instinctual drive is considered by Freud
to be '*normal*'. Freud continues: 'But even in the most normal sexual
process we may detect rudiments which, if they had developed, would
have led to the deviations described as "perversions"' (2001a, p. 149). At
a causal level perversion disrupts the A to B undertaking of satisfaction
and describes a deviation in the form of A going not to B but to either
C, D, E, F, and so on. Perversions are thus 'sexual activities which either
(a) extend, in an anatomical sense, beyond the regions of the body that
are designed for sexual union, or (b) linger over the intermediate relations to the sexual object which should normally be traversed rapidly on
the path towards the final sexual aim' (Freud 2001a, p. 150). It is amid
this description of perversion that Freud first situates fetishism as cases 'in
which the normal sexual object is replaced by another which bears some
relation to it, but is entirely unsuited to serve the normal sexual aim'
(2001a, p. 153).

   As stated previously, this book does not settle on Freud's initial formulation of fetishism in the *Three Essays* but draws instead on his work on
fetishism from 1927 onwards. It is important to understand how, if at

all, Freud's notion of perversion changed. It is important to understand that perversion transcends description only in terms of sexual practices. We can talk about perversions in terms of the sublimation of broader social practices and as a meta-psychology, even though, as Freud argued, sublimation is an outcome of sexual instincts and drives. We can see a link between Marx and Freud when Freud himself, in *Civilisation and Its Discontents*, offers a bridge between the personal (psychic) economy of the subject and the economic structure of society (supported by the private property order) across which perversion leaves its mark in the form of often subtle aberrations from the norm (2001c). To revert briefly to Freud's earlier formulations of perversion, non-pathological forms of perversion that exist alongside the norm rather than ousting it (2001a, p. 161).

The later Freud, in ways of particular note here, locates perversion sublimated into the realm of property (whether tangible or intangible) and specifically 'the attraction in general of forbidden things' that countermands 'an undeniable diminution in the potentialities of enjoyment' brought about by a greater surrendering by the subject to the reality principle (2001c, p. 79). In search of enjoyment, the subject turns in fantasy to the 'irresistibility of perverse instincts' to satisfy desires (Freud 2001c, p. 79). This enables a negotiation of the frustrations presented by the external world, by unlocking forms of satisfaction and enjoyment that, even when not satisfactory possess a 'special quality' that seems 'finer and higher' than the norm (Freud 2001c, p. 79). That generates a fetishistic inversion akin, as Žižek suggests, to the commodity form in Marx's analysis. In the commodity form, as Žižek maintains, there is 'definitely more at stake than the commodity-form itself' (1989, p. 9). In terms of Equity fetishism, as with other examples of fetishism that help explain the vagaries of social relations in fields beyond the economic interpretation offered by Marx, it is the 'more' that Žižek highlights that is key to understanding what he calls 'the fascinating power of attraction' wielded by the fetish over many fields of social relations (1989, p. 10).

Where definitions of perversion mean a deviation from normality, despite Marx not using the term himself, it is possible to make the case that Marx's use of fetishism relies on a reading of socioeconomic structures that are, in themselves, perverse. This is because, as Marx says, we base these relations in the 'very queer' nature of the commodity which is 'full of metaphysical subtleties and theological whimsies' (1930,

p. 44). Inversely Marx's use of fetishism is anything but perverse precisely because it posits objectively the normal socioeconomic conditions as they exist under capitalism. For Marx, there is no escaping the fetishistic character of the commodity form because it mirrors fundamental social relations. Similarly, I claim, Equity fetishism is a product of the *normal* functioning of civil justice, where its function accords with economic reason and logic.

Following Marx, we can see that Equity fetishism begins from a point in which the fetishistic character at the heart of private property order represents the *status quo*. And it is possible to understand the perversion of Equity fetishism in this sense by reconsidering Gray and Gray's definition of property not as a thing but a *power relationship*, whereby 'a relationship of social and legal legitimacy' exists 'between a person and a valued resource (whether tangible or intangible)' (2009, p. 87). Because the relationship Gray and Gray highlight mirrors the nature of commodity fetishism outlined by Marx, then it is normatively fetishistic in nature. We can adjust Gray and Gray's outline to read, 'a relationship of social […] legitimacy existing between a person and a valued resource (whether tangible or intangible)'. A relationship that keeps or emphasizes only the *social* dimension of the property order's legitimacy.

The perversion of Equity fetishism thus lies in interventions in civil justice by Equity that pervert a purely social legitimacy existing between a person and a valued resource by constructing or imposing the fantasy (latent in capitalism) of complete justice and Equity's legitimacy onto the private property order. In this instance, the focus is on the point at which property and law intersect and establish, in Gray and Gray's terms, 'legitimacy', and in the terms of this book, Equity fetishism. Further, if the 'theory of fetishism demonstrates the *economic, everyday* basis of the *philosophical* theories of mystification and alienation' as Lefebvre claims, then we can also say that the perversity of Equity fetishism lies in Equity's alienation of already alienated commodity (property) forms (2014, p. 199). This means that Equity fetishism enacts a further masking of the immediacy of economic and social realities beyond that already maintained by the commodity form and thus further envelops and disguises the human relations that make up the property form (Lefebvre 2014, p. 199).

At stake from this deeper mystification of social relations enacted by Equity fetishism is precisely that which describes the difference between the economic (Marxist) and (meta)psychological (Freudian) fetish. Namely, suspension of the social link and an increased atomization of the subject that reflects the notion that the economic fetish 'may be the privileged embodiment of value, but it is also the support of exchange', as Samo Tomšič explains, whilst the fetish in Freudian terms 'excludes the economy exchange and bends the libidinal economy back onto itself' (2015, p. 154). As a result, it is 'strictly private' perverse subjects who recognize only themselves in the property form as 'selfish' litigant and de-socialized (de-humanized) individuals, in ways that equally accord with the concept of narcissism, as discussed shortly (Jolowicz 1983; Tomšič 2015, p. 154). So, whilst 'man has developed and has raised himself above the animal and biological condition of his lowly beginnings via socio-economic fetishism and self-alienation', as Lefebvre contends, it has resulted in very particular outcomes in terms of the concept of the subject of capitalism, namely, '*the human has been formed through dehumaniza-tion* – dialectically' (2014, p. 200). As Tomšič states: 'Capitalism is *not* perversion, but it *demands* perversion from its subjects', and via Equity fetishism, the stakeholder can realize this perverse duty (2015, p. 151).

Castration

Castration is a central theme in fetishism, as it was for much of Freud's work. Given the notable privileging of the male gender in his formulation of theories of sexuality, Freud often evokes a literal sense of castration (the cutting off of the penis) in his discussions. This literality occurs in Freud's discussion of fetishism, as elsewhere in his work (the basis of the anxiety that starts the latency period in boys and which informs the *castration complex*), when, for example, the fetishist (Freud refers to the 'patient') confronts the 'proof of the possibility of his being castrated himself' because females have no penis (1964, p. 202). In her book on the erotics of markets, Jeanne Schroeder discusses the particular gendered aspects of castration. 'The two sexes are two positions one can take with respect to castration', claims Schroeder, 'denial and acceptance. The masculine, which feels that he has lost a precious part of himself, falsely claims to possess and exchange the object of desire. The feminine, which feels that she has lost her selfhood, accepts the role of identification with the enjoy-ment of the object of desire' (2004, p. 241). Freud considers castration a male concern (the patient 'who is almost always male'), albeit in dialogue with a corresponding discovery of anatomical difference to the female body (1964, p. 202). This point of difference is important because of the *threat* of parity. The fact (the threat) that castration may make the male female-like, adding further to the anxiety of the subject. For the fetishist, the fetish object serves partly to dispel or displace this anxiety. 'The creation of the fetish', says Freud, 'was due to an intention to destroy the evidence for the possibility of castration, so the fear of castration could be avoided' (1964, p. 203).

Whilst Freud often evokes a literal sense of castration through direct reference to the penis, his reliance on myth (namely the Oedipus myth) as a basis for much of his aetiology betrays him not meaning castration and the particular reference to anatomical organ (penis) literally as *the* site of primal desire central to the development of human sexuality. Rather, as Henry Krips suggests, 'in the case of fetishism staged within the Oedipus myth, as for fetishism generally, the object of desire must reside somewhere other than the fetish' (1999, p. 69). Hence, as the paradigm of negativity ('the symbolic operation that constitutes the subject as split and decentralised') castration corresponds closely with psychic functions such as fantasy and the concept of loss (Tomšič 2015, p. 152). Or, given the terms of the present discussion, 'the capitalist fantasy of an uncastrated subject' (Tomšič 2015, p. 152). The castration and Oedipus complexes both focus on the child's fantasy concerning his father, or as Freud frames it in *Totem and Taboo*, 'the part of a dreaded enemy to the sexual interests of childhood', who threatens to punish the child by castration 'or its substitute, blinding' (2001b, p. 130). The threat, therefore, further to that discussed above, relates to fantasy to deflect the trauma of castration whilst facilitating the repetition of primal desires structured around the infliction of loss (Freud 2006, p. 94).

The connection between castration and the inauguration of the super-ego function has particular resonance regarding the language of Equity because it is through the super-ego that Freud traces the roots of conscience (2001c, p. 125). The super-ego function, the internalized inheritance of the parental influence, that 'garrison in a conquered city' that 'takes the father's place, depersonalizing the father figure and incorporating it in the subject in the form of a higher and punitive law' (Freud 2001c, p. 124; Aristodemou 2014, p. 55). Regarding legal critique, this makes castration an important theme because it talks to the social (externalized) function of law. In a description of conscience that would befit historical narratives of Equity relating to a time when Equity was the preserve of Roman Catholic lawyers such as Thomas More (see, Herian 2020), Freud maintains that, 'As long as things go well with a man his conscience is lenient and lets the ego do all sorts of things; but when misfortune befalls him, he searches his soul, acknowledges his sinfulness, heightens the demands of his conscience, imposes abstinences on himself and punishes himself with penances' (2001c, p. 126). The function of the super-ego, whilst important to a critique of Equity, takes the matter of castration away from the central theme of fetishism and is therefore not overly relevant here. It warrants mention, however, because, as Freud maintains, the 'super-ego is in fact the heir to the Oedipus complex and is only established after the complex has been disposed of', which, as a description of the psychic basis to the formation of subjective conscience, is significant for understanding the extension of conscience as a juridical mechanism within Equity (1964, p. 205).

Above all, we need to read castration as a symbolic gesture. Under these terms castration ceases to represent anatomy (the penis) and instead describes the loss of an object of desire, namely the phallus which the subject is always searching for. So, whilst Freud states on the one hand that 'the fetish is a penis substitute', it is also a substitute for 'the woman's (mother's) phallus' (2006, pp. 90–91). We will consider in Chapter 8 the structuring of fetishism around the symbolic gesture of castration—how, for example, 'the fetishist denies [disavows] the unwelcome fact of female castration' (Freud 2006, p. 93). It is worth noting at this point however that castration is central to compromise as a vital feature of memorialization in fetishism. A compromise, as Böhme maintains, 'that is made in the unconscious between the fear of castration and the saviour of the phallus' (2014, p. 319).

Phallus

Regarding fetishism, a crucial question is, as the quote from Freud above suggests, the extent to which the phallus and penis are interchangeable. Where a strictly anatomical reference ends and symbolism begins; a shift in reference between genitalia males possess and females lacks, a gap in which (in the in-between) the subject imagines a substitute in fantasy for the penis, one capable of preventing them from trembling 'for the continued possession of one's own penis' (Freud 1964, p. 203). For Freud, the phallic phase of sexual development signals a divergence between the sexes from the premise of 'the universal presence of the penis' (1964, p. 154). This divergence lies at the root of Freud's particularly patriarchal distinction between the development of male sexuality versus the vain attempts of female sexuality to 'do the same as the boy', which for Freud ultimately leads to (penis) envy, a sense of inferiority, and the 'first disappointment in rivalry' for the girl against the boy (1964, pp. 154–155).

Post-Freud, and most notably in the work of Jacques Lacan, the phallus ceases to be a mere synonym for the penis, and functions instead, as Böhme maintains, as 'the symbolic counterpart to castration' (2014, p. 297). This Lacanian shift in phallic status shows the significance of the organ to fantasy and in distinction to Freud 'that the accession to subjectivity involves introducing the subject into an economy of lack defined in relation to the phallus' (Krips 1999, p. 8). Henry Krips calls this the 'omnihistorical' significance that Lacan gives to the phallus helps to further distinguish the penis from the phallus, and thus, as Krips further argues, 'Lacan's reworking of the Freudian architectonic promises to avoid' the privileged place Freud's theory of castration gives to 'the penis in the constitution of the human psychic economy' (1999, p. 8). For Krips, the 'Lacanian reworking of the Freudian architectonic enables a reconceptualization of the fetish', most notably in terms of Lacan's desig-nation of the object of desire (*objet a*) *qua* phallus (1999, p. 9). However, some have argued that Lacan's designation of the phallus 'responds to the logic implicit in Freud's formulations on the penis', and, therefore, 'Lacan's terminological innovation simply clarifies certain distinctions that were already implicit in Freud's work' (Evans 1996, pp. 140–141).

The distinction Lacan makes between the penis and phallus is impor-tant, especially where it allows for a conceptualization of the socioe-conomic significance and function of the phallus that highlights the importance of lack in understanding, not only certain motivations under-pinning fetishism, but the broader ideological effects that lack is complicit in defining. For example, how the phallus is conceptually important to a critique of law *qua* bureaucratic systems, administrations and institu-tions of authority. The 'phallus as the signifier of lack in the Other, where the place of the Other (which may be occupied by the mother, a policeman, or any other authority figure) is', Krips maintains, 'the exter-nally projected position from which the subject looks for an answer to the question of his or her own desire' (1999, p. 8).

Translated into the terms of the present book: Equity or ECJ as a substitute phallus (fetish) is a response to the lack in complete justice (Other), which is the externally projected position of desire for the economic subject. Specifically, it is a position engendered by the displace-ment onto individual or atomized private property or the private property order of a primal subjective desire for the lost object. Whether as an abstract socio-legal concept, a politico-economic institution (a sedimentation of long-standing customs and traditions) or order (something that is both organized at the social level and organizes the social), in private property the subject has a site to which they can return repeatedly in search of the lost object and an answer to their own desire. As a mediator of this interaction between the stakeholder and property Equity occupies the position of the (substitute) phallus, a position in fantasy that points to a fundamental lack in complete justice, whilst staving off the anxieties of stakeholders locked into a pattern of repeating their own primal lack with no hope of resolution or satisfaction.

Narcissism

Freud introduces narcissism as a perversion ('an individual treats his own body in the same way in which he might treat that of any other sexual object'), an analytic status that might more readily explain its relationship to fetishism (as itself a perverse mechanism). He is also quick to acknowledge that, via what he calls 'the difficulties encountered in the psychoanalytical treatment of neurotics', we also find narcissism in 'the normal sexual development of human beings' (2006, p. 358). Further supported by the same biological inferences that Freud applies to his theory of the drives, notably the object-cathexis discussed earlier in this chapter, Freud offers two statements in *On the Introduction of Narcissism* that will structure the definition deemed appropriate here.

First, Freud's notion of the double-existence of the individual 'both as an end in himself, and as a link in a chain he serves against his will, or at any rate regardless of his will'; he continues (finally summarizing his point with an uncanny reference to property law),

> He even supposes sexuality to be one of his own designs – whereas on alternative view he appears as a mere appendage of his germ-plasm, to whose purposes he devotes all his energies in return for the reward of a mere sensation of pleasure. On this view, he is but the mortal vehicle of a - perhaps – immortal essence; like the lord of an entailed estate, he is but the temporary occupant of an institution that will outlast him. (2006, pp. 362–363)

Second, that the 'development of the ego consists in an ever-increasing separation from one's primary narcissism, and gives rise to an intense struggle to retrieve it'; Freud continues,

> This separation occurs through the displacement of libido on to an ego-ideal imposed from without; gratification occurs through fulfilment of that ideal. At the same time, the ego sends forth libidinal object-cathexes. It becomes depleted for the sake of these cathexes and for the sake of the ego-ideal, but replenishes itself through object-gratifications and through fulfilment of the ideal. (2006, p. 386)

Both statements turn upon an account of narcissism predicated on the subject's investment in an object other to the self. Further, investment in the object as an external conductor (material or ideal) through which to channel what Freud refers to as the 'intense struggle to retrieve' a primary narcissism being lost relative to 'an ever-increasing separation' (2006, p. 386). Narcissism is not a process without consequences for the internal psychic structure of the subject. That the second statement focuses so intently on the ego betrays Freud's orientation of narcissism simultaneously across internal and external worlds. As the two statements suggest, narcissism is a far-reaching concept in Freud's work that intersects with his other formulations. To ensure that the consideration of narcissism undertaken here remains within the margins of the concept of fetishism, we must return to Freud's direct reference to narcissism in his mature formulation of fetishism. Here is the passage in full in which Freud applies the concept of narcissism to fetishism,

> [A] fetish is a substitute for the woman's (mother's) phallus, which the little boy once believed in and which – for reasons well known to us – he does not want to give up. What has happened, then, is this: the boy has refused to acknowledge the fact that he has perceived that women have no penis. No, this cannot be true, because if women have been castrated, then his own penis is in danger, *and the piece of narcissism, with which nature providently equips this very organ, recoils at the thought* [my emphasis]. (2006, p. 91)

Here Freud applies narcissism in a very similar vein to that regarding the child's reconciliation of the ego and sexual drives in the body (breast) of the mother. On the matter of that formative stage in the development of the drives Freud maintains that, 'There is no doubt that, to begin with, the child does not distinguish between the breast and its own body; when the breast has to be separated from the body and shifted to the *"outside"* because the child so often finds it absent, it carries with it as an *"object"* a part of the original narcissistic libidinal cathexis' (1964, p. 188).

That Freud conceptually connects the organ (penis) equipped with 'a piece of narcissism' and the external object (breast) as a part of the original narcissistic libidinal cathexis is entirely accurate given the proximity of the two as stages in Freud's development of human sexuality: the mother is the child's first seducer and the 'prototype of all later love-relations' (1964, p. 188). Thus it is from the object-breast to object-penis and the child's manipulation of each to satisfy a need and derive pleasure that translates narcissism along the chain of sexual development, eventually finding its way into the theory of fetishism as and when a perverse shift occurs in sexual development. As maintained above, therefore, it is across both internal and external worlds that narcissism features in fetishism and in particular at the point of the ego's recoiling at the thought of castration, allowing the fetish to inhabit a space in fantasy 'opened up by the demise of primary narcissism' (Gemerchak 2004a, p. 39).

Narcissism in terms of fetishism plays a vital role on two successive counts. First, as a sign of a primary inseparable unity or totality (the child with the mother). It directly relates this primary narcissism to the primal desire *qua* mother-child relation, hence why it is so powerful a force acting on the psychic economy of the subject long after childhood. Therefore, the subject repeatedly invests a great deal of energy trying to find the lost object and restore a sense of unity and completeness that they believe the object represents. That restoration of the primal unity is an impossible task explains why the subject willingly invests so much energy (time, money, property, exposure to risk, and so on) in trying to recreate the unity or instituting fetishes able to support the fantasy of completeness. Complete justice, as described, is symptomatic of this attempt at replication of primary narcissism within the complementary fields of private property and civil justice. Second, a secondary narcissism emerges as alienation that constantly reminds the subject that they have settled for less than their heart's desire. They have not, and never will return to primary narcissism because the lost object is, by definition, always already lost and unrecoverable. This secondary (traumatic) narcissism is central to fetishism because the fetish offers the subject a belief in the possibility of a return to primary narcissism, albeit a fantastical belief accompanied by a necessary process of disavowal that at once sustains the fantasy and mitigates the subject's anxiety concerning the lost object of desire.

REFERENCES

BOOKS & ARTICLES

Althusser, L. *On Ideology*. 2008. London: Verso.

Althusser, L., Balibar, E. *Reading Capital*. Translated by Ben Brewster. 2009. London: Verso.

Aristodemou, M. *Law, Psychoanalysis, Society: Taking the Unconscious Seriously*. 2014. Abingdon: Routledge.

Baudrillard, J. *For a Critique of the Political Economy of the Sign*. Translated by Charles Levin. 1981. St. Louis: Telos Press Ltd.

Böhme, H. *Fetishism and Culture: A Different Theory of Modernity*. Translated by Anna Galt. 2014. Berlin: De Gruyter.

Evans, D. *An Introductory Dictionary of Lacanian Psychoanalysis*. 1996. London: Routledge.

Freud, S. *Moses and Monotheism, an Outline of Psycho-Analysis and Other Works: The Standard Edition Volume XXIII (1937–1939)*. Translated and Edited by James Strachey. 1964. London: The Hogarth Press.

Freud, S. *A Case of Hysteria, Three Essays on Sexuality and Other Works: The Standard Edition Volume VII (1901–1905)*. Translated and Edited by James Strachey. 2001a. London: Vintage.

Freud, S. *Totem and Taboo and Other Works: The Standard Edition Volume XIII (1913–1914)*. Translated and Edited by James Strachey. 2001b. London: Vintage.

Freud, S. *The Future of an Illusion, Civilization and Its Discontents and Other Works: The Standard Edition Volume XXI (1927–1931)*. Translated and Edited by James Strachey. 2001c. London: Vintage.

Freud, S. *The Penguin Freud Reader*. Edited by Adam Phillips. 2006. London: Penguin Classics.

Gemerchak, C.M. (ed.). *Everyday Extraordinary: Encountering Fetishism with Marx, Freud and Lacan*. 2004a. Leuven: Leuven University Press.

Gemerchak, C.M. Fetishism and Bad Faith: A Freudian Rebuttal to Sartre. *Janus Head*, Vol. 7, No. 2 (2004b), pp. 248–269.

Gray, K., Gray, S.F. *Elements of Land Law*. 5th Edition. 2009. Oxford: Oxford University Press.

Herian, R. The Conscience of Thomas More: An Introduction to Equity in Modernity. *The Heythrop Journal* (early access), 2020, pp. 1–12.

Hudson, A. Law as Capitalist Technique. *King's Law Journal*, Vol. 29, No. 1 (2018), pp. 58–87.

Jolowicz, J.A. General Ideas and the Reform of Civil Procedure. *Legal Studies*, Vol. 3, No. 3 (November 1983), pp. 295–314.

Krips, H. *Fetish: An Erotics of Culture*. 1999. Ithaca: Cornell University Press.

Lefebvre, H. *Critique of Everyday Life*. 2014. London: Verso.

Marx, K. *Capital Volume 1*. 1930. London: J.M. Dent & Sons Ltd.
McGowan, T. *Capitalism and Desire: The Psychic Cost of Free* Markets. 2016. New York: Columbia University Press.
Meagher, R.P., Gummow, W.M.C., Lehane, J.R.F. *Equity Doctrines & Remedies*. 3rd edition. 1992. Sydney: Butterworths.
Schroeder, J.L. *The Triumph of Venus: The Erotics of the Market*. 2004. Berkeley: University of California Press.
Tomšič, S. *The Capitalist Unconscious: Marx and Lacan*. 2015. London: Verso.
Žižek, S. *The Sublime Object of Ideology*. 1989. London: Verso.

Equity Fetishism

INTRODUCTION

Previous chapters have discussed the theoretical and material foundations of Equity fetishism, which can be summarized in the following three points that tell us an important story. To echo Robert Stoller, when he says that, 'An object (inanimate thing, animal, or body part) becomes a fetish when it stands for – condenses in itself – meanings that are, wholly or in crucial parts of the text, unconscious: a fetish is a story masquerading as an object' (Stoller 1985, p. 155). First, Equity fetishism draws upon and combines key elements of the work of both Marx and Freud, and is a phenomenon particularly associated with the psycho-juridical existence of stakeholders within capitalism. Second, central to Equity fetishism (as with all forms of fetishism) is a subject qua stakeholder whose search for complete justice is a response in fantasy to the traumatic fact of castration and the need to disavow it. And third, the private property order overseen by civil justice is where stakeholder's Equity fetishism is located and where it plays out. A site in which the stakeholder finds particular, perverse enjoyment in the form and substance of civil justice, including a vindication of property rights as a basis to support a culture of ownership and wealth provision. Building on these three foundations, the following chapter will return to Freud's formulation of fetishism to complete my theoretical outline and give a clearer picture of why it is Freud's and not only Marx's interpretation of fetishism that ultimately counts. This exploration will concentrate on three of the main psychical functions that structure fetishism and which, to paraphrase Freud, make it a very energetic action to maintain denial of castration: *belief, disavowal, and memorialization* (2006, p. 91).

BELIEF

Freud's core statement on fetishism involves a crucial instance of belief that occurs within the broader Oedipal aetiology and thus turns on the fundamental issue of castration and loss. 'A fetish is a substitute for the woman's (mother's) phallus, which', claims Freud, 'the little boy once believed in and which – for reasons well known to us – he does not want to give up' (2006, p. 91). The nature of the belief that Freud highlights is one which prevails in order for the fetish to function. Belief marks the subject (little boy) in the past, the present, and enduring into the future. Holding onto belief vouchsafes it for the subject into the future, endowing it with a certain narcissistic quality that Freud also attributes to the general function of the fetish (2006, p. 91).

Belief exists within the oedipal aetiology as complicit in an unavoidable confrontation that reveals a further important dimension to the belief in question. It is always already primed for a confrontation with a reality in which loss has occurred and one we expect the fetish to mask. Following Freud's 'little boy', Christopher Gemerchak maintains that 'because reality does not conform to what he hopes and expects it will be, he simply prefers it otherwise. He chooses, in effect, not to know what he knows' (2004b, p. 262). Whilst Gemerchak is pointing to the importance of disavowal to the fetish structure in his statement, it equally reveals a deliberate and, importantly, conscious commitment to belief made by the subject.

'At its most fundamental', Žižek argues, 'authentic belief does not concern facts, but gives expression to an unconditional ethical commitment' (2007, p. 117). Žižek's evaluation of belief here is not one derived from an analysis of fetishism. Yet, the ethical commitment of which Žižek speaks is one that resonates with the belief evoked by the fetish as a counterfactual function that we expect to mask the duality of the traumatic reality of castration and loss on behalf of the stakeholder. The commitment of the fetishist is precisely not ethical, but belief, consciously determined and thus not ignorant, maintains that it is. Kant arguably predicted (or vouchsafed) 'authentic belief' as a basis of Equity fetishism via his notion of *reverence*. 'What I recognise immediately as a law for me' claims Kant, 'I recognise with reverence, which means merely consciousness of the *subordination* of my will to a law without the mediation of external influences on my senses'. He continues: 'Immediate determination of the will by the law and consciousness of this determination is called *"reverence"*, so that reverence is regarded as the *effect* of the law on the subject and not as the *cause* of the law [...] The *object* of reverence is the *law* alone – that law which we impose *on ourselves* but yet as necessary in itself [...] All moral *interest*, so-called, consists solely in *reverence* for the law' (2005, p. 73). As far as there is a perverse ethical commitment within the structure of fetishism, therefore, it is a commitment that the subject reserves for or turns back (imposes) upon themselves. Self-commitment contained within a closed circuit of desire that exists only between the fetishist and the object.

Whilst there is no absolution of ethical responsibility for the fetishist, albeit a responsibility to themselves (to that piece of narcissism within the subject), it is a commitment that manifests as loyalty to the self or a self-regarding ethics, one that speaks to Freud's concept of the *ideal ego* which in transferring the individual's narcissism, 'finds itself possessed of every estimable perfection' (2006, p. 380). Freud also highlights the importance of distinguishing between *idealization* and *sublimation*. The former, as suggested above, is a more relevant associate of fetishism. As Freud maintains, 'To the extent [...] that sublimation has to do with drives whereas idealization has to do with objects, the two concepts need to be clearly distinguished from each other' (2006, p. 381). Self-regarding ethics and an associated belief structure that helps support it find particular form in private property and the corresponding alienation of the self that occurs with the desire to have rights and to own what is 'mine' (Davies 1999, p. 328). On this matter, we can again see how Equity fetishism marries two of the most significant contributions on the sociocultural and economic impact of fetishism, namely the commodity fetishism of Marx and the psychology of Freud. The alienation caused by the great ascendancy in the social sphere of the status of property rights and ownership beyond all but the wealthiest during the nineteenth century was a product of parallel sociocultural and economic shift. Pashukanis maintains that the 'dialectical development of the fundamental juridical concepts not only provides us with the legal form as a fully developed and articulated structure, but also reflects the actual process of historical development, a process which is synonymous with the process of development of bourgeois society itself' (1989, p. 59). Hence, I argue, it is important to consider Equity in that century, and thereafter, in terms of fetishism, and why we cannot overlook the significance of the Judicature reform agenda as conceived *within* the ambit of capitalism.

'It can be argued', says Böhme, 'that the nineteenth century is […] *the* saeculum of things' (2014, p. 5). He continues,

> Statistics about things show that compared to the eighteenth century, the number of available things, for example in a household, vastly increased. Industrialisation led to the proliferation of artificial things in daily use and consumption, and not just in the upper classes. Newly appearing department stores were described as cathedrals of commodities, displaying hundreds of thousands of things to bewitch the customer in an almost ritually staged presentation […] The average person extended the borders of his or her self into more and more object-spheres too. Stronger forms of capitalism promoted the pursuit of property, which often led to, for example, the bourgeois apartments of the *Gründrzeit*, stuffed with an almost unimaginable number of things […] People collected, traded, procured, desired, exhibited, consumed, used, bought and sold, hoarded and wasted, ordered and classified, evaluated and valued things with a mania and intensity unprecedented in the history of everyday life. (2014, p. 5)

The forms of fetishism that Böhme directly attributes to the proliferation of material property, and which I argue extends equally over a desire for property (and personal) rights, reveals the root system of self-regarding ethics and belief in contemporary capitalist society. And it explains why Equity fetishism is central to the economic life of self-respecting (and self-regarding) stakeholders. Further, Equity fetishism aptly fits the measure of this belief where we can view it in terms of 'premodern forms and institutions of magic, myth and cult, religion and festivities', which, as Böhme maintains, 'begin to disappear in the modern era', although 'the energies and needs bound up in them does not' (2014, p. 8). Instead, Böhme argues, 'they are released and now pervade all levels of modern social systems', a view that, whilst speaking to a far broader considera- tion of fetishism, nevertheless captures a sense of Equity and specifically the legacy of ecclesiastical conscience on its jurisprudence and procedure (2014, p. 8; Herian 2020).

DISAVOWAL

To develop the role played by belief in structuring fetishism it is vital to consider disavowal, understood here as a 'simultaneous acknowledgment and denial' (Gemerchak 2004b, p. 262). Disavowal is key to explaining why fetishism engages conscious processes as much if not more than those of the unconscious and why an analysis of fetishism does not begin and end with the unconscious. 'The first movement of disavowal is avowal', states Gemerchak, hence there is 'no disavowal without prior knowledge, and so it is clear that one cannot claim [retention] of belief out of ignorance' (2004b, p. 262). For present purposes, the significance of disavowal in fetishism begins with Octave Mannoni's well-known formulation (Je sais bien, mais quand-même), in which the fetishist knows very well that the fetish is not *the thing* (*das ding*), but turns away from such a reality by believing otherwise. For Mannoni the question at the heart of fetishism is, therefore, one of 'the possibility of simultaneously embracing two contrary beliefs, one official and one secret', which triggers a subjective paradox in the fetishist (2015, p. 151). On Mannoni's account, this simultaneous abandonment and retention of belief is an everyday, perhaps even banal occurrence, rather than the perverse undercurrent of life, which further adds to the notion of Equity fetishism as normative. A key difference that Mannoni highlights between the belief found in Freud's formulation of fetishism and other psychic mechanisms for the repression and negation of ideas is precisely the fact that the belief is repudiated but not repressed nor denied (2015, p. 151). In short, Mannoni points to the importance of disavowal in maintaining both the structure of belief and by extension the structure of the fetish itself.

Gemerchak echoes Mannoni in viewing disavowal as responsible for fetishism. 'Only by expanding Freud's notion of disavowal', argues Gemerchak, 'will we be able to understand fetishism as a fundamental possibility for the human subject' (2004a, p. 16). Disavowal is, Gemerchak further explains, 'the psychic anomaly that underpins Freud's mature conception of fetishism [...] an anomaly which henceforth served as a model for analysing structures as diverse as Marxist commodity fetishism, the Lacanian *objet a*, and primitive belief' (2004b, pp. 249–250). Disavowal is thus crucial for several but interrelated reasons, all of which explain certain forms of subjective existence in society. The outline of split ego defence with which Freud further developed his 'mature' understanding of fetishism speaks to divisions within the subject which not only bring to bear a certain belief but also sets in motion a *partial repression* of that belief in which disavowal plays a key role. Recalling the point made earlier, disavowal begins with an avowal and thus we find a sign of the split at a pivotal point in the fetish's establishment. The partial repression of belief and the turning away from reality that simultaneously forms that belief structure does not occur in ignorance of the hitherto disavowed reality. It does not qualify, so to speak, for (full) repression where there does not exist an overriding motive of avoiding unpleasure (Freud 2005, p. 36). The repression of belief is partial precisely because it occurs after a *conscious* avowal of the knowledge held by the subject. The content of the avowal remains in consciousness and is not turned away from it (Freud 2005, p. 360).

We can illustrate the particular repression of belief important to an understanding of Equity fetishism more clearly if contrasted with another corresponding fetish structure that represses knowledge. Following Žižek, consider the position in which the subject proclaims, '"(I know that God exists, but nevertheless) I act as though I believe that there is no God" – what he represses', claims Žižek referring to the part in brackets, 'is the *knowledge* of the existence of God' (2008, p. 243). We can contrast this with repression of belief, whereby, as Žižek explains, a 'gap between (real) knowledge and (symbolic) belief determines our everyday ideological attitude: "I know that there is no God, but nevertheless I operate as if (I believe that) he exists"—the part in brackets is repressed (belief in a God whom we witness through our activity is unconscious)' (2008, p. 243). If we rewrite this example to take the perspective of a stakeholder, then the result is: I know that there is no such thing as complete justice, but I conduct my business as if there is, and Equity is proof of it.

Disavowal enables the stakeholder to enjoy that existence, which again highlights the peculiarly perverse instead of neurotic structure of fetishism, the latter being that part of Equity fetishism provided by the legal community as purveyors of legal expertise, knowledge and meaning. In making his distinction, Freud posits neuroses as 'the *negative* of perversion', and that like a 'stream of water which meets with an obstacle in the river-bed', the motive forces leading to the formation of hysterical symptoms in neurotics 'draw their strength not only from repressed *normal* sexuality but also from unconscious perverse activities' (2001, pp. 50–51). In terms of the stakeholder's belief in the reality of complete justice as a basis from which to pursue their interests, the distinction between perversity à la fetishism and neurosis adheres to the problem a neurotic stakeholder would have in committing to the belief. This is because, where there is only partial repression of the avowed belief in fetishism, repression in cases of neuroses is more vigorous. This means it is less likely that the stakeholder would or could form the belief because the unconscious material cannot be rendered conscious and thus form the basis for the initial avowal, the 'I know' that precedes the 'nevertheless' in Mannoni's formulation, and why the perverse stakeholder needs the neurotic lawyer as complement.

'Belief can survive its own denial by reality', and, explains Gemerchak, 'belief can persist even after the believer has been disillusioned, and therefore knows the belief is false' (2004a, p. 43). This helps explain how belief can function in prescribed circumstances because it persists 'without the subject even knowing about it, simply because of a projection that allows someone else to believe in one's place' (Gemerchak 2004a, p. 43). Trusts provide a good example of a bureaucracy that involves the split central to disavowal mimicked in the split between legal interest in the trustee and beneficial interest in the beneficiaries. The office of the trustee alone offers further examples of that 'someone else' able to believe in one's place that Gemerchak highlights.

There are various modern instantiations of the office of trustee in which, to varying degrees, we find forms of disavowal that correspond to the notion of conscious partial repression that structures belief. In the parlance of Equity jurisprudence, this disavowal and repression of belief takes different forms but is perhaps most notably in what Sarah Worthington refers to as 'restrictions on personal autonomy' in the trustee's office (and fiduciary) (2006, pp. 127–156). Doctrines of self-denial always already assume that trustees will commit breaches for personal gain, and therefore the loyalty basis of the fiduciary duty, which is also of note in the more specific field of trusts, is a good example of the source of such fictions (Worthington 2006, p. 131). Like other remedial modes that form part of Equity's trust jurisprudence, constructive trusts, for example, they interpolate a legal fiction predicated on the notion of conscience into the social transaction, but which point, I argue, to a formalization of disavowal and repression. Echoing the early twentieth-century American jurist Roscoe Pound, Margaret Halliwell describes the role of conscience vis-à-vis legal fiction in the following way: 'Because the general rules are based on abstraction and the disregard of the variable and less material element in affairs, the legal element is mechanical in its operation. Equity, or good conscience, operates as an element via the judicial modification or supplementing of existing rules of law by reference to current conditions and circumstances. It is antagonistic to the legal element because it is not technical but discretionary' (Halliwell 2004, p. 5). Meanwhile, Irit Samet explains that,

> By invoking this rich concept of loyalty the courts of equity advise fiduciaries that the serious commitment they took upon themselves calls for the adoption of an unusual disposition. A detached and purely instrumental approach to her relationship with the principal may get the fiduciary to abide by her legal duties. But this unique position of great power over other people, combined with an information gap that renders detection of abuse quite unlikely, *generates a temptation for wrongdoing that can be very hard to overcome*. And this is true for an honest, well-intentioned fiduciary. (2004, p. 140)

As well as disavowal there is also an important compromise by the stakeholder. The stakeholder, as trustee, for instance, disavows opportunities for personal gain. In doing so, however, she equally reaches a compromise regarding ways of continuing to enjoy the process, the bureaucracy, of which she forms so vital a part. This includes an enjoyment of the process that extends over the moral character of the trustee. Hence, trusteeship has long secured social and moral status for the stakeholder instead of personal financial gains. Discussing trusteeship during the nineteenth century, Chantal Stebbings remarks that, 'trusteeship was an act of true affection and esteem, a demonstrable adherence to the social and moral codes, and as such it ensured the respect of the trustee's own social class. Moreover, since this ethos was reinforced and encouraged by the teaching of the Christian Church, a man falling short of the expected moral code would have to answer ultimately to God. In the context of the intense religious fervour in Victorian England, trusteeship was significant. It showed, no less, the moral standing of a man: to his family, his fellows, and to God' (Stebbings 2002, p. 9). The compromise would appear to be part of the function of disavowal. Both compromise and disavowal relate to the fundamental split in the subject that sets in motion the establishment of the fetish and the associated belief structure that supports it based upon the ambivalence of the subject's 'simultaneous acknowledgement and denial' (Gemerchak 2004a, p. 37). Compromise warrants examination on its own terms as it involves processes distinguished from disavowal and thus serves to further define what disavowal is and why it is so important to fetishism. Freud introduces compromise as follows,

> It is not true that the child's belief in the female phallus remains unchanged after he observed a woman. He both retains this belief and renounces it; in the conflict between the force of the unwelcome perception and the intensity of his aversion to it, a compromise is reached such as is possible only under the laws of unconscious thought, the primary processes. In his psyche, yes, the woman still has a penis, but this penis is no longer the same thing as before. Something else has taken its place, has been appointed its successor, so to speak, and this now inherits all the interest previously devoted to its predecessor. But because the horror of castration has been immortalized in the creation of this substitute, this interest also becomes intensified to an extraordinary degree. (2006, pp. 91–92)

This rich passage covers a lot of ground. The final sentence talks of immortalization and conveys the notion of a temporality that attaches to the fetish structure. I will deal with what underscores immortalization and the subject's forward movement in time, accompanied by their fetish in the following section on memorialization. Where we can more readily distinguish between compromise and disavowal is in the processes following the retention and renouncement of belief. As discussed regarding disavowal, there is in that process a necessary conscious stage of avowal whereby the subject has the knowledge they consciously turn away from, which maintains that belief does not derive from ignorance.

Compromise, as Freud suggests, concerns primary processes of repression at the level of the unconscious. There is no conscious stage of compromise, no compromise in ignorance, which ultimately structures the fetish object as a structure of ambivalence. The compromise is instead a direct result of a conflict in the subject's psyche 'between the force of the unwelcome perception and the intensity of his aversion to it' (Freud 2006, p. 91). 'In sexual fetish worship', Böhme claims, 'things must always be kept in balance: the annihilation of identity by castration, which can no longer be expunged from the world (the sacrifice), must be represented in a new form, must mask itself as the love object that warrants all feelings of lust being focused on it' (2014, p. 319). Böhme concludes, 'in the strict sense, the fetish is a *compromise* that is made in the unconscious between the fear of castration and the saviour of the phallus' (2014, p. 319).

Again, the following section on memorialization will draw out the importance attributed to the 'new form' that emerges in fetishism, one which is apposite to Equity fetishism in terms, notably, of post-Judicature mobilization in the wider field of Common law of complete justice. The procedure that John Sorabji summarizes as Chancery's ability to 'disapply procedural rules where abiding by them would frustrate its over-riding objective of doing complete justice', which itself signals a form of comprise occurring within the machinations of civil procedure (2014, p. 45). Compromise returns the discussion to unconscious conflicts over the universal nature of justice and fairness and a relationship to Equity at a corresponding unconscious social and institutional level. 'The fetish makes the unconscious fantasy that there is "nothing but the phallus" possible', says Böhme, whilst at the same time and in adherence to compromise preserving, 'the repressed fantasy that there is such a thing as castration' (2014, p. 318). Thus, Equity fetishism serves to maintain the structure of the capitalist fantasy of completeness, whilst also preserving a certain limit that serves as a reminder to the stakeholder that the fantasy is always already compromised.

Civil justice reform, as a form of institutional compromise, is, I argue, driven by capitalism. Nineteenth-century Judicature involved the creation of a form of civil justice that preserved Chancery's overriding aim of doing complete justice without the corresponding problems that rendered 'its process both expensive and time-consuming' (Sorabji 2014, p. 42). Equity fetishism emerged from the nineteenth-century reform agenda as a perverse and fantastical response to stakeholder demand for a different form of the civil justice system to the one that predominated during the earlier periods of capitalism, largely because the old system did not satisfy their desires. Despite the fusion of the court system and creation of a new and arguably more efficient way of doing civil justice, stakeholders did not achieve an infallible system of justice, and the recent Woolf and Jackson reforms, whilst responses to changes in socioeconomic conditions under capitalism since the nineteenth century, are equally a testament to the impossibility of perfectibility. In Freudian terms, compromise *qua* civil justice reform continues because a 'particular and quite special penis' only lives in fantasy and will never manifest in reality.

MEMORIALIZATION

The memorialization of Equity as an object is central to understanding its significance and value as a fetish in the contemporary civil justice system. A notable product of analyses of Equity (including the present one) is the proliferation of historical references, each of which records and recounts a piece of Equity. All are complicit, therefore, although to varying degrees of a memorialization symptomatic of Equity fetishism. For instance, memorialization of Equity, as previously argued, is traceable to the effects of the nineteenth-century Judicature reforms which included securing the supremacy of Equity over Common Law and placing it, as Robert Pearce and Warren Barr maintain, 'on a statutory footing' (2015, p. 9). And the cementing of memorialization in subsequent pieces of Judicature legislation in 1925 and 1981, and via the Rules of the Supreme Court (RSC).

Memorialization of Equity via each stage of Judicature has looked to the past as much as to the future. The modern foundations of Equity's 'supremacy' continue to live in the notion that its rules prevail over those of Common Law in the event of a conflict. We can trace this idea to the *Earl of Oxford's Case*, in which the Lord Chief Justice of the King's Bench, Sir Edward Coke, and the Lord Chancellor, Lord Ellesmere, failed to agree as to the status of Chancery injunctions respecting Common Law judgements. 'This jurisdictional civil war', Pearce and Barr claim, 'was finally ended in 1616, when James I issued an order in favour of the Chancery Court and the common injunctions' (2015, p. 7). Despite attempts by Common Lawyers to reverse the outcome of the extraordinary intervention of the monarch by a Parliamentary Bill in 1690, which was eventually dropped 'when it was shown that it would make equity unworkable' and lead to injustice, 'the primacy of the Chancery Courts was well established by the end of the [seventeenth] century' and continued through the Woolf reforms at the end of the twentieth century as a further memorialization of the notion of complete justice as the normative means for achieving civil justice outcomes (Woolf 1996; Pearce and Barr 2015, p. 7).

Key to fetishism, memorialization involves temporality which engages the subject in considerations of both the past and future in their structuring of the fetish object. Beginning with Freud we can see that the structure of the fetish requires a special something that the subject believed in once upon a time (in the past), but, crucially, does not want to give up (in the present or future) (Freud 2006, p. 91). As part of Freud's aetiology, the memorialization that helps establish the fetish is, as Böhme maintains, 'the perverse memorial to an archaic time in which there was a *"male* gender, but not a *female* one"' (2014, p. 322). The fetish locks the subject into a specific temporality in which it ties the past tense to the future tense of the object in a cyclical yet historically contingent masking of loss *qua* castration. Or, more accurately, a re-signifying or re-symbolizing that allows the meaning the object holds for the subject to endlessly (re)form in a chain of signification implies castration never occurred or has to occur in the fantasy life of the subject. 'It goes without saying', argues Böhme, 'that things also acquire meaning as memorial objects [...] Here meaning is understood as an extra layer, a material patina. The cultural part of things is put on them like a dress, which then gradually becomes a second skin. This becoming historical and biographical of things makes them into archives of memory, in which individual people and collectives find security' (2014, p. 81).

Regarding the interrelation between Equity and Chancery in the structure of Equity fetishism, memorialization involves a coalescence of both materiality and temporality. The Court of Chancery represented and represents an archive of the materiality of Equity; Equity sustained through an architecture of stone, bricks and cement. Whilst the name of Chancery is carried forward, as a homology, through time on the signifying chain as the "Chancery" Division. Therefore, a materiality (the weight of the stone, brick and cement) associated with the long-dead court remains part of how we continue to interept and understand Equity. The divisional preservation of Chancery was thus, I argue, no accident and preservation of the name post-Judicature deliberately considered and memorialized that which Equity had been, but, importantly, could not close-off what Equity was to become, a commercially astute and adaptable mode of civil justice capable of bearing more children. That some say Equity is not past the age of childbearing is yet another reference to its flexibility, where it can bring forth new rules and principles as required by given situation. Lord Denning was a famous proponent of the idea in relation to his "new model" constructive trust in *Eves v Eves* [1975] 1 WLR 1338 at 1341. 'The essence of institutional equity is the creation of a special court, distinct from the courts administering the general law, having the power to modify or correct the general law', state Bryan and Vann, although, as they further maintain in full acknowledgement of memorialization, 'the paradox of institutional equity is that it is premised on the existence of a court which no longer exists' (2012, p. 4).

Because of the withering status of the Court of Chancery by the time of its closure, preservation also had to account for what Equity or civil justice must never be again. Not least because a return to costliness and inefficiency of the magnitude attributed to the Court of Chancery by stakeholders and reformers during the nineteenth century would contradict the spirit of capitalist ideology that had made the case for systemic reform of civil justice a necessity and a reality. Accordingly, memorialization with Equity fetishism reflects stakeholder's desire for complete justice, but also of certainty and stability in terms of the overarching procedural functionality of the courts. A desire driven by stakeholder's anxieties regarding the loss of ground on which they have staked certainty, the same ground from which the fetish emerges. As Kevin and Susan Francis Gray maintain regarding real property (land), 'The English law of real property [...] confirms', in a mantra-like formula, that 'in matters relating to title to land, certainty is of prime importance. To permit any uncertainty as to the impact of land transactions on various subsidiary claims is to place an intolerable burden on the process of land transfer and the long-term planning of land use' (2009, p. 136). The fetish captivates the subject in a constant present that parallels an otherwise developing experience, and around which the arms of the past and future are wrapped. Gravestones, war memorials and other non-functioning objects that, made from organic or natural materials, decay (are subject to forces of entropy), are examples that give the subject a sense of fixity and immovability. The tended grave in particular, visited, cleaned, repaired and maintained, is an example of the captivation of living subjects by objects and by stasis. Engaged in memorializing, these subjects affect a constant return to the *once upon a time*. Instead of the actual reincarnation of the body in the grave, the cleaning and renewal of the headstone can represent this re-enactment of the moment or event signalling the living subject's loss.

To "*tend*" is a ritual, therefore, that institutes forms of renewal and a sense of return to an earlier point in time where the special object remained, at least symbolically, intact. We then translate meaning into the present and projected into the future, raised up and celebrated. A process succinctly put in the infamous memorialization of the war dead: *lest we forget*. 'This is always about overcoming death or the dead (things) that mark themselves as absent and a void', argues Böhme, 'fetishism can thus be described as an animating force that is taken from a memory that masks its origin and yet in the fetish becomes an event in the here and now' (2014, p. 312). Central to this aspect of memorialization are, I claim, also aesthetic and atmospheric considerations. It is important to explain how these considerations further define fetishism. That fetishism has an aesthetic dimension is axiomatic. Böhme posits the relationship between fetishism and aesthetics as prehistoric and fundamental to the human condition itself (Böhme 2014, p. 82). Fetishism, Böhme maintains, apprehends basic human considerations for and concerns with beauty and ugliness, pleasure and aversion (2014, p. 82). The suggestion is that we can trace the ethnographic and cultural anthropology of fetishism to a set of aesthetic values, which far from being fixed are in fact developing with human experience and reason in the form of, for example, fashions, tastes, techniques, institutions and so on. Considering Freud's aetiology, we can link the relationship of aesthetics to fetishism to the substitutional value and the substantive qualities and characteristics of the fetish object itself. The substantive *thingness* of the fetish speaks to the notion that fetishism involves reification and a freezing or stalling, temporally, at the point of the fragmentation and loss of the primal object of desire. Hence the purpose of the fetish, as Freud states, is to 'prevent this loss from occurring', something that goes to the heart of memorialization as a key feature of fetishism (2006, p. 91). The fetish generates enjoyment for and happiness in the subject because it is not just any object but 'a specific and very special one' (Freud 2006, p. 90). Integral to its ability to sustain belief, therefore, the fetish possesses for the subject an aesthetic quality that makes it special.

In being the special thing that provides enjoyment for the subject and makes him or her happy, the substantive aesthetic quality of the fetish equally exists in or rather generates a certain atmosphere for the subject. To sustain belief there remains extant for the duration (life) of that belief in the fetish a commitment to a certain atmospheric (and aesthetic) quality, making it a vital component in structuring the fetish. For example, the genital construction performed by the little boy apropos his mother's special phallus is, for Freud more than just an aesthetic concern—what we may consider a concern for the penis as an aesthetic, functional object itself, and for the functional integrity of that penis vis-à-vis the threat of castration. Freud integrates aesthetic considerations into his discussion of fetishism both in the 1927 essay ('Fetishism'), and shortly after in his short 1938 essay entitled, 'The splitting of the ego in defence processes'

(Freud 2006, pp. 64–67). We can trace what is special about the object
able to fulfil this genital construction to an atmosphere that surrounds it,
what Böhme refers to as 'the matrix of beauty', which at once 'arouses
pleasure or dislike, attraction or revulsion' in the subject (2014, pp. 81–
82). Atmosphere akin to a symptomology, manifests aesthetic effects
which generate their own material. Atmosphere can also involve something more subtle, such as a gesture made in and through space, which
describes or determines a causal outcome or consequence. The historical
view of Equity as a court of conscience signal juridical gestures of discretion and contemplation that illustrate an atmosphere of justice on the
terms described here. An atmosphere of civil process in which the court
seeks less to know the defendant's conscience, than for the defendant
to have self-regard for their own conscience. Or, rather, for the court to
reach a point at which it can interpolate a fiction of conscientiousness into
proceedings in order, for instance, to guarantee the legitimacy of property
rights claims.

The Aesthetic atmosphere produced by the fetish always derives from
a position of subjective desire. It is not something that can be objectively
or scientifically measured. That does not mean that the subject cannot
relay or communicate to others the particular qualities of a fetish that
trigger enjoyment and happiness for them. Take, for example, the deeply
affective aesthetic representations of the Court of Chancery during its
demise in the nineteenth century. And in particular the reformist portrait
painted by Charles Dickens in *Bleak House* that deliberately cast Chancery
cloaked in fog as an arcane and dysfunctional institution. As an example
from Dickens shows, 'On such an afternoon, some score of members of
the High Court of Chancery bar ought to be – as here they are – mistily
engaged in one of the ten thousand stages of an endless cause, tripping
one another up on slippery precedents, groping knee-deep in technicalities, running their goat-hair and horse-hair warded heads against walls
of words, and making a pretence of Equity with serious faces, as players
might' (2011, p. 14). The problems surrounding Chancery were, like
Dickens' fog, all-pervasive and much debated by the nineteenth-century
reformers. Also, these problems were cast as much in aesthetic as ethical
terms. The role commentators such as Dickens had in shaping perceptions
of the civil justice system were important, therefore, not least because they
helped determine the fate of Chancery as a material place and an idea.
And with the demise of Chancery came the reconfiguration of the system,
as Gary Watt maintains: 'Dickens added high-grade fuel to the existing

fire of chancery law reform' (2012, p. 56). And as part of an aesthetic commitment the aim of reform was to satisfy, if not exactly a cultural need for the (fetid) atmosphere of Chancery, then at the very least the need for an acknowledgement and appreciation of an atmosphere from which to salvage something functional, namely Equity. Together with an aesthetic discourse, atmosphere describes how belief in Equity was shaped by a memorialization of Chancery despite its ruin and closure.

Complete justice post-Judicature (and post-Chancery) involved the interlinked desires for concurrency with the Common Law and for the procedural approach of Equity to prevail. Chancery remained an important part of civil justice not only as a homology linking the name of the old court to the new, post-Judicature division, but in a ghostly and memorial form. When Anthony Mason talks of Equity in the contemporary Common Law world in which he focuses specifically on 'equity's incursions into the area of commerce', he, therefore, insists on 'the distinctive concepts, doctrines, principles and remedies which were developed and applied by the old Court of Chancery, as they have been refined and elaborated since' (1994, pp. 245 and 238). Mason's 'old' Court of Chancery is a jurisprudential *archive* maintained for practical and systematic reasons under the heading of the post-Judicature Chancery Division, but equally a certain persistent spectre of Chancery that continues to haunt the moment of civil justice adjudication.

Reformers and stakeholders imputed what was worthwhile about Equity and necessary to preserve and memorialize post-Judicature fashioned from the atmosphere of Chancery. Mason describes, once again, the nature this dominant form of procedure took as the 'underlying values of equity centred on good conscience', that, 'will almost certainly continue to be a driving force in the shaping of the law unless the underlying values and expectations of society undergo a fairly radical alteration' (1994, p. 258). Mason does not expand on the 'underlying values and expectations of society' he refers to, but the juridical-economic *status quo* of capitalism underpinned by the civil justice system is not an unreasonable implication. For Sorabji, the shift in underlying values and expectations came not in the form of a social so much as a juridical alteration. Namely, a theory of civil justice planned at the end of the twentieth century by the Woolf reforms based on the determination of an 'overriding objective', which echoed Benthamite utilitarianism and promoted economy and efficiency as necessary traits of the litigation process (Sorabji 2014, pp. 148–150). It is interesting that both Mason and Sorabji imply that the same forces are at work in shaping civil justice—economic reason and capitalist ideology. That neither name capitalism but rely on euphemism is, I argue, testament to the depth of capitalist ideology; as Jodi Dean argues, in getting us to think only in terms of capitalist logics of competition and efficiency (2012, p. 73).

Equity's (former) relationship to the Court of Chancery indelibly marks Equity fetishism. What I place in brackets in the previous sentence is deliberate and to highlight the temporality at play, and that, actually, to consider the relationship between Equity and the Court of Chancery to be 'former', finished or in the past is, as discussed above, inaccurate. Memorialization of the (dead) Court of Chancery occurs in the (living) Chancery Division as a homology (in name), but also as a tending of the graves. An analogy which adheres to Mason's suggestion that Equity makes up not only a reference to the old Court but the constant refinement and elaboration since of the rules and doctrines originated in Chancery. Variations of the memorialization on the signifying chain of Chancery ('tending of the grave'), in terms put forward by Mason, naturally manifests in judicial statements. For example, Bagnall J. in *Cowcher v Cowcher* [1972] 1 WLR 425, a case concerning matrimonial property, in which he stated that,

> In any individual case the application of these propositions may produce a result which appears unfair. So be it; in my view that is not injustice. I am convinced that in determining rights, particularly, property rights, the only justice that can be obtained by mortals, who are fallible and not omniscient, is justice according to law; the justice which flows from the application of sure and settled principles to proved or admitted facts. So in the field of equity, the length of the Chancellor's foot has been measured or is capable of measurement. This does not mean that equity is past child-bearing; simply that its progeny must be legitimate – by precedent out of principle. (at 430)

For Bagnall J. Equity was what the Court of Chancery *did* until Judicature and any development thereafter belonged only within the margins and cognizance of the Common Law. Following a broader school of thought on integrating Equity and Common Law led by Peter Birks, and which continues to live through the development of other bodies of law, namely the law of restitution and unjust enrichment, Sarah Worthington shows that, 'Integration is possible. Integration is also desirable in the interests of better justice. It facilitates the aim of treating like cases alike. It also facilitates the sort of *rational evolution* of the law that is only possible if courts can draw distinctions based on meaningful differences rather than accidental jurisdictional divides' [my emphasis] (2006, p. 335). Regarding a complete system of civil justice, it was important to sustain absolute coherence between the ways and means of Common law and Equity. Sarah Worthington sums up the dogmatic insistence shown by Bagnall J, who has equally performed the remarkable (fetishistic) task of writing in-depth and with exceptional clarity about Equity, only to conclude that, as a body of law, it has no rational place in the future of the Common Law system of civil justice. 'History cannot', Worthington argues, 'go on to convincingly vindicate what is unquestionably a counter-intuitive choice [...] Comprehensive, rational integration of Common Law and Equity doctrines appears to be the only defensible modern option in pursuing principled legal development' (2006, p. 335).

The integration that Worthington advocates is arguably memorialization *par excellence regarding* Equity fetishism. This is because its aim is to dissolve Equity as a body of laws into the Common Law to make it unclear to stakeholders where one law begins and another ends—Peter Birks remarks on the ultimate failure to achieve this: 'Although the institutional separation of law and equity finally came to an end in 1871, the inheritance of intellectual duality has proved difficult to overcome' (2005, p. 292). Whilst at the same time preserving Equity as a distinguished and distinguishable other of the Common Law. 'Comprehensive doctrinal integration must surely be the grand plan for *Equity and the Common Law*', states Worthington, 'it is certainly the best plan for *Equity in the common law*' [my emphasis] (2006, p. 336). Whether this is a typographic error by the author or publisher, it remains the case even as Worthington seeks to shift Equity from a parallel status with the Common Law ('and'), to an integrated position of subservience 'in' the Common Law, it is Equity that remains capitalized, remains supreme, and thus ultimately prevails as the fetish object of complete justice. As a commentary on the victory of Equity over Common Law that implementing complete justice post-judicature signifies, Worthington's slip, whether intended, is, therefore, instructive.

SUMMARY

Having outlined three of the major features of fetishism in Freud's mature theory of the concept, it is now possible to summarize the notion of

Equity fetishism before moving on. Fetishism as discussed, regarding disavowal, is not a function restricted to the level of the unconscious. Instead, fetishism occurs in plain view, so to speak, as normative conscious (real) knowledge, which, by constructing mechanisms of belief, contradicts unconscious desires that manifest in the subject as unwelcome perceptions (Gemerchak 2004b, p. 243). Hence, different manifestations of fetishism, including Equity fetishism, do not amount to mere fantasy but maintain a basis in reality that allows them, as with complete justice, to invite objective evaluation. To appear rooted in objective reason rather than subjective desire. As Gemerchak maintains: 'The mystery of fetishism is that the closed circuit of desire and the belief in the satisfying nature of the object may be shattered, and consciously so, but the belief in the exclusive fulfilling object remains' (2004a, p. 41).

As a condition of capitalist society in which ECJ corresponds to 'the institutionalized structuring of social consciousness so as to create social reality as a comprehensive system of objective illusion', Equity fetishism manifests in the fixation of stakeholders on 'empty signs rather than material substance' (Gemerchak 2004a, pp. 24–25). Equity fetishism involves producing more profound symbolic meanings. This takes the form of sustaining belief in the fantasy of a complete and thus certain system of civil justice, predicated on the post-Judicature unity or fusion of Common Law and Equity. In this context, Equity fetishism sustains stakeholder belief in, for example, the coherence and rationality of the private property order in particular and capitalist ideology. 'The fetish', says Gemerchak, 'not only serves to disavow a lack and assert a presence, but as well to incarnate a lack, to simultaneously veil and unveil an essential absence' (2004a, p. 38). Reemphasizing aspects of the discussion above on memorialization, I argue that, as a product of the nineteenth-century reform agenda, the Court of Chancery indelibly marks Equity fetishism. As a particular site of loss and negativity from which the notion of complete justice continues to speak. 'At the heart of fetishism, both on the side of the fetish object and the fetishisitic subject', argues Gemerchak, 'there is an internal contradiction between brute materiality and evanescent dissimulation, essence and appearance, which makes it flow' (2004a, p. 13). As the exclusive material embodiment of Equity, the physical site of the practice and dissemination of Equity's ideas and reason, and thus the source and repository of the language of Equity, Chancery remains central to the notion and practice of Equity fetishism post-Judicature.

In whatever context Equity arises, language is key. As a feature of Equity fetishism the means of testifying to its 'enduring presence' occurs not only through the evocation of Chancery, in the homology between Court and Division, but also in the language of Equity. The centrality and solemnity of the language of conscience in shaping complete justice, including the oft-used reflexive, unconscionability, has since the time of John Selden's Table Talk assumed the very particular form of a foot fetish. Selden remarked, 'Equity is a Roguish thing: for Law we have a measure, know what to trust to; Equity is according to the Conscience of him that is Chancellor, and as that is larger or narrower, so is Equity. Tis all one if they should make the Standard for the measure, we call a Foot, the Chancellor's Foot; what an uncertain measure this would be? One Chancellor has a long Foot, another a short Foot, a Third and indifferent Foot: Tis the same thing in the Chancellor's Conscience' (1856, p. 49). 'We focus on language', states Geoffrey Galt Harpham in his general analysis of language-as-fetish, 'as a way of reassuring ourselves, albeit indirectly, of our special place in the order of things, our singular endowments and high destiny', a statement which speaks to the status and absoluteness afforded to justice, flexibility (adaptability), and fairness, and the various ways that Equity aims to apply these in various contexts for stakeholders (2002, p. 66).

Equity fetishism is key to the fantasy of the need for legal certainty (among many other fantasies) that capitalism promulgates to satisfy the stakeholder and guarantee the sanctity of economic reason. The fantasy of legal certainty engages and captivates stakeholders. It makes them want to invest, invite risk and competition and litigate over property rights and interests. Underlying this fantasy (what the fantasy and fetishism mask) is the message capitalism wishes to communicate to the stakeholder: that castration is avoidable and complete satisfaction possible. And communicating this message involves the language of Equity as we record it in case-law, legislation and other modes of juridical discourse that give credence to a culture of rights and the broader notion of a private property order. Where the language of Equity concerns penetrating or engaging the mystique of Equity, there have perhaps been no more desiring stakeholders than those members of the Chancery Bar who, in the lead up to Judicature and throughout the nineteenth century, fought to keep Equity distinct from the Common Law, and did so predicated on their special knowledge of that jurisdiction. Through language Equity structures belief in complete and certain justice. As a desirable legal end certainty is not exclusive to Equity, but to the concurrent system of civil justice. Certainty is itself contingent, therefore, upon the integrity of the whole. In the notion of certainty, it is possible to discern yet another dimension of Equity fetishism regarding the uncastrated fantasies of capitalism. Equity fetishism turns upon, as Valerie Kerruish claims regarding 'rights fetishism', certainties in 'legal practice of deciding particular cases by general rules, of coercive enforcement of those decisions, and of claiming that such judgments and their enforcement are objectively or uniquely right' (1991, p. 194). As a result, Equity fetishism allows thoughtful subjects to lose themselves 'in and to their own product: their thought and their laws' (Kerruish 1991, p. 194).

It ought to be clear by now that this book maintains that complete justice demanded by the stakeholder in Equity is never the thing (is never complete), but only ever a banal instant manufactured by a neurotic legal counterpart in and by language to defeat a negativity, a lack, at the core of the stakeholder. It is more accurate to think of Equity fetishism therefore as a totalizing and fantastical means through which civil justice appears complete in the stakeholder's eye, as that which the stakeholder seeks, when they seek justice *in* Equity. Civil justice contingent upon the language of Equity, even where that engenders a closed and discrete field of knowledge and expertise, only serves to further alienate the stakeholder, where the language is tied to an already alienating process of property. The fetishization of the language of Equity, as a more precise description of how Equity fetishism manifests, disguises endless chains of signification that are always inconclusive and which reveal in the stakeholder a certain commitment to and investment in the materiality of the sign. But a sign mistaken for complete justice, certainty or both. Language lives at the heart of what it means for Equity fetishism to prevail, rather than mere Equity. In its prevailing, the centrality of Equity to legal consciousness established by Lord Ellesmere in the *Earl of Oxford's Case* which continues in the present via s.49(1) of the *Senior Courts Act* 1981 marks the temporal record and legal consciousness of law in England and Wales. And for Equity fetishism to continue formatting scenes of complete justice in property on behalf of stakeholders who need to believe, not only in the fantastic possibility that justice is complete and will legitimize their rights to property and thus make them good economic subjects under capitalism, but that the primal loss associated with castration never occurred and does not apply to them.

References

Books and Articles

Böhme, H. *Fetishism and Culture: A Different Theory of Modernity*. Translated by Anna Galt. 2014. Berlin: De Gruyter.

Bryan, M.W., Vann, V.J. *Equity & Trusts in Australia*. 2012. Cambridge: Cambridge University Press.

Davies, M. Queer Property, Queer Persons: Self-Ownership and Beyond. *Social & Legal Studies*, Vol. 8, No. 3 (September 1999), pp. 327–352.

Dean, J. *The Communist Horizon*. 2012. London: Verso.

Freud, S. *A Case of Hysteria, Three Essays on Sexuality and Other Works: The Standard Edition Volume VII (1901–1905)*. Translated and Edited by James Strachey. 2001. London: Vintage.

Freud, S. *The Unconscious*. Translated by Graham Frankland. 2005. London: Penguin Modern Classics.

Freud, S. *The Penguin Freud Reader*. Edited by Adam Phillips. 2006. London: Penguin Classics.

Gemerchak, C.M. (ed.). *Everyday Extraordinary: Encountering Fetishism with Marx, Freud and Lacan*. 2004a. Leuven: Leuven University Press.

Gemerchak, C.M. Fetishism and Bad Faith: A Freudian Rebuttal to Sartre. *Janus Head*, Vol. 7, No. 2 (2004b), pp. 248–269.

Gray, K., Gray, S.F. *Elements of Land Law*. 5th Edition. 2009. Oxford: Oxford University Press.

Halliwell, M. *Equity and Good Conscience*. 2nd Edition. 2004. London: Old Bailey Press.

Harpham, G.G. *Language Alone: The Critical Fetish of Modernity*. 2002. London: Routledge.

Herian, R. The Conscience of Thomas More: An Introduction to Equity in Modernity. *The Heythrop Journal* (early access), 2020, pp. 1–12.

Kant, I. *The Moral Law*. Translated by H. J. Paton. 2005. London: Routledge Classics.

Kerruish, V. *Jurisprudence as Ideology*. 1991. London: Routledge.

Mannoni, O. *Freud: Theory of the Unconscious*. Translated by Renaud Bruce. 2015. London: Verso.

Mason, A. The Place of Equity and Equitable Remedies in the Contemporary Common Law World. *Law Quarterly Review*, Vol. 110 (April 1994), pp. 238–259.

Pashukanis, E.B. *Law & Marxism: A General Theory Towards a Critique of the Fundamental Juridical Concepts*. Translated by Barbara Einhorn. Edited by Chris Arthur. 1989. London: Pluto Press.

Pearce, R., Barr, W. *Pearce & Stevens' Trusts and Equitable Obligations*. 6th Edition. 2015. Oxford: Oxford University Press.

Sorabji, J. *English Civil Justice After the Woolf and Jackson Reforms: A Critical Analysis*. 2014. Cambridge: Cambridge University Press.
Stebbings, C. *The Private Trustee in Victorian England*. 2002. Cambridge: Cambridge University Press.
Stoller, R.J. *Observing the Erotic Imagination*. 1985. New Haven: Yale University Press.
Watt, G. *Equity Stirring: The Story of Justice Beyond Law*. 2012. Oxford: Hart Publishing.
Worthington, S. *Equity*. 2nd Edition. 2006. Oxford: Oxford University Press.
Woolf, L. *Access to Justice: Final Report*. 1996. http://webarchive.nationalarch ives.gov.uk/20060213223540/http://www.dca.gov.uk/civil/final/contents. htm.
Žižek, S. *How to Read Lacan*. 2007. New York: W.W. Norton & Company.
Žižek, S. *For They Know Not What They Do: Enjoyment as a Political Factor*. 2008. London: Verso.

CHAPTER 9

Neoliberalism and Equity Fetishism

INTRODUCTION

During this chapter, I will discuss Equity fetishism in the contemporary neoliberal capitalist age. Between Judicature and the *Senior Courts Act* 1981, the role and place of Equity has often been restated in the civil justice system. Significant reform programmes in England and Wales have further shifted the onus of civil justice, I argue, towards an alignment of economic principles to Equity's deontological imperative, or rather, *vice versa*. In his final report on access to justice Lord Woolf remarked that civil justice should be 'just in the results it delivers; fair in the way it treats litigants; offer appropriate procedures at a reasonable cost, and be responsive to the needs of those who use it' (1996). The Woolf Reforms echo the debates that informed the Judicature reforms during the nineteenth century where cost and speed, especially regarding Chancery, were key themes and significant problems needing solving. However, the notable alignment of principles of fairness and justice with economic injunctions for civil justice to perform with greater efficiency, flexibility (adaptability and responsiveness), and cost-effectiveness are entirely contemporary justifications made within and native to neoliberal capitalism. The Woolf reforms accord with a notion and ideal of common-sense justice native to neoliberal reason. We have already explored the impact of Chicago School and the law and economics of Richard Posner. Reforms to civil justice,

© The Author(s), under exclusive license to Springer Nature Switzerland AG 2021
R. Herian, *Capitalism and the Equity Fetish*,
https://doi.org/10.1007/978-3-030-66523-4_9

conducted by the likes of Lord Woolf, whilst redolent of the nineteenth-century project to tidy up the legal field littered with the most venerable survivals from bygone ages, is most recognizable as a further fusion of law and economics such that efficiency becomes a proxy for justice.

This chapter will describe two key areas. First, the place of Equity and civil justice within neoliberal thought. This will involve considering the impact of neoliberalism on notions of complete justice that I described previously as the basis for 'selfishness' in contemporary civil litigation in defence of private interests (Jolowicz 1983). Second, I will consider Equity fetishism and the emphasis placed on strategy and strategizing within neoliberal capitalism; the propensity for stakeholders to combine various social, political, moral, economic and legal options into strategies to support selfish interests. As part of this strategizing, there is, I argue, a reliance on fantasies of efficient commutative justice capable of soothing the stakeholder-as-engaged economic subject within neoliberal capitalism. Fantasies that turn on ECJ, but which now also embody models of adjudication such as Alternative Dispute Resolution (ADR) that extend, and have thus rendered porous, traditional boundaries of civil justice 'as a way of resolving disputes that does not require the use of court resources' (Gearey et al. 2009, p. 383; Main 2005, pp. 329–404; Stychin and Mulcahy 2007; Rai et al. 2008, pp. 74–91). Whilst this book has identified Equity fetishism as broadly related to the notion of complete justice to describe Equity fetishism under neoliberalism, this chapter will further examine unconscionability as a specific symptom of the demand placed on the subject by neoliberal capitalism to be flexible and agile. How unconscionability *qua* flexibility itself assumes the status of fetish, and stakeholders engaging under the aegis of neoliberal thought in both contexts of high-level economic risk and everyday bargaining come to rely on it both conceptually and materially in civil justice events, including forms of adjudication both in and out of court.

THE LAW OF NEOLIBERALISM

The drift towards socialist economic policies as an attenuation of capitalism during the first half and middle of the twentieth century in Western capitalist societies produced programmes such as the New Deal in the United States and the Welfare State in Great Britain. But these have arguably been politico-economic aberrations in government policies otherwise caught within the ambit of capital since the late eighteenth century. It is important to note that the monumental crises of capitalism, for example, in the form of the 1929 'Wall Street crash' and the subsequent Great Depression in the United States that American historian Howard Zinn claims were symptomatic of 'a sick and undependable system', reveal that capitalism is configured to reach points of logical impasse and crisis (1996, p. 378). Fantasies of complete justice are, therefore, vital to stakeholders if they are to maintain a belief in an unstable and illogical form of social organization, and a parallel belief that capitalism holds the key to endlessly deferring the trauma of castration.

During the middle of the twentieth century, leading academics of the time and thinkers from a variety of different fields established the Mont Pelerin Society. The Society's founding statement, quoted below, laid the foundations for a resurgence of late nineteenth-century neoclassical economics and the desire to disseminate economic reason across Anglo-American post-war capitalist societies seen as under threat from socialism.

> The central values of civilization are in danger. Over large stretches of the Earth's surface the essential conditions of human dignity and freedom have already disappeared. In others they are under constant menace from the development of current tendencies of policy. The position of the individual and the voluntary group are progressively undermined by extensions of arbitrary power. Even that most precious possession of Western Man, freedom of thought and expression, is threatened by the spread of creeds which, claiming the privilege of tolerance when in the position of a minority, seek only to establish a position of power in which they can suppress and obliterate all views but their own.
>
> The group holds that these developments have been fostered by the growth of a view of history which denies all absolute moral standards and by the growth of theories which question the desirability of the rule of law. It holds further that they have been fostered by a decline of belief in private property and the competitive market; for without the diffused power and initiative associated with these institutions it is difficult to imagine a society in which freedom may be effectively preserved. (Mont Pelerin Society, April 8 1947)

Central to the conceptual foundations of neoliberalism are juridical and, I argue, fetishistic concerns: 'the desirability of the rule of law' and 'belief in private property'. And, as Alastair Hudson suggests, 'The effect on the rule of law is complex' (2018, p. 79). 'In international financial markets', Hudson maintains, 'law' has been 'privatised',

> That is, the law has had its most useful features extracted from it by the lawyers who facilitate it. These are lawyers in the largest international law firms, lawyers employed in-house in investment banks and lawyers who work in tax havens. They work alongside accountants, public relations specialists, professional lobbyists, investment bankers and traders. Those legal techniques, taken principally form the creative incubators of common law jurisdictions, are then deployed as part of a closed system by legal professionals who want to achieve clear goals for their clients: such as the protections of assets, the acquisition of preferential rates of funding through financial engineering, and the avoidance of regulatory oversight. (2018, p. 79)

Further to Hudson's outline, what the analysis later in this chapter will aim to describe is how Equity fetishism relates to the contemporary socioeconomic and legal moment, enabling stakeholders, to paraphrase Sir Henry Maine, to 'strive to recover a lost perfection' and sustain their fantasies of uncastrated unity and through private property, wealth and complete civil justice (1972, p. 41). This train of thought reflects the work of Frederick Hayek as one of the major architects of law's place in neoliberal thought, and which led him to make the case for the new super-charged competitive and market-driven form of capitalism in his infamous diatribe against, what he saw as, the perils of socialism, *The Road to Serfdom* (2001). It is not unreasonable given the sheer amount of times he references the notion in his work to suggest that the key aspect for Hayek was competition, and the strategic nature of competitive practices in particular. He directs his furious defence of competition not only against the centralizing tendencies of economic organization that he regarded as key to an unfavourable socialism, but equally against the prevailing threat of the capitalist who would promote the eventual collapse of free markets into a state of monopoly (2001, p. 42).

Hayek's reimagining of capitalism gave particular prominence to the legal system in ensuring the legitimacy and effectiveness of the competitive market structure that he desired and predicted. 'The functioning of competition not only requires adequate organisation of certain institutions like money, markets, and channels of information', argued Hayek, 'but it depends above all on the existence of an appropriate legal system, a legal system designed both to preserve competition and to make it operate as beneficially as possible' (2001, p. 39). In Hayek's scheme, and for commentators and stakeholders of libertarian capitalism such as Ludwig Von Mises and Milton Friedman that formed part of what Mirowski calls 'the Neoliberal Thought Collective (NTC)', law (and *we* must include Equity within that definition when discussing a Common Law system) had a very particular role to play (2013). Civil justice that, akin to the stakeholders who relied upon it, was always already subordinate to a need for risk contained deep within the internal logic of neoliberalism. All forms of law and legal institution within a neoliberal superstructure predicated on so-called 'free-market' competition, on the maximum deregulation and minimum state intervention, as the primary mode of socioeconomic organization had to achieve one overriding aim: efficient and effective competition and more risk as the essential platforms for maximum capital accumulation and profit (Hayek 2001, p. 39). In his critique of neoliberalism Paddy Ireland exposes the role of competition in fermenting Hayek vision, stating that, 'not only is it perfectly "natural" for people to seek to bend or avoid rules [something Equity has facilitated in one form or another for centuries] and to circumvent social obligations if tis generates market and/or material advantage, competition may compel them to do so' [my addition] (2018, p. 7).

Hayek's vision prompted a system of law and civil justice that had to be agile, flexible and creative. We have seen all the features idealised in Hayek's justice system as particular attributes of an Equity jurisdiction that 'balances out the need for certainty in rule-making with the need to achieve fair results in individual circumstances' (Hudson 2017, p. 4). Equity offers a valuable lens through which to view the work of Hayek and in particular the basis of the neoliberal programme he ultimately unleashed. And whilst Hayek does not expressly discuss Equity, he comes very close to ECJ in his notion of the 'rules of just conduct'. In particular, he attaches this notion of conduct to what he calls 'end-independent rules which serve the formation of a spontaneous order' (the potent concept behind the proliferation of free-market liberty), in contrast with 'end-dependent rules of organization', namely the basis of the unfavourable and inflexible central economic organization found under socialism that relies on high levels of government intervention and control of the economy through robust regulation (2013, p. 197). Rules of just conduct, as end-independent rules, are like the discretionary attributes of ECJ unconscionability as 'the *nomos* which is at the basis of a "private law society" and makes an Open Society possible' (Hayek 2013, p. 197).

For Hayek, private law as *nomos*, as a modality of individual utility and obligation, was necessary to foster independence and just conduct able to prevent stakeholder conflict and facilitate co-operation 'by eliminating some sources of uncertainty' (2013, p. 204). As I have described, the private law domain, especially regarding property, is one in which Equity facilitates precisely this conduct through ECJ, and through the finer detail of its principles, doctrines, and remedies. Equity cannot, as with any laws, eliminate uncertainty, but regarding the property rights framework and the private property order, can, echoing Hayek, 'create certainty [...] to the extent that they protect [proprietary] means against the interference by others, and thus enable the individual to treat those means as being at his disposal' [my addition] (2013, p. 204).

Equity Within Neoliberal Thought

I do not consider neoliberalism as an abstract mode of social organization but an outgrowth of economic reason, and in particular a set of *strategies* that broadly follow and adhere to the ideology of capitalism. Yet the strategic nature of neoliberalism is also that which ultimately differentiates it from classical forms of capitalism, and places requirements on stakeholders to redefine themselves and society imaginatively as economic ecosystems. As Byung-Chul Han claims, within neoliberalism, 'we do not deem ourselves subjugated *subjects*, but rather *projects*: always refashioning and reinventing ourselves' (2017, p. 1). David Harvey defines neoliberalism as follows,

> Neoliberalism is in the first instance a theory of political economic practices that proposes that human well-being can best be advanced by liberating individual entrepreneurial freedoms and skills within an institutional framework characterised by strong private property rights, free market s, and free trade. The role of the state is to create and preserve an institutional framework appropriate to such practices. The state has to guarantee, for example, the quality and integrity of money. It must also set up those military, defence, police, and legal structures and functions required to secure private property rights and to guarantee, by force if need be, the proper functioning of markets [...] In so far as neoliberalism values market exchange as 'an ethic in itself, capable of acting as a guide to all human action, and substituting for all previously held ethical beliefs', it emphasizes the significance of contractual relations in the marketplace. It holds that the social good will be maximised by maximising the reach and frequency of

market transactions, and it seeks to bring all human action into the domain of the market. (2005, pp. 2–3)

Central to neoliberalism are interpellated economic subjects (stakeholders) who, despite subtle shifts in the exercise of economic reason that neoliberalism entails nevertheless remain entirely and unreservedly focused on achieving the aims of capitalism. These stakeholders strive for individual accumulation (profit and wealth) and the reproduction of class power through the variegated ways and means of commercial and personal self-interest and entrepreneurialism, as we might find in traditional capitalism. As a species of rather than a reinvention of capitalism, neoliberalism relies upon the same (super)structural arrangements and forces that feed the economic base of classical capitalism, notably markets and competition. Hence, a body law that promotes the following of one's conscience 'even when dealing with strangers in the market' is sure to resonate with stakeholders (Samet 2020, p. 13).

Neoliberalism is little more than a new name for a reconfigured form of capitalism that has pushed society towards an unreserved acceptance of the God-like nature of the market system and the forces of competition that lure stakeholders into engagement, action, and investment, both economically and psychically. And yet neoliberalism differs from traditional capitalism where it claims a moral project and a set of ethical imperatives that, as the Mont Pelerine statement shows, adhere to pure classical economic ideals that predate the brutal turn of capitalism in its high industrial and imperialist forms, but also in its general expansion of global inequality. Thus neoliberalism, almost as a perverse complement to communism's critique of capitalism, offers a way to reset history in order not to mask the reality of capitalism's failures and brutality, but to denude the influence of socialism and communism as a critical and sociopolitical alternative. The apparent ability of neoliberalism to be all things to all people, both on the left and right of politics, is a key strategy within what Philip Mirowski calls the 'neoliberal playbook' (2013, pp. 325–358).

As keys to understanding neoliberalism, competition and an overriding emphasis on markets and marketization prefigure the greater risk that stakeholders must assume compared with their capitalist predecessors. Risk is not a marginal consideration in neoliberal thought, it is the fuel for the engine of neoliberal progress. But as Anthony Giddens claims, this emphasis on risk no longer reflects the truth of the external world in shaping human behaviour but is instead 'manufactured' to satisfy certain prescribed political ends (1999, p. 4). But he also sees it as positive where risk provides an apparently greater degree or expansion of choice within the social domain (1999, p. 5). Meanwhile, Philip Mirowski views risk as the sine qua non of neoliberal agency, precisely what defines stakeholders in the contemporary age of capitalism,

> A denizen of modern neoliberal society has not demonstrated real flexibility of personal identity until they have prostrated themselves before the capricious god of risk [...] Salvation through the market comes not from solidarity with any delusional social class or occupational category, but instead bold assertions of individuality through capitulation to a life of risk [...] the modern culture of risk is the very embodiment of the neoliberal commandment: there is no such thing as commutative justice, and consequently, the participant must simply acquiesce in the verdict of the market. (2013, pp. 120–121)

Mirowski's claim is of particular significance here because, if, as he states, 'there is no such thing as commutative justice' then how do we account for the type of civil justice system discussed throughout the book so far as a key component of the socioeconomic existence of stakeholders? The answer lies in the first part of the quote: the reliance on and demand for flexibility. This defines a civil justice model tailored to meet economic and market principles that the likes of the Woolf reforms describe, and within this model unconscionability assumes the fetishistic role it does in the neoliberal age. We will return to this matter in more depth shortly.

Risk, like economic reason, has become a standard by which we measure the value of many if not all domains of social activity and behaviour in contemporary neoliberal societies. And neoliberalism, although arguably relying on civil justice to administer a robust private property order as capitalism did during the nineteenth and much of the twentieth century, inherits the doctrine of unconscionability as a particular strategic juridical form through which stakeholders can navigate their exposure to and, I argue, enjoyment of the uncertainties (and risks) of contemporary economic life. Viewed through the prism of Equity fetishism, the tension between certainty in law and uncertainty in (economic) life that engenders risk is in many senses to neoliberal stakeholders what material forms of property were to their nineteenth-century capitalist counterparts. The contemporary neoliberal stakeholder seeks-out material property and corresponding property rights under the logic of capitalism. But risk provides a patina and layer of enjoyment that induces stakeholder engagement and investment in juridical-economic activity, as described in previous chapters, and signifies the augmentation and extension of enjoyment sought by fetishistic stakeholders. As the prevailing dominant socioeconomic ideology, the entrenchment, reproduction, and dissemination of neoliberal capitalism is enabled by and conducted through flexible and permissive laws and modes of civil justice. Since the 1873 Act a transition in civil justice and thus Equity's role in the administration of it occurred because of implementing the Rules of the Supreme Court (RSC) and further reform programmes, and did so, I argue, with the shifting nature of capitalism.

As a set of juridical strategies within neoliberalism, civil justice no longer involves the exclusive practices, reasoning and dominion of the courts but often occurs in the shadow of the courts (Alfini and McCabe 2001, pp. 171–206; Stychin and Mulcahy 2007, pp. 363–368). The contemporary rise of alternative 'out of court' forms of settlement and bargaining, especially ADR and mediation to maximise flexibility, cost-effectiveness and efficiency in civil procedure, has arguably augmented Equity's role in contemporary civil justice by 'standing in the breach created by the merger of Law and Equity', and 'reincarnating' Equity (Main 2005, pp. 329–330). Flexibility and 'the need to adapt procedures to the circumstances of the particular case is a common theme' begins Sir Rupert Jackson in his lecture to the Chartered Institute of Arbitrators, that is 'the purpose of the "tracks" which Lord Woolf introduced in 1999' (Jackson 2016). ADR and civil justice reform more broadly has, under the terms of this book, given new life to the fetishization of Equity, not least because it has reemphasised and re-energised the role of flexibility in law and civil justice procedure. 'ADR is more flexible and adapts to the specific needs and demands of the case', claim Robert B. Moberly and Judith Kilpatrick,

> With ADR the parties can utilize creative remedies and a broader range of solutions. Because the courts use a relatively structured approach, the range of remedies available may be quite limited. Lawyers may be required to reframe the issues so as to fit a particular legal doctrine and, thus, the nature of the dispute. As a result, the real issues and tailor an appropriate remedy. When using ADR instead of the court system, judicial precedent may not be as important. ADR often provides for relaxed rules of evidence

and procedure, which can enhance flexibility and make the process more streamlined than a judicial proceeding. (2001, p. 167)

Further, and perhaps unsurprisingly given the role we have seen neuroses play in the life of a legal community faced by the gradual colonization of law by economics, Equity fetishism on ADR has been met by neurotic counteraction. Lord Neuberger, for example, has argued both a defence of formal court-based civil justice, and, in a starkly anti-neoliberal move, for a rejection of consumerist justice (2010; also see Genn 2012, pp. 397–417). Also, Neuberger's particular neuroses exemplify an opposition between reality and fantasy that we explored in earlier chapters, as he equivocates between the reality of law's colonization by economics, and fantasy in the form of lamenting the effect of economics on the 'value' of justice (Freud 2001, p. 110). We can see the former in the following passage from his lecture to representatives of the Chancery bar,

> A successful capitalist economy, as Adam Smith pointed out, depends on a trusted and effective legal system. That is particularly true of an emphasis on financial and associated services. In that connection, the high reputation of our legal services, our courts and our law has served us very well since the 18th century. But we cannot afford to sit on our laurels. High legal costs do not always present the same problem for large businesses and a few very rich individuals, but legal costs are rarely an irrelevant factor even to them. So competition from other jurisdictions must always be in our minds. And it's not just arbitration and the new courts in Singapore, Dubai, Qatar and the like: there are now courts in Germany and the Netherlands which offer English language hearings. The threat to the British economy if we cease to be pre-eminent in the commercial legal world is self-evident. (2012, at 5)

The latter from Neuberger's keynote address to a civil mediation conference,

> Provided we acknowledge and take into account the disadvantages of mediation and do our best to cater for them or to neutralise them, I think we can and should be pretty uninhibited about supporting the idea of mediation in civil and family disputes. Since 1999, with the Woolf reforms, and even more since 2012 with the Jackson reforms, there is a very strong presumption that the court time and the legal costs involved in any civil case should be proportionate to the value of what is at issue in the case.

*Of course, the "value" of a case in this context is not limited to pure finan-
cial value, but normally and inevitably financial value is a major factor,
and, frankly, sometimes the only factor, when one is assessing proportionality*
[emphasis added]. (2015, at 13)

Echoing the notion of civil justice expansion beyond the court as a
neoliberal strategy, Gabel and Feinman state in their assessment of the
relationship between contract and ideology that, 'most of the time the
socioeconomic system operates without any need for law as such because
people at every level have been imbued with its inevitability and necessity'
(1998, p. 508). Gabel and Feinman's claim here is, I argue, reflective
of the particular shift in civil justice caused by neoliberalism that moti-
vates Lord Neuberger but ultimately struggles to reconcile. The effect
of neoliberalism on modalities of civil justice (like justice more broadly
conceived) has been not only to subject them to programmes of calculable efficiency (the 'value' problem that Neuberger laments), but also
to provoke hand-wringing regarding the (im)possibility of justice in an
unjust world that inevitably leads, as Simon Critchley says, to 'contempla-
tive withdrawal [...] a sort of drift, disbelief and slackening that is both
institutional and moral' and thus ultimately to submission to the dictates
of neoliberal capital, hence Neuberger's concern for the reputation and
relative competitiveness of British legal services (2012, pp. 38–39).

Neoliberalism has sped up the capitalist agenda during the last forty
years by broadening capitalist logic and reason to include wider and more
personalized pursuit of self-interest. If, as David Harvey suggests, neoliberalism produces a chaos of individual interests, and, as William Davies
claims, the 'economist's vocational and epistemological distance from
moral reasoning is the crucial ingredient in neoliberal legal authority',
then the civil justice required to meet neoliberal interests, unless deliberately geared towards forms of restraint against those interests, must flow
with and work in the shadows of that chaos and amorality (Harvey 2005,
p. 83; Davies 2017, p. 101). If we can interpret if this as relating to
laws that are systemized and encompass rule compliance whilst remaining
agile, flexible and discretionary, then the civil justice implied matches
conceptualizations of ECJ. Neoliberal approaches to civil justice take seriously, and arguably more so than during the nineteenth century, the
flexible and imaginative tenets of ECJ that allow more discretion and a
greater free play of enterprise around the fringes of legislation, regulation

and the core of rule compliance at the heart of the property rights regime (Millett 1998; Neuberger 2009; Ahern 2012, pp. 114–139).

Equity fetishism, whilst a product of nineteenth-century capitalism, was primed for the coming of the neoliberal age and a time in which 'remedies to any problems have to be sought by individuals through the legal system', and conceptions of fairness and equality are merely 'atavistic holdovers of old images of justice that must be extirpated from the modern mind-set' (Harvey 2005, p. 67; Mirowski 2013, p. 63). As Paddy Ireland argues, 'Unlike many of its rivals, capitalism is free from moral self-deception: it accords with and reflects human nature, and recognises the egoism of *homo economicus* and insatiable appetite to consume' (2018, p. 6). What we have seen regarding civil justice as representative of the legal system within neoliberalism, however, is a stretching and manipulation of the traditional boundaries of civil justice to ensure that flexibility no longer applies to the application of rules and doctrines alone, but also to modes of adjudication and the moral fabric in which these are wrapped. This is, I argue, a validation of ECJ's flexibly within the legal system and to civil justice, made by neoliberal stakeholders. Where neoliberalism recreates and memorializes principles of the free-market neoclassical economics that 'emerged in the second half of the nineteenth century (thanks to the work of Alfred Marshall, William Stanley Jevons, and Leon Walras) to displace the classical theories of Adam Smith, David Ricardo, and Karl Marx', seeing how Equity fetishism translates from the late nineteenth to late twentieth century with relative conceptual ease becomes clearer (Harvey 2005, p. 20). Regarding unconscionability as a remedy primed to support commercial stakeholder transactions, Equity fetishism points to the belief that there is a fix for every problem that might arise, including those in other areas and competences of the law.

In her discussion of the need to 'fill gaps' in the *Companies Act* 2006 for instance, Deirdre Ahern remarks that the 'flexibility of broad, principle-based judge-made rules facilitated judicial revitalisation of the duties where required to move with the changing world view in relation to corporate standards. Age-old principles proved capable of yielding new applications and new perspectives and this was instrumental in ensuring that the duties retained both credibility and relevance' (2012, p. 134). Despite the neoliberal reinvigoration or reincarnation of Equity, Equity fetishism is a testament to the reality capitalism has failed and cannot universalize complete justice. 'When universal law is recognized, idols are destroyed', argues Jean-Joseph Goux, 'this law is what enables the subject at last to bear the emptiness of the sanctuary without needing to furnish it with fetishes and images' (1990, p. 159). Captured in the concept of Equity fetishism, there is a sign that stakeholders cannot bear such emptiness. The existence of Equity fetishism thus reveals an even greater monument to the castration that stakeholders deny is central to subjectivity within neoliberalism, than during earlier points in Equity's history within capitalism.

The repetitive equivocation between crisis and failure that requires the re-imagination of capitalism fits broadly with what Joseph Schumpeter referred to as 'the essential point to grasp' when dealing with capitalism: that it is a fundamentally evolutionary system that can 'never be stationary' (2010, p. 72). The non-stationary nature of capital celebrated by the likes of Schumpeter abhors the inflexible rule and instead favours discretion and merit as modes of adjudication. The flexibility of Equity thus favours neoliberal civil justice, and the stakeholders invested in it who demand rules that bend to their will and self-interest. Discretion is not the court's alone however, as when regulatory standards of, for example, taxation become too onerous for stakeholders to bear, and they and their capital take flight offshore or hide behind obscure concentrations of economic power, such as trusts (Harrington 2016, p. 13). The 'versatility' of trusts, as described by Jonathan Garton, meets the versatility of modern private capital in its ability to flow freely to where it is less threatened by public or state interference (2015, p. 5). As John Christensen explains: 'If the trustee, the beneficiary, and the trust assets are located in the right combination of jurisdictions, tax can often be avoided altogether without technically breaking the law' (2015, p. 141).

Capitalism never leaves nor surrenders its grip on the domain of the social, despite appearances or claims to the contrary. As John Maynard Keynes remarked: 'It [capitalism] is a method for bringing the most successful profit-makers to the top by a ruthless struggle for survival, which selects the most efficient by the bankruptcy of the less efficient. It does not count the cost of the struggle, but looks only to the benefits of the final result which are assumed to be permanent' (2015, p. 50). The dominance of capitalism throughout the twentieth century and beyond shows it is a project of such resilience as to appear all but complete and victorious in its aims—'permanent', to echo Keynes. The many guises capitalist class power assumes (including neoliberalism) mask and detracts from what is otherwise an unrelenting and durable set of core ideological practices and tendencies. For stakeholders seeking to deflect the trauma of castration, through private property, the versatility of trusts to create wealth and so on, capitalism's endurance explains its appeal. It explains why stakeholders are keen to mobilize the legitimating forces of law and civil justice in support and defence of capitalist ideology, and how this project has spread. The neoliberal vision of law and justice now forms the basis of much-uncontested wisdom espoused, for example, in legal education textbooks that view competition as normative and a central tenet of legal common sense. Consider, for example, the following passage from a textbook on Competition Law,

> Competition means a struggle or contention for superiority, and in the commercial world this means a striving for the custom and business of people in the market place [...] The ideological struggle between capitalism and communism was a dominant feature of the twentieth century. Many countries had the greatest suspicion of competitive markets and saw, instead, benefits in state planning and management of the economy. However enormous changes took place as the millennium approached, leading to widespread demonopolisation, liberalisation and privatisation. These phenomena, coupled with rapid technological changes and the opening up of international trade, unleashed unprecedentedly powerful economic forces. These changes impact upon individuals and societies in different ways, and sometimes the effects can be uncomfortable. Underlying them, however, is a growing consensus that, on the whole, markets deliver better outcomes than state planning; and central to the idea of a market is the process of competition. (Whish and Bailey 2015, p. 4)

At a general level, Mirowski refers to this as 'a whole panoply of diverse "policy" responses' (2013, p. 336). For the purposes of this book we see it as far more specific: the application of ECJ to provide the flexible and agile civil justice system needed to complement and shadow the evolution of never stationary capital.

Legal Contortionism as Neoliberal Strategy

Equity fetishism is symptomatic of the fullest capability of legal contortionism: flexibility, adaptability, efficiency and agility, all of which stakeholders require and demand within neoliberalism to manage uncertainty and negotiate risk in personal and commercial settings alike. I agree with Irit Samet, therefore, that Equity 'is a live body of law that safeguards the legal system from the dangers of a myopic focus on rule-of-law values of certainty and predictability', but differ from him on the reasons and, perhaps more importantly, the motivations behind this (2020, p. 15). For me, such legal contortions as we find contemporary equity performing and which are applied at the level of civil justice, are not merely instrumental to more efficient and effective juridical-economic ontologies but part of the fabric of neoliberal existence. 'Flexible specialisation can be seized upon by capital', argues David Harvey, 'as a handy way to procure more flexible means of accumulation' (2005, p. 76). In terms of civil justice this includes leaving open the possibility that the courts will have discretion concerning remedies and the path to remedies, namely unconscionability, and the need for 'versatility', as we have previously seen regarding trusts (Hopkins 2007, p. 4). Mark Pawlowski maintains that adoption by the English courts of unconscionability has been far broader in recent years, and has, I argue, under the ideological aegis of neoliberalism proven a suitably wide-ranging and agile counterpart to the socioeconomic activities of competitive risk-inclined stakeholders (2001, p. 79).

Whilst we examined unconscionability in earlier chapters, it is important to restate some characteristics of the doctrine here, as it forms the backdrop to this section of the chapter. We can define unconscionability in a variety of ways that appeal to neoliberal thought. These definitions include highlighting the moral scope and content of the doctrine, and the ability to foster flexible and complete justice between parties. Drawing on a formulation of the doctrine in the nineteenth century, notably the case of *Fry v Lane* (1888) 40 Ch D 312, unconscionability has been defined as the intervention by Equity 'to set aside unfair transactions made with "poor and ignorant" persons' (Martin 2012, p. 911; Harpum et al. 2012, pp. 284–285). Following the more recent decision in *Hart v O'Connor* [1985] AC 1000 a 'preferable interpretation' of unconscionability has been viewed as being in cases where the court is able to show 'that the defendant acted in a morally reprehensible manner' (Virgo 2015, p. 280). Meanwhile, flexibility and adaptability are necessary, as Peter Birks maintained, to meet 'constant change in pursuit of justice', because 'it is important to remember that we do live in a legal world where continual and rapid change is an inescapable reality' (1996, p. 4).

I do not claim capitalism invented unconscionability—the *long durée* of Equity discussed throughout this book shows this is not the case. Instead, neoliberalism has seized upon unconscionability as a formal and legitimate mode of legal reason, remedy and adjudication that also engenders the requisite flexibility neoliberalism demands. 'Unconscionability *is* equity's jurisprudence', argues Gary Watt, 'since the word identifies that very species of wrongdoing which it is the peculiar function of equity to remedy, that wrongdoing being any conduct which, having no substantial justification, turns the common law into an instrument of harm by taking advantage of a general provision or general omission of the common law to oppress a party in the particular case' (2007, p. 128). For Graham Virgo statutory intervention via the *Consumer Credit Act* 1974 is the 'most important statutory provision relating to unconscionable conduct' (2015, p. 286). The Act 'gives the court extensive powers to deal with credit agreements where the relationship between the creditor and the debtor arising from the agreement is unfair to the debtor because of the terms of the agreement, the way in which the creditor enforced his rights under the agreement or anything else which the creditor has done or failed to do' (Virgo 2015, p. 286).

Organizing civil justice considering the demands of economic advantage enables stakeholders to secure the favourable legal system highlighted by Hayek: an all-pervasive form of economic reason that, as Philip Mirowski maintains, insists 'upon the thoroughgoing ignorance of everyone in the face of the all-knowing market', one built on a platform of the chaotic free play of economics (2013, p. 119). Economic reason that is purposefully and superficially nebulous and shape-shifting, yet still reliant on formalism and rule compliance. The privileging of Equity's notion of conscience in civil justice, channelled through the doctrine and language of unconscionability, engenders the essence of the flexible approach to civil justice favoured by neoliberalism. One which perversely disrupts neurotic concerns that the language of unconscionability can only ever be capable of 'sensible application' and a 'useful role in the story of property law [...] provided it is kept distant from infractions of moral conscience and social mores' (Watt 2007, p. 137).

As with Virgo's example of the *Consumer Credit Act*, it is important to note that the Act, like unconscionability, does not enforce an imperative of fair dealing among parties who may be unequal in terms of social or economic power, but foregrounds a morality that is always already economized in the neoliberal sense of ideological strategy (Gorz 1989, p. 2; Brown 2015, p. 151; Davies 2017, pp. 21–28). On these terms, unconscionability has, as Simon Chesterman has argued, affected 'change at a level deeper than the application of doctrine', under neoliberalism, it has helped change 'the structure of justice itself' (1997, p. 2). As Watt reminds us the 'language of unconscionability arises from the long saga of law's relationship to morality and in this sense borders on fiction and has the potential to engage with extra-legal notions of moral or ecclesiastical conscience' (2007, p. 128). Although he also adds, as if to negate any perverse estimations of the true value of conscience in law that 'most jurists long familiarity has bred healthy caution' for the possibility of extending the moral virtues of Equity beyond the margins of the legal context (Watt 2007, p. 128).

Unconscionability plays a significant role in sustaining the fantasy of complete justice by appearing to offer stakeholders more than a mere procedural framework in which to conduct and navigate their existence within society. They make the very notion of a procedural framework elastic within the terms of neoliberal justice, and unconscionability provides an effective means of following the contours of such nebulous juridical conditions. More than that perhaps, Equity fetishism offers stakeholders a 'spiritual duty in the form of what were termed moral obligations' but are an 'equitable diversion of positive norms', and unconscionability is a good solution for stakeholders on these terms (Goodrich 1996, p. 26). And The diversionary nature of unconscionability in this context further points to fetishism (Balibar 2017, p. 73). Under neoliberalism, unconscionability helps transform 'the ideology of "freedom and equality" [...] into a new image that might retain the legitimating power of the older images while modifying them to conform more closely to the actual organization of daily life in the modern era' (Gabel and Feinman 1998, p. 505). In contrast to the capitalism discussed it is no longer a project of complete justice that Equity is engaged with but under neoliberalism a far broader, nebulous and more pervasive social project that, to echo Wendy Brown, reaches for the very soul of the stakeholder (2005, p. 39). A project, as we have already seen, fuelled not by stakeholder desire for property rights, but equally by the need for flexibility and agility to navigate the risks that accompany the accumulation of property rights and a competitive struggle for wealth within contemporary neoliberal capitalist societies.

So, Gary Watt's claims concerning unconscionability—that 'if the retention of the language of unconscionability happens incidentally to perpetuate humane and aspirational virtues of conscience, that is well and good, but there is no room for the promotion of transcendental moral notions of "good conscience" as a basis for enforcing and allocating rights in property'—might ring true from the point of view of the law's neurotic protection of its own internal logic (2007, p. 118).

But from the point of view of perverse, fetishistic neoliberal stakeholders a doctrine such as unconscionability is precisely that which possesses a degree of the transcendental as a spiritual duty reproduced through the banal yet flexible diversion that ECJ offers from the risk-averse restraint of law's positive norms. David Harvey claims that under neoliberalism 'remedies to any problems have to be sought by individuals through the legal system', yet, and albeit given a far more specific analysis of the legal context, it is important to consider this simple idea alongside Watt's claim that any 'judge who employs the language of unconscionability as a means of ditching property rules in favour of moral intuition is abusing the name of conscience' (2005, p. 67; 2007, p. 118). Harvey paints a picture of the legal context in which perverse stakeholders conduct themselves and perform their contractual social relations. That stakeholders expect to use the legal system to remedy what are predominately contractual *qua* economic and financial issues, points directly to the call of the neoliberal founders to respect the rule of law and the ramifications that flow from it. Yet we must also consider that the 'highly financialised, neoliberal capitalism that has emerged is singularly unconducive to socially responsible or ethical behaviour' (Ireland 2018, p. 24). Through a further demonstration of the neurotic defence of legal principles that coloured the Judicature reform process by attempting to stave off the influence of stakeholders in shaping civil justice post-Judicature, Watt reveals the strategic value that unconscionability holds for fetishistic neoliberal stakeholders.

A clear and, I argue, a deliberate contradiction exists, therefore, between the value neoliberal thought places on stakeholder engagement with risk and the function the civil justice structure has in appearing to mollify uncertainties. It is through a privileging of doctrines such as unconscionability within the civil justice system that judges actually 'justify the normal', capitalist, 'functioning of the system' by resolving the conflict through fetishized legal forms that promise to fix the failure of, for example, contracts to suitably facilitate social relations between stakeholders (Gabel and Feinman 1998, p. 508). In response to Harvey's claim, therefore, I further argue that stakeholders substitute personal conscience for both a contract and the remedy of unconscionability that interjects at the point of the failure of that contract, and this enables certain freedom from the restraints of conscience. ECJ, broadly, thus serves as the de facto conscience of neoliberal stakeholders, a fundamental strategic significance and purpose of ECJ and specifically the doctrine of unconscionability. Neoliberalism demands that stakeholders walk a fine line between 'success' (profit, accumulation) and 'failure' because of its privileging of risk, and civil justice must, therefore, offer a safety-net for stakeholders. As Mirowski argues, 'accepting risk is not the fine balancing of probabilities, the planning for foreseen exigencies and the exercise of prudential restraint; rather it is wanton ecstasy: the utter subjection of the self to the market by offering oneself up to powers greater than we can ever fully comprehend' (2013, p. 119). For stakeholders to have a sense that remedies insulate them for exposing themselves to risk in everyday economic life, or that their individual economic conditions can somehow be 'reset' by remedies is important.

Citing P. S. Atiyah's view on risk and contract considering Lord Woolf's recommendations for the application of remedies in Equity to address a commercial financial loss—although he does not agree with it whole-heartedly—Hudson highlights how unconscionability is used to shape more effective commercial practices (2017, p. 912). This involves ECJ in commercial contracts being used to promote 'greater economic efficiency by requiring commercial people to become better at evaluating such risks before forming contracts' (Hudson 2017, p. 912). We might interpret the preparedness and due diligence that Atiyah appears to advocate for stakeholders engaging in contractual relations as common sense. If you can understand the ramifications of what you are contractually agreeing to, Atiyah appears to say, then you have successfully evaluated the risks that naturally accompany the contractual process. As, arguably, a neurotic response to risk, however, and not the response we would expect from the perverse fetishistic stakeholder, the contractual regime Atiyah is advocating does not account for the lure that risk has for stakeholders. Thus it is a desire *for* rather than protection *against* risk that justifies stakeholder evaluation of the contractual regime in which they commit to socioeconomic transactions. What we could easily interpret here as either legal instrumentalism or a 'baptism by fire' for commercial actors who fail to suitably (or rationally) evaluate the risks before committing to a commercial transaction, is in actuality entirely in tune with the normative forms of competitive risk-taking contained within the ethos that neoliberalism promotes. So, whilst Hudson feels it necessary to undertake a 'defence of Equity' regarding commercial actors who may see it as a body of law that works against their interest by unreasonably restraining their exposure to risk, considered through the lens of neoliberal reason the opposite is instead true. For stakeholders, Equity is absolutely the *thing* as a strategy embedded within economic risk-taking, because it inoculates against economic failure whilst fostering belief in a culture of risk.

As long as the stakeholder is economically active and, importantly, acting competitively by exposing themselves to risk, they have, in strict neoliberal terms, already proven themselves successful. As Atiyah maintains, in an overtly neoliberal voice, 'The whole point of the free market bargaining approach was to give full rein to the greater skill and knowledge of those who calculated risks better [...] He who failed to calculate a risk properly when making a contract would lose by it, and next time would calculate more efficiently' (1979, p. 437). In short, the stakeholder always comes back for more, and the protection offered by discretionary remedies saturated in the deontological imperatives of conscience is a significant way to guarantee this. The emphasis on the remedial *qua* conscience here, therefore, accords with neoliberalism's normative construction and interpellation of the individual as an economic and entrepreneurial actor in every sphere of life. By acting as the de facto conscience of stakeholders, so they need not concern themselves with restrictions their own conscience may place on the elision between the self and economic activity, unconscionability soothes stakeholder exposure to the harsh realities of what Wendy Brown calls, '"mismanaged life", the neoliberal appellation for failure to navigate impediments to prosperity' (2005, p. 42).

In a discussion not only of unconscionability but of the more general concept of compensation, Roberto Esposito says that as a remedy compensation 'implies, and reproduces, what it seeks to make up for' (2011, p. 82). For the stakeholder unconscionability, like Esposito's notion of compensation, implies a desire to fill a particular lack that exists, for example, regarding a financial loss, albeit less in terms of bare economic calculation than through subjective or personal (psychic) restitution. Yet in filling this lack the stakeholder equally maintains their belief in the fantasy of complete fulfilment: financial and psychic fulfilment as the same. Remedy defined in these terms, much like the broader conception of Equity that holds within its jurisprudence these forms of remedial action, performs the basic requirement of the fetish to substitute and thus deflect from the fact of loss even as actual economic or financial loss might occur (Freud 2006, pp. 90–91). 'What else is a surrogate, or prosthesis, if not a device that substitutes a presence, thereby reaffirming its absence?' asks Esposito, and in his question, we can once again discern the basic outline of fantasy and fetishism traceable to Equity and ECJ (2011,

p. 82). Fantasy 'denotes a framing device which subjects use to "protect" themselves from the anxiety associated with the idea that there is no ultimate guarantee or law underlying and guiding our social existence', argues Jason Glynos, 'this guarantee has been given many names, certainly when one takes the long historical view: God, Reason, the Senses, the Laws of History, and so on. But this guarantee – conceived as a key part of the fantasmatic device used to defend against a form of "Cartesian anxiety" – can take any guise whatsoever' (2012, p. 2405). We have, for instance, discussed this previously regarding Equity's development of the law of fiduciaries, and it also concerns protecting vulnerable parties via the doctrine of undue influence (*Bank of Credit and Commerce International S.A. v. Aboody and another* [1990] 1 Q.B. 923; also see, Millet 1998, p. 220).

CONCLUSION

Unconscionability is an example of what Hartmut Böhme calls 'fetishistic synecdoche'—'a figure through which the signifier completely substitutes the object it refers to, thereby becoming independent of this object' (2014, p. 311). Unconscionability *qua* Equity fetishism is a function of a culture of legal contortionism and remedial strategizing used by stakeholders against a backdrop of risk, competition and market engagement as requirements in contemporary economic life. Neoliberal emphasis on competition, risk and strategies to manage the two, gives civil justice purpose, and makes ECJ an economic consideration foremost. As Davies maintains: 'as a replacement for the pursuit of justice itself, neoliberalism offers the goal of competition as a form of quasi-justice, which lacks a substantive concept of the common good' (2017, p. 107). And so, because of the recurrent neoliberal problematic of 'how to represent or stabilize uncertainty, without determining it through political dictat', civil justice as a set of strategies 'offer to solve this' (Davies 2017, p. 115). The neoliberal notion of having a strategy (Wendy Brown talks of the neoliberal citizen 'who strategizes for her- or himself among various social, political, and economic options') begins with remedies assuming the object thingness of Equity fetishism (2005, p. 43). The unknown purpose of the object thingness of Equity-as-remedy transforms into an adaptable strategy and assumes a known purpose 'developed because it made people who operated under it more effective in the pursuit of their purposes' (Hayek 2013, p. 107). Unconscionability gives stakeholders a formalized conscience and within a semantics of perverse neoliberal stakeholder fantasy, complete justice *qua* Equity fetishism re-emerge as object(tive) strategies always already indexed to the stakeholder's fate in a society beholden to competitive and risky market activity and conduct.

Unconscionability marks a significant point of expansion of the traditional basis of the relief proffered by Equity (Mason 1994, p. 238). 'The transformations seen in the equitable jurisdiction', claims Simon Chesterman, 'mark a deeper transformation not merely in the formal (procedural) dispensation of justice, nor indeed the substantive rights of parties, but in the structure of justice itself' (1997, p. 357). ECJ *à la* unconscionability speaks to a particular emphasis given by stakeholders to judicial discretion. Specifically, forms of discretion that impose upon the neurotic judge, not the perverse stakeholder, the genuine risk of injustice. As a flexible, imaginative and discretionary invention unconscionability assumes the characteristic of a combination of certainty and uncertainty, 'the known and the unknown' and 'the experience of a limit' (Chesterman 1997, p. 363). It is a point of fantastical ecstasy that always already engenders the actions of neoliberal stakeholders in pursuit of the enjoyment of their economic and proprietary interests, and the corresponding pleasure and relief felt by them because of the remedial intervention that denies failure and thus denies lack. As Bernard Harcourt maintains, 'The element of desire in the notion of "fantasy", naturally, emphasizes wish fulfilment in the Freudian sense, but also an idea of playfulness. There is something enjoyable, often libidinal, which satisfies the person who believes' (2012, p. 2417).

REFERENCES

BOOKS AND ARTICLES

Ahern, D. Directors' Duties, Dry Ink and the Accessibility Agenda. *Law Quarterly Review*, Vol. 128 (January 2012), pp. 114–139.

Alfini, J.J., McCabe, C.G. Mediating in the Shadow of the Courts: A Survey of the Emerging Case Law. *Arkansas Law Review*, Vol. 54, No. 2 (2001), pp. 171–206.

Atiyah, P.S. *The Rise and Fall of Freedom of Contract*. 1979. Oxford: Clarendon Press.

Balibar, E. *The Philosophy of Marx*. Translated by Chris Turner. 2017. London: Verso.

Birks, P. Equity in the Modern Law: An Exercise in Taxonomy. *Western Australian Law Review*, Vol. 26, No. 1 (July 1996), pp. 1–99.

Böhme, H. *Fetishism and Culture: A Different Theory of Modernity*. Translated by Anna Galt. 2014. Berlin: De Gruyter.

Brown, W. *Edgework: Critical Essays on Knowledge and Politics*. 2005. Princeton: Princeton University Press.

Brown, W. *Undoing the Demos: Neoliberalism's Stealth Revolution*. 2015. New York: Zone Books.

Chesterman, S. Beyond Fusion Fallacy: The Transformation of Equity and Derrida's 'The Force of Law'. *Journal of Law and Society*, Vol. 24, No. 3 (September 1997), pp. 350–376.

Christensen, J. *The Greatest Invention: Tax and the Campaign for a Just Society*. A Tax Justice Network Production. 2015. Margate: Commonwealth Publishing.

Critchley, S. *Infinitely Demanding: Ethics of Commitment, Politics of Resistance*. 2012. London: Verso.

Davies, W. *The Limits of Neoliberalism: Authority, Sovereignty and the Logic of Competition*. 2017. London: Sage.

Esposito, R. *Immunitas: The Protection and Negation of Life*. 2011. Cambridge: Polity Press.

Freud, S. *A Case of Hysteria, Three Essays on Sexuality and Other Works: The Standard Edition Volume VII (1901–1905)*. Translated and Edited by James Strachey. 2001. London: Vintage.

Freud, S. *The Penguin Freud Reader*. Edited by Adam Phillips. 2006. London: Penguin Classics.

Gabel, P., Feinman, J. Contract Law as Ideology. *The Politics of Law: A Progressive Critique*. 3rd Edition. Edited by David Kairys. 1998. New York: Basic Books, pp. 497–510.

Garton, J. *Moffat's Trusts Law, Text and Materials*. 6th Edition. 2015. Cambridge: Cambridge University Press.

Gearey, A., Morrison, W., Jago, R. *The Politics of the Common Law: Perspectives, Rights, Processes, Institutions*. 2009. London: Routledge.

Genn, H. What Is Civil Justice for? Reform, ADR, and Access to Justice. *Yale Journal of Law & the Humanities*, Vol. 24, No. 1, Article 18 (2012), pp. 397–417.

Giddens, A. Risk and Responsibility. *Modern Law Review*, Vol. 62, No. 1 (January 1999), pp. 1–10.

Glynos, J. The Place of Fantasy in a Critical Political Economy: The Case of Market Boundaries. *Cardoza Law Review*, Vol. 33, No. 6 (August 2012), pp. 2373–2411.

Goodrich, P. *Law in the Courts of Love: Literature and Other Minor Jurisprudences*. 1996. London: Routledge.

Gorz, A. *Critique of Economic Reason*. 1989. London: Verso.

Goux, J.J. *Symbolic Economies: After Marx and Freud*. Translated by Jennifer Curtiss Gage. 1990. Ithaca: Cornell University Press.

Han, B.C. *Psycho-Politics: Neoliberalism and New Technologies of Power*. Translated by Erik Butler. 2017. London: Verso.

Harcourt, B.E. Fantasies and Illusions: On Liberty, Order, and Free Markets. *Cardoza Law Review*, Vol. 33, No. 6 (August 2012), pp. 2413–2428.

Harpum, C., Bridge, S., Dixon, M. *The Law of Real Property*. 8th Edition. 2012. London: Sweet & Maxwell.

Harrington, B. *Capital Without Borders: Wealth Managers and the One Percent*. 2016. Cambridge: Harvard University Press.

Harvey, D. *A Brief History of Neoliberalism*. 2005. Oxford: Oxford University Press.

Hayek, F.A. *The Road to Serfdom*. 2001. London: Routledge Classics.

Hayek, F.A. *Law, Legislation and Liberty*. 2013. London: Routledge Classics.

Hudson, A. *Equity and Trusts*. 9th Edition. 2017. London: Routledge.

Hopkins, N. How Should We Respond to Unconscionability? Unpacking the Relationship between Conscience and the Constructive Trust. *Contemporary Perspectives on Property, Equity and Trusts Law*. Edited by Martin Dixon and Gerwyn LL H Griffiths. 2007. Oxford: Oxford University Press, pp. 3–18.

Hudson, A. Law as Capitalist Technique. *King's Law Journal*, Vol. 29, No. 1 (2018), pp. 58–87.

Ireland, P. From Lonrho to BHS; The Changing Character of Corporate Governance in Contemporary Capitalism. *King's Law Journal*, Vol. 29, No. 1 (2018), pp. 3–35.

Jackson, R. Civil Justices Reform and Alternative Dispute Resolution. *Judiciary of England and Wales*, 20 September 2016. https://www.judiciary.uk/wp-content/uploads/2013/03/lj-jackson-cjreform-adr.pdf.

Jolowicz, J.A. General Ideas and the Reform of Civil Procedure. *Legal Studies*, Vol. 3, No. 3 (November 1983), pp. 295–314.

Keynes, J.M. *The Essential Keynes*. Edited by Robert Skidelsky. 2015. London: Penguin Classics.

Main, T.O. ADR: The New Equity. *University of Cincinnati Law Review*, Vol. 74 (2005), pp. 329–404.

Maine, H. *Ancient Law*. 1972. London: J.M. Dent & Sons Ltd.

Martin, J.E. *Modern Equity*. 19th Edition. 2012. London: Sweet & Maxwell.

Mason, A. The Place of Equity and Equitable Remedies in the Contemporary Common Law World. *Law Quarterly Review*, Vol. 110 (April 1994), pp. 238–259.

Millett, P.J. Equity's Place in the Law of Commerce. *Law Quarterly Review*, Vol. 114 (April 1998), pp. 214–227.

Mirowski, P. *Never Let a Serious Crisis Go to Waste*. 2013. London: Verso.

Moberly, R.B., Kilpatrick, J. Introduction: The Arkansas Law Review Symposium on Alternative Dispute Resolution. *Arkansas Law Review*, Vol. 54, No. 2 (2001), pp. 161–170.

Neuberger, L. The Stuffing of Minerva's Owl–Taxonomy and Taxidermy in Equity. *Cambridge Law Journal*, Vol. 68, No. 3 (November 2009), pp. 537–549.

Neuberger, L. *Equity, ADR, Arbitration and the Law: Different Dimension of Justice*. The Fourth Keating Lecture. 19 May 2010. http://www.civilmediation.org/downloads-get?id=98.

Neuberger, L. *Developing Equity—A View from the Court of Appeal*. Chancery Bar Association Conference, London. 20 January 2012. www.judiciary.uk/wp-content/uploads/JCO/Documents/Speeches/mr-speech-chancery-bar-assoc-lecture-jan12.pdf.

Neuberger, L. *Keynote Address: A View from on High*. Civil Mediation Conference. 12 May 2015. www.supremecourt.uk/docs/speech-150512-civil-mediation-conference-2015.pdf.

Pawlowski, M. Unconscionability as a Unifying Concept in Equity. *The Denning Law Journal*, Vol. 16 (2001), pp. 79–96.

Rai, S., Chandra, S., Mullick, S. ADR Processes: A Jurisprudential Understanding. *The Icfai University Journal of Alternative Dispute Resolution*, Vol. 7, No. 4 (2008), pp. 74–91.

Samet, I. Equity. *Research Handbook on Private Law Theories, Hanoch Dagan & Benjamin Zipursky eds., Forthcoming*. 2020. https://papers.ssrn.com/sol3/papers.cfm?abstract_id=3600193.

Schumpeter, J.A. *Capitalism, Socialism and Democracy*. 2010. London: Routledge Classics.

Stychin, C.F., Mulcahy, L. *Legal Methods and Systems*. 3rd Edition. 2007. London: Sweet & Maxwell.

Virgo, G. *The Principles of the Law of Restitution*. 3rd Edition. 2015. Oxford: Oxford University Press.

Watt, G. Unconscionability in Property Law: A Fairy-Tale Ending? *Contemporary Perspectives on Property, Equity and Trusts Law*. Edited by Martin Dixon and Gerwyn LL H Griffiths. 2007. Oxford: Oxford University Press, pp. 117–138.

Whish, R., Bailey, D. *Competition Law*. 8th Edition. 2015. Oxford: Oxford University Press.

Woolf, L. *Access to Justice: Final Report*. 1996. http://webarchive.nationalarchives.gov.uk/20060213223540/http://www.dca.gov.uk/civil/final/contents.htm.

Zinn, H. *A People's History of the United States from 1492 to the Present*. 2nd Edition. 1996. London: Longman.

CHAPTER 10

Law and the Reality It Masks

INTRODUCTION

The following statement from Lord Chancellor Campbell at the second reading of the Law and Equity Bill in 1860, one of the many stepping stones towards Judicature reform, is univocal in its appraisal of what is required to remedy the perceived ills in pre-Judicature civil justice.

> We have arrived at the conclusion that without abolishing the distinction between law and equity, or blending the Courts into one Court of universal jurisdiction, a practical and effectual remedy for many of the evils in question may be found in such a transfer, or blending of jurisdiction, coupled with such other practical amendments as will render each Court competent to administer complete justice in the cases which fall under its cognizance. We think that the jurisdiction now exercised by the Courts of equity may be conferred upon Courts of law, and that the jurisdiction now exercised by Courts of law may be conferred upon Courts of equity to such an extent as to render both Courts competent to administer entire justice without the parties in the one Court being obliged to resort to the aid of the other. (*HC Deb 24 April 1860 Vol. 158 cc1-211*)

Latent in Campbell's remedy 'for many of the evils' were serious questions regarding the future of the Court of Chancery: questions crucial in shaping the idea that civil justice ought to be more competent to achieve complete justice. For Lord Campbell or many lawyers, whether in the

R. Herian, *Capitalism and the Equity Fetish*,
https://doi.org/10.1007/978-3-030-66523-4_10

nineteenth century or in history, a competent justice system able to show not its own competence so much as that of the legal community who operate within it, makes it a vital consideration for civil justice reform.

What amounts to competence for the lawyer who must defend the ways and means of law with neurotic determination is, however, not necessarily the same interpretation of competence arrived at by stakeholders for whom the civil justice system must work in particular ways and produce particular and economically valid results. As Duncan Kennedy claims: 'If the cardinal principle, the legal foundation of capitalism, was that the state must respect the will of private parties concerning property and contracts, and if the cardinal principle rigidly controlled the particular subrules, then it was much more plausible to describe the economic process as "free"' (1985, p. 956). By ensuring economic reason as determinative of freedom through a regime of rights in and over property, in personal and commercial contexts, civil justice facilitates enjoyment for the stakeholder around a set of fantastical and perverse interests. As Alison Dunn maintains, 'In the commercial setting, equity's armoury is particularly attractive. The increasing complexity of the commercial world, with its diverse forms of property transactions, dictates a more direct and far-reaching approach to the recovery of assets than the common law can provide' (1999, p. 149). This is one example of Equity as competent in the eyes of the stakeholder, and, therefore, equally an 'attractive' object of desire and devotion. Given the discussion throughout this book, it is important to ask what competence represents or what realities it ultimately masks in terms of complete justice, the nature of civil justice more broadly, and the relationship of these to the existence and psychic life of stakeholders.

Competence is not a word or idea used expansively by this book and specifically not in relation to the theorization of the Judicature reforms and the results that flowed from them in the years of civil justice reform and evolution under capitalism that followed. The intention here is not to introduce a novel principle that will steer the critique along an alternative path. Instead, the notion or ideal of competence posited by Lord Campbell is relevant because it provides a means of summarizing and reconciling the key themes addressed during this book.

(IN)COMPETENT JUSTICE

Competence as we understand it here spans two planes. First, the transcendentalism of ECJ, as a stakeholder fetish charged with the authorial promise of guaranteeing private property rights to legitimate engagement in the private property order and bind stakeholders to the promise of the accumulation of wealth, and, ultimately, the belief in the future perfect of the secular and Godless 'thou will be done' of economic reason. Second, the utter banality, bureaucracy, and utility of civil justice that threatens to anchor the stakeholder 'in the drudgery of daily life' (McGowan 2016, p. 224). Presented by Lord Campbell during a period of rapid growth in capitalism during the mid-nineteenth century, the notion of competence echoed one of Sir John Mitford's earlier key determinations of the role of Equity's 'extraordinary jurisdiction', namely that the Court of Chancery assumed control over Common law jurisdictions by 'removing from them suits' which they were 'incompetent to determine' (1876, p. 106). What I claim are determinations of complete justice based on notions of competence that engender a marriage of the transcendental with the bureaucratic in harmony with neoliberal thought; what we might otherwise call a 'super-banality' (Baudrillard 2001, p. 203). The competence of which Lord Campbell spoke continues to resonate as a contemporary idea more than a century and a half later.

Like the excessive packaging that accompanies many contemporary commodities and often elicits the ire of the consumer who must negotiate it before they can get to the sweet fruit of the commodity inside, the complexities civil justice wraps around the private property order (that appear to restrain the free play of stakeholder economic interests), that signal competence, Equity transforms into a tantalizing prospect for stakeholder enjoyment. This is notable in ideas of fairness and conscience, and within the doctrine of unconscionability, which Alastair Hudson says is illustrative of Equity's engagement 'on a deontological, moral project, which it does by reference to the doctrine of precedent and centuries of careful worrying at its core' (2014, p. 61). And yet conscience in this context bears no relation to the 'sense of guilt' that, as Freud tells us, is a vital ingredient in understanding conscience as a tension between the harsh super-ego and the ego of the subject (2001, p. 123). Guilt is, instead, reserved for the criminal law where it justifies particular forms of sanction that society applies to guilty minds and acts. In contrast, defendants and claimants emerge from the civil justice system as either winners or losers determined not by a morality or ethics that is human, but one that is economic. Regardless of the outcome, conscience remains devoid of any genuine sense of guilt because it is vouchsafed from elsewhere, as a deferred systemic conscience, rather than a personal one. Conscience masquerades like the fetish object as a mere prosthesis, acting as a placeholder for what is lacking in the subject.

Further, Equity and ECJ are not suggestive of a moral project with centuries of 'worrying at its core' as Hudson claims, but are instead, and perhaps most notably within neoliberal capitalism, strategies predicated on a one-dimensional consideration that conscience is and ought to be economically determinative (Hudson 2014, p. 61). R. H. Tawney points to enforced reappraisal of the role of conscience in the life of Christendom because of the rise of capitalism as a need to come to terms with an 'obstinate refusal to revise old formulae in the light of new facts' in which the 'whole fabric of their philosophy, truth and fantasy alike, was overwhelmed together' (1990, p. 276). Max Weber talks of the particular recalibration of conscience in the construction of a 'style of life according to the dictates' of the spirit of capitalism' (2002, p. 295). Whilst Herbert Marcuse describes people 'led to find in the productive apparatus [of capitalism] the effective agent of thought and action to which their personal thought and action can and must be surrendered. And in this transfer, the apparatus also assumes the role of moral agent. Conscience is absolved by reification, by the general necessity of things' (2002, p. 82). Conscience as a basis for a better and more competent civil justice is, therefore, I argue, part of the expectation of systems and institutions to work towards and achieve deeper and stronger capitalism, including fluid capital market economies that privilege the exchange value of property and the favouring of tradable forms of ownership *qua* proprietary rights and interests. 'At a theoretical level, the association of conscience with moral values, social standards, fairness and justice serves to sustain the quintessential nature of equity or *epieikeia*', argues Alison Dunn, 'on a more practical level, the doctrine's inherent pliability enables a flexible approach to be taken not just to the remedy it affords, but also to its triggering requirements – two important characteristics in the face of a changing society' (1999, p. 142). Dunn's outline of Equity describes the clash of apparent supraeconomic (moral) and economic concerns indicative of the super-banality I associate, echoing Baudrillard, with the meta-psychological effects of Equity fetishism, but which, as Tawney, Weber, and Marcuse show, is an inescapable part of the construction of social expectations that correspond with the machinations of capital—a conjunction which also recalls the earlier discussion in this book of Marx with Freud.

We have seen that ECJ and in particular conscience are for stakeholders both objects of desire, in the form of remedies, vindication of rights and so on, and object *causes* of desire because of being an added layer of banal bureaucracy that ensures the stakeholder maintains a certain motivating distance in the form of a future promise of finding the lost object *qua* private property and wealth. 'It is precisely the status of being out of reach', as Todd McGowan claims, 'that serves to animate the subject' (2016, p. 215). ECJ never fulfils the promise of competence nor has to, but, to paraphrase McGowan, 'the act of promising itself has a creative power' that ensures stakeholders remain engaged and continue to invest economically and psychically in property under the demands of capitalist ideology (2016, p. 225). Yet Equity, ECJ, property rights or wealth can or will ever reunite the stakeholder with the lost object, and the stakeholder as a contemporary economic subject must perpetually negotiate the trauma of castration through a variety of substitutions in fantasy. And from the point of view of fetishism, in particular, a disavowal that a loss has ever occurred or that the subject is fundamentally constituted around a lack.

What for stakeholders is a competent civil justice system, therefore, one capable of producing so-called good results in terms of economic reason (improved efficiency, favourable cost-benefit analyses of case-load disposal, and so on), is arguably incompetent by any measure that does not insist upon economic reason as the primary or only determining factor of civil justice. This is because a competent civil justice system in the eyes of the stakeholder is one that masks the messy, human reality at the core of civil justice and brings the stakeholder into a more immediate and ecstatic union with economics as objective reality. One in which the reality of the failure of civil justice to realise the incomprehensibility of human relations through property and the accumulation of personal wealth, by instead promoting the property order as, for example, morally determinative, hides behind a thick tradition of neurotically defined language and principles that help structure stakeholder belief in the fantasies promulgated by capitalist ideology. As a result, competence is not only a measure of the distance between the transcendental and banal but also a clear sign of the influence of capitalist ideology and its colonization of the intertwined discourses of consolidation and reform that have shaped civil justice, piecemeal, since Judicature.

THE POLITICS OF EQUITY

David Kennedy argues that,

> The only way the nineteenth century judges could choose, and the only way we can choose a background regime is by making a vast multiplicity of detailed distributive and other ethical choices about right and wrong in

human interaction. The actual choice of the supposed "free market regime" of the late nineteenth century just could not be justified, then or now, on the basis of economic or legal science. The choice of that particular free market system over the other possibilities was inescapably political. (1985, p. 965)

My theory and analysis of Equity fetishism presents a case that does not consider capitalism or neoliberal capitalism good facilitators of justice in the public interest. Prevailing forms of justice within capitalism befit a narrow cohort of stakeholders able to show the privilege necessary to gain access to justice because of substantial private interest and wealth. But that justice also defines and legitimatises forms of economic subjectivity in Western Common Law societies judged, almost only, by an ability to own, to transact, and ultimately to perform and conduct oneself in a common-sense *qua* neoliberal capitalist juridical-economic fashion. The deontological imperatives that defined Equity through the ideas of Jeremy Bentham and up to Judicature are long gone in substance but preserved and fetishized in name and ideal as the discretion of judicial reason and the flexibility of unconscionability that bends a utilitarian law to points of fairness demanded and defined by the economic will.

R. H. Tawney offers a useful summary of the course this book has followed, where, notwithstanding the early modern conjunction of law and religion in the life and work of Thomas More and thereafter, Tawney's references to departmentalization of religion within economics apply equally, I suggest, to the fate of Equity and the Common Law,

> When the age of the Reformation begins, economics is still a branch of ethics, and ethics of theology; all human activities are treated as falling within a single scheme, whose character is determined by the spiritual destiny of mankind; the appeal of theorists is to natural law, not to utility; the legitimacy of economic transactions is tried by reference, less to the movements of the market, than to moral standards derived from the traditional teaching of the Christian Church; the Church itself is regarded as a society wielding theoretical, and sometimes practical, authority in social affairs. The secularization of political thought, which was to be the work of the next two centuries, had profound reactions on social speculation, and by the Restoration the whole perspective, at least in England, has been revolutionized. *Religion has been converted from the keystone which holds together the social edifice into one department within it, and the idea of a*

rule of right is replaced by economic expediency as the arbiter of policy and the criterion of conduct [emphasis added]. (1990, p. 273)

The notion of privilege is apposite here because it describes what both divides communities and creates the strange glue that binds them within capitalism, through aspiration and the bourgeois desire for private property and belief that it will lift them to a place of privilege. 'Private property has made us stupid and one-sided that an object is only *ours* when we have it – when it exists for us as capital', argues Marx, 'when it is directed possessed, eaten drunk, worn, inhabited, etc. – in short, when it is used by us. In the place of *all* physical and mental senses there has therefore come the sheer estrangement of *all* these senses, the sense of *having*. The human being had to be reduced to this absolute poverty in order that he might yield his inner wealth to the outer world' (Marx and Engels 1975, p. 300). In contrast, Hayek claims that private property is not a privilege (and socialists, among others, are therefore wrong to refer to it), precisely because all are free to acquire it. Therefore, even if only a few actually do so, because of a privileged relationship with civil justice, this does not make property nor any means of attaining it, privilege (Hayek 2001, pp. 83–84). Yet that all are free to acquire property is contestable, if not just wrong. But, then again, this is exactly the fantasy alluded to throughout this book: a fantasy promulgated by capitalism and sustained by neoliberalism that promises the stakeholder so much and delivers, at least in terms of a satiation of unconscious desires and often also in the material, proprietary substitutions they inhabit, so little.

To take political economy seriously, and perhaps more the necessity of its critique, in terms of Equity and civil justice is a message this book has attempted to communicate by bringing to the centre of the discussion the influence of capitalism on that field of juridical reason and practice. Capitalism, I have argued, promulgates fantasies, demands particular forms of subjectivity and conduct, and shapes the nature and institutions of civil justice in harmony with 'the idolatry of wealth […] the practical religion of capitalist societies' (Tawney 1990, p. 280). Equity is, therefore, political, although this is systematically and often obscured by shifts in sociopolitical dynamics that ultimately lead to the de-politicization of economic subjects *qua* 'the Dictatorship of Capital' (Han 2017, p. 6). 'The equity that most dominates the late capitalist imagination', argues Fortier, 'is equity as wealth' (2005, p. 186). He continues,

"What is your equity?" is an economic and not a moral question. This notion of equity is well-grounded in legal precedent: common law recognizes only the rights of ownership; equity, out of fairness, recognizes property rights other than ownership. Thus we can purchase equitable property rights in things (companies, etc.) that we don't actually own. Equity has always been in large part about property rights. But the elision of the principle of fairness at work, so that when we now speak of equity we don't mean the principle of fairness that demands a recognition of certain property rights but only of the monetary value involved, seems something like the elision of the creation of value that Marx sees in the notion of capital itself. Such an elision of principle and right, even as it speaks of wealth, cheapens equity as a moral idea. (Fortier 2005, p. 186)

Neither the super-banality of civil justice nor the 'elision of the principle of fairness' as a peculiar contribution that Equity makes to the field of civil justice can ultimately mask the political or the brutal and uncompromising core of competitiveness and self-interest that is the *sine qua non* of modern capitalist society. One which capitalism would rather the stakeholder did not see or concern themselves with for it might undermine the legitimacy of the capitalist project. 'Capitalism portends the end of the sacred or sublime location that could continue to reside outside of the system of exchange', argues McGowan, and accordingly everything 'becomes secular and quotidian because everything can be exchanged for the right price. This is the universe we continue to inhabit today' he concludes, 'a universe in which value is reducible to exchange value and in which nothing transcends the gravitational pull of exchange – not honor, not loyalty, not even love' (McGowan 2016, p. 218) Instead, the fetishization of Equity structures a fantasy of fairness through civil justice and private property and presents it to the stakeholder as a coherent and complete moral project that masks reality and disavows the traumatic core of capitalist subjectivity.

In the fetishist's mind, as Freud tells us in his 1927 formulation of the concept, 'the woman *has* got a penis, in spite of everything; but this penis is no longer the same as it was before' (2001, p. 154). For Freud (and Lacan), the first major change that occurs regarding the penis in theoretical terms is its transformation into the phallus, what Jean-Joseph Goux describes in his own work conducted at the intersection between Marx and Freud as 'the general equivalent of objects' (1990, p. 4). For the fetishist, all objects are open to fetishization where they can take the place of the penis (the object cause of desire) and as a result inherit 'the interest which was formerly directed to its predecessor [the penis]' (Freud 2001, p. 154). The last twist in Freud's aetiology being that with the fetish the subject's interest 'suffers an extraordinary increase [...] because the horror of castration has set up a memorial to itself in the creation of this substitute' (2001, p. 154). All attempts made by the subject to deflect the trauma of castration ultimately fail, leaving the subject only one conceivable option: learning to enjoy the limitations of human social existence and therefore what they do not have (McGowan 2013). Equity fetishism thus points to not competent civil justice, but its inverse and endlessly resisted form—especially by a neurotic legal community—*incompetent justice*.

'Facts never speak for themselves. Meaning is always imposed on them', says Roger Cotterrell, a reality that has rebounded throughout the topics discussed in this book. His solution (and mine) is the study of law in its broader social and political context and a call to theory that is both able and necessary 'to examine the coherence of the meanings we attach to what we observe about law and the context in which it exists' (Cotterrell 1987, p. 80). No shortage of critical work has achieved these aims. But Equity has not enjoyed quite the same level of attention. This book has described Equity and civil justice as products of capitalist reason and fetishism as a response within civil justice to capitalism. Within this complex of psycho-juridical and economic associations we find Equity prevailing, not because legislation mandates it, but because it is essential to satisfying powerful stakeholder desires within capitalism. Equity not only offers a good economic life for those who seek it, but a good fantasy life for those who demand it.

REFERENCES

BOOKS & ARTICLES

Baudrillard, J. *Jean Baudrillard Selected Writings*. Edited by Mark Poster. 2001. Cambridge: Polity Press.

Cotterrell, R. Power, Property and the Law of Trusts: A Partial Agenda for Critical Legal Scholarship. *Journal of Law and Society*, Vol. 14, No. 1 (Spring 1987), pp. 77–90.

Dunn, A. Equity Is Dead. Long Live Equity! *The Modern Law Review*, Vol. 62, No. 1 (January 1999), pp. 140–150.

Fortier, M. *The Culture of Equity in Early Modern England*. 2005. Farnham: Ashgate.

Freud, S. *The Future of an Illusion, Civilization and Its Discontents and Other Works: The Standard Edition Volume XXI (1927–1931)*. Translated and Edited by James Strachey. 2001. London: Vintage.

Goux, J.J. *Symbolic Economies: After Marx and Freud*. Translated by Jennifer Curtiss Gage. 1990. Ithaca: Cornell University Press.

Han, B.C. *Psycho-Politics: Neoliberalism and New Technologies of Power*. Translated by Erik Butler. 2017. London: Verso.

Hayek, F.A. *The Road to Serfdom*. 2001. London: Routledge Classics.

Hudson, A. *Great Debates in Equity and Trusts*. 2014. London: Palgrave.

Kennedy, D. The Role of Law in Economic Thought: Essays on the Fetishism of Commodities. *The American University Law Review*, Vol. 34, No. 4 (Summer 1985), pp. 939–1001.

Marcuse, H. *One-Dimensional Man: Studies in the Ideology of Advanced Industrial Society*. 2002. London: Routledge.

Marx, K., Engels, F. *Collected Works, Volume 3 1843–1844*. 1975. London: Lawrence & Wishart.

McGowan, T. *Enjoying What We Don't Have: The Political Project of Psychoanalysis*. 2013. Lincoln: University of Nebraska Press.

McGowan, T. *Capitalism and Desire: The Psychic Cost of Free* Markets. 2016. New York: Columbia University Press.

Mitford, J. *A Treatise on the Pleadings in Suits in the Court of Chancery by English Bill*. 1876. New York: Baker, Voorhis & Co. Publishers. http://www.mindserpent.com/American_History/reference/equity/1876_mitford_by_jeremy_equity_pleading.pdf.

Tawney, R.H. *Religion and the Rise of Capitalism*. 1990. London: Penguin Books.

Weber, M. *The Protestant Ethic and the "Spirit" of Capitalism and Other Writings*. Edited and Translated by Peter Baehr. 2002 London: Penguin Books.

REFERENCES

BOOKS AND ARTICLES

Ahern, D. Directors' Duties, Dry Ink and the Accessibility Agenda. *Law Quarterly Review*, Vol. 128 (January 2012), pp. 114–139.

Alexander, G.S., Peñalver, E.M. *An Introduction to Property Theory*. 2012. Cambridge: Cambridge University Press.

Alfini, J.J., McCabe, C.G. Mediating in the Shadow of the Courts: A Survey of the Emerging Case Law. *Arkansas Law Review*, Vol. 54, No. 2 (2001), pp. 171–206.

Althusser, L. *On Ideology*. 2008. London: Verso.

Althusser, L., Balibar, E. *Reading Capital*. Translated by Ben Brewster. 2009. London: Verso.

Anderson, T.L., McChesney, F.S. (eds.). *Property Rights: Cooperation, Conflict, and Law*. 2003. Princeton: Princeton University Press.

Arendt, H. *The Portable Hannah Arendt*. Edited by Peter Baehr. 2000. London: Penguin Books.

Aristodemou, M. *Law, Psychoanalysis, Society: Taking the Unconscious Seriously*. 2014. Abingdon: Routledge.

Aristotle. *Rhetoric*. Translated by W. Rhys Roberts. 2004. New York: Dover Publications.

Aristotle. *The Nicomachean Ethics*. Translated by David Ross. 2009. Oxford: Oxford World Classics.

Arndt, H.W. The 'Trickle Down' Myth. *Economic Development & Cultural Change*, Vol. 32, No. 1 (1983), pp. 1–10.

Atiyah, P.S. *The Rise and Fall of Freedom of Contract*. 1979. Oxford: Clarendon Press.

Atkins, S. *Equity and Trusts*. 2013. London: Routledge.

Atkinson, A.B. *Inequality: What Can Be Done?* 2015. Cambridge: Harvard University Press.

Auchmuty, R. Law and the Power of Feminism: How Marriage Lost Its Power to Oppress Women. *Feminist Legal Studies*, Vol. 20, No. 2 (August 2012), pp. 71–87.

Baldissone, R. From Helen's Pharmacy to the Multiverse of Equities: Difference, Opposition, *Différance*. *Pólemos*, Vol. 10, No. 2 (September 2016), pp. 137–157.

Balibar, E. *The Philosophy of Marx*. Translated by Chris Turner. 2017. London: Verso.

Barthes, R. *Mythologies*. 2000. London: Vintage.

Baudrillard, J. *For a Critique of the Political Economy of the Sign*. Translated by Charles Levin. 1981. St. Louis: Telos Press Ltd.

Baudrillard, J. *Jean Baudrillard Selected Writings*. Edited by Mark Poster. 2001. Cambridge: Polity Press.

Baudrillard, J. *The System of Objects*. Translated by James Benedict. 2005. London: Verso.

Beale, H., Bridge, M., Gullifer, L., Lomnicka, E. *The Law of Security and Title Based Financing*. 2nd Edition. 2012. Oxford: Oxford University Press.

Benjamin, W. *Walter Benjamin Selected Writings, Volume 1, 1913–1926*. Edited by Marcus Bullock and Michael W. Jennings. 1996. Cambridge: The Belknap Press of Harvard University Press.

Bentham, J. *Theory of Legislation*. Translated from the French of Etienne Dumont by R. Hildreth. 1864. London: Trüber & Co.

Bentham, J. *A Fragment on Government*. 1891. Oxford: Clarendon Press.

Bingham, T. *The Rule of Law*. 2011. London: Penguin Books.

Birks, P. Equity in the Modern Law: An Exercise in Taxonomy. *Western Australian Law Review*, Vol. 26, No. 1 (July 1996), pp. 1–99.

Birks, P. *Unjust Enrichment*. 2nd Edition. 2005. Oxford: Oxford University Press.

Blackstone, W. *Commentaries on the Laws of England Book I*. 2009. https://www.gutenberg.org/files/30802/30802-h/30802-h.htm.

Böhme, H. *Fetishism and Culture: A Different Theory of Modernity*. Translated by Anna Galt. 2014. Berlin: De Gruyter.

Bostaph, S. Utopia from and Economist's Perspective. *Thomas More Studies 1: Utopia*. 2006, pp. 196–198.

Bosteels, B. *The Actuality of Communism*. 2011. London: Verso.

Bottomley, A. (ed.). *Feminist Perspectives on the Foundational Subjects of Law*. 1996. London: Cavendish Publishing.

Boucher, D., Kelly, P. (eds.). Bentham. *Political Thinkers from Socrates to the Present*. 2003. Oxford: Oxford University Press.

Brown, W. *Edgework: Critical Essays on Knowledge and Politics*. 2005. Princeton: Princeton University Press.

Brown, W. *Undoing the Demos: Neoliberalism's Stealth Revolution*. 2015. New York: Zone Books.

Brown, W., Halley, J. (eds.). *Left Legalism/Left Critique*. 2002. Durham: Duke University Press.

Bryan, M.W., Vann, V.J. *Equity & Trusts in Australia*. 2012. Cambridge: Cambridge University Press.

Burn, E.H., Virgo, G.J. *Maudsley & Burn's Trusts & Trustees, Cases & Materials*. 7th Edition. 2008. Oxford: Oxford University Press.

Cahill, K. The Great Property Swindle: Why Do So Few People in Britain Own So Much of Our Land? *The New Statesmen*. 11 March 2011. http://www. newstatesman.com/life-and-society/2011/03/million-acres-land-ownership.

Campbell, D. Welfare Economics for Capitalists: The Economic Consequences of Judge Posner. *Cardoza Law Review*, Vol. 33, No. 6 (August 2012), pp. 2233–2274.

Chesterman, S. Beyond Fusion Fallacy: The Transformation of Equity and Derrida's 'The Force of Law'. *Journal of Law and Society*, Vol. 24, No. 3 (September 1997), pp. 350–376.

Chiesa, L., Toscano, A. Agape and the Anonymous Religion of Atheism. *Angelaki Journal of Theoretical Humanities*, Vol. 12, No. 1 (April 2007), pp. 113–126.

Christensen, J. In Trusts We Trust. *The Greatest Invention: Tax and the Campaign for a Just Society*. 2015. Margate: Commonwealth Publishing.

Cohen, M.R. *Law and the Social Order: Essays in Legal Philosophy*. 1982. New Brunswick: Transaction Books.

Coleman, J.L (ed.). *Readings in the Philosophy of Law*. 2013. New York: Routledge.

Cooter, R., Freedman, B.J. The Fiduciary Relationship: Its Economic Character and Legal Consequences. *New York University Law Review*, Vol. 66 (October 1991), pp. 1045–1075.

Cotterrell, R. Power, Property and the Law of Trusts: A Partial Agenda for Critical Legal Scholarship. *Journal of Law and Society*, Vol. 14, No. 1 (Spring 1987), pp. 77–90.

Cotterrell, R. *The Politics of Jurisprudence: A Critical Introduction to Legal Philosophy*. 1989. London: Butterworths.

Crimmins, James E. Jeremy Bentham. *The Stanford Encyclopedia of Philosophy*. Edited by Edward N. Zalta. 2018. [Online] Available at: https://plato.sta nford.edu/archives/sum2018/entries/bentham/.

Critchley, S. *Infinitely Demanding: Ethics of Commitment, Politics of Resistance.* 2012. London: Verso.

Davies, M. Queer Property, Queer Persons: Self-Ownership and Beyond. *Social & Legal Studies*, Vol. 8, No. 3 (September 1999), pp. 327–352.

Davies, W. *The Limits of Neoliberalism: Authority, Sovereignty and the Logic of Competition.* 2017. London: Sage.

Dean, J. *Democracy and Other Neoliberal Fantasies: Communicative Capitalism and Left Politics.* 2009. Durham: Duke University Press.

Dean, J. *The Communist Horizon.* 2012. London: Verso.

Deaton, A. *The Great Escape: Health, Wealth, and the Origins of Inequality.* 2013. Princeton: Princeton University Press.

de Chardin, P.T. *Le Milieu Divin: An Essay on the Interior Life.* 1964. London: Fontana.

Denning, A. The Need for a New Equity. *Current Legal Problems*, Vol. 5, No. 1 (January 1952), pp. 1–10.

Dickens, C. *Bleak House.* 2011. London: Penguin Classics.

Dinwiddy, J.R. Adjudication Under Bentham's Pannomion. *Utilitas*, Vol. 1, No. 2 (October 1989), pp. 283–289.

Dixon, M., Griffiths, G.L.L.H. (eds.). *Contemporary Perspectives on Property, Equity and Trusts Law.* 2007. Oxford: Oxford University Press.

Douzinas, C., Gearey, A. Critical Jurisprudence: The Political Philosophy of Justice. 2005. Oxford: Hart.

Dunn, A. Equity Is Dead. Long Live Equity! *The Modern Law Review*, Vol. 62, No. 1 (January 1999), pp. 140–150.

Easterbrook, F.H., Fischel, D.R. Contract and Fiduciary Duty. *The Journal of Law and Economics*, Vol. 36 (April 1993), pp. 425–446.

Endicott, Timothy O. The Conscience of the King: Christopher St. German and Thomas More and the Development of English Equity. *Toronto, Faculty of Law Review*, Vol. 47, No. 2 (1989), pp. 549–570.

Ensor, R. *England 1870–1914.* 1936. Oxford: Clarendon Press.

Esposito, R. *Immunitas: The Protection and Negation of Life.* 2011. Cambridge: Polity Press.

Evans, D. *An Introductory Dictionary of Lacanian Psychoanalysis.* 1996. London: Routledge.

Evershed, R. Reflections on the Fusion of Law and Equity After 75 Years. *The Law Quarterly Review*, Vol. 70 (July 1954), pp. 326–341.

Ferraro, F. Direct and Indirect Utilitarianism in Bentham's Theory of Adjudication. *Journal of Bentham Studies*, Vol. 12 (2010), pp. 1–24.

Fortier, M. *The Culture of Equity in Early Modern England.* 2005. Farnham: Ashgate.

Fortier, M. *The Culture of Equity in Restoration and Eighteenth-Century Britain and America.* 2015. Farnham: Ashgate.

Frankel, T. Watering Down Fiduciary Duties. *Philosophical Foundations of Fiduciary Law*. Edited by Andrew S. Gold and Paul B. Miller. 2014. Oxford: Oxford University Press, pp. 242–260.

Franklin, M. Book Reviews. *Tulane Law Review*, Vol. 8, No. 3 (April 1934), pp. 473–476.

Fraser, N., Jaeggi, R. *Capitalism: A Conversation in Critical Theory*. 2018. Cambridge: Polity Press.

Freud, S. *Moses and Monotheism, an Outline of Psycho-Analysis and Other Works: The Standard Edition Volume XXIII (1937–1939)*. Translated and Edited by James Strachey. 1964. London: The Hogarth Press.

Freud, S. *A Case of Hysteria, Three Essays on Sexuality and Other Works: The Standard Edition Volume VII (1901–1905)*. Translated and Edited by James Strachey. 2001a. London: Vintage.

Freud, S. *Jensen's 'Gradiva' and Other Works: The Standard Edition Volume IX (1906–1908)*. Translated and Edited by James Strachey. 2001b. London: Vintage.

Freud, S. *Five Lecturers on Psychoanalysis, Leonardo De Vinci and Other Works: The Standard Edition Volume XI (1910)*. Translated and Edited by James Strachey. 2001c. London: Vintage.

Freud, S. *Totem and Taboo and Other Works: The Standard Edition Volume XIII (1913–1914)*. Translated and Edited by James Strachey. 2001d. London: Vintage.

Freud, S. *The Future of an Illusion, Civilization and Its Discontents and Other Works: The Standard Edition Volume XXI (1927–1931)*. Translated and Edited by James Strachey. 2001e. London: Vintage.

Freud, S. *The Unconscious*. Translated by Graham Frankland. 2005. London: Penguin Modern Classics.

Freud, S. *The Penguin Freud Reader*. Edited by Adam Phillips. 2006. London: Penguin Classics.

Friedman, M. *Capitalism and Freedom*. 2002. Chicago: University of Chicago Press.

Funk, K. Equity Without Chancery: The Fusion of Law and Equity in the Field Code of Civil Procedure, New York 1846–76. *Journal of Legal History*, Vol. 36, No. 2 (2015). http://ssrn.com/abstract=2600201.

Gabel, P, Feinman, J. Contract Law as Ideology. *The Politics of Law: A Progressive Critique*. 3rd Edition. Edited by David Kairys. 1998. New York: Basic Books, pp. 497–510.

Galsworthy, J. *Forsyte Saga, Volume 1: The Man of Property, in Chancery, and To Let*. 2001. London Penguin Classics.

Garton, J. *Moffat's Trusts Law, Text and Materials*. 6th Edition. 2015. Cambridge: Cambridge University Press.

Gautreau, J.R.M. Demystifying the Fiduciary Mystique. *The Canadian Bar Review*, Vol. 68, No. 1 (March 1989), pp. 14–18.

Gearey, A., Morrison, W., Jago, R. *The Politics of the Common Law: Perspectives, Rights, Processes, Institutions.* 2009. London: Routledge.

Gemerchak, C.M. (ed.). *Everyday Extraordinary: Encountering Fetishism with Marx, Freud and Lacan.* 2004a. Leuven: Leuven University Press.

Gemerchak, C.M. Fetishism and Bad Faith: A Freudian Rebuttal to Sartre. *Janus Head*, Vol. 7, No. 2 (2004b), pp. 248–269.

Genn, H. What Is Civil Justice for? Reform, ADR, and Access to Justice. *Yale Journal of Law & the Humanities*, Vol. 24, No. 1, Article 18 (2012), pp. 397–417.

Giddens, A. *The Consequences of Modernity.* 1991. Cambridge: Polity Press.

Giddens, A. Risk and Responsibility. *Modern Law Review*, Vol. 62, No. 1 (January 1999), pp. 1–10.

Gilvarry, E. Lawyer of the Millennium: Gazette Survey. *The Law Society Gazette*, 24 November 1999.

Glynos, J. The Place of Fantasy in a Critical Political Economy: The Case of Market Boundaries. *Cardoza Law Review*, Vol. 33, No. 6 (August 2012), pp. 2373–2411.

Gold, A.S., Miller, P.B. (eds.). *Philosophical Foundations of Fiduciary Law.* 2014. Oxford: Oxford University Press.

Goodrich, P. *Law in the Courts of Love: Literature and Other Minor Jurisprudences.* 1996. London: Routledge.

Gorz, A. *Critique of Economic Reason.* 1989. London: Verso.

Goux, J.J. *Symbolic Economies: After Marx and Freud.* Translated by Jennifer Curtiss Gage. 1990. Ithaca: Cornell University Press.

Gramsci, A. *Selections from the Prison Notebook.* Edited and Translated by Quintin Hoare and Geoffrey Nowell Smith. 1971. London: Lawrence & Wishart.

Gray, K., Gray, S.F. *Elements of Land Law.* 5th Edition. 2009. Oxford: Oxford University Press.

Graziadei, M. Virtue and Utility. *Philosophical Foundations of Fiduciary Law.* Edited by Andrew S. Gold and Paul B. Miller. 2014. Oxford: Oxford University Press, pp. 287–301.

Grey, T.C. The Disintegration of Property. *Nomos*, Vol. 22, Property, 1980, pp. 69–85.

Gupta, S. *Corporate Capitalism and Political Philosophy: Corporate Capitalism and Political Philosophy.* 2001. London: Pluto Press.

Haldar, P. Equity as a Question of Decorum and Manners: Conscience as Vision. *Pólemos*, Vol. 10, No. 2 (September 2016), pp. 311–328.

Haley, M., McMurty, L. *Equity & Trusts.* 3rd Edition. 2011. London: Sweet & Maxwell.

Hall, S. *Cultural Studies 1983: A Theoretical History*. Edited by Jennifer Daryl Slack and Lawrence Grossberg. 2016. Durham: Duke University Press.

Hall, S. *Selected Political Writings: The Great Moving Right Show and Other Essays*. Edited by Sally Davidson, David Featherstone, Michael Rustin, and Bill Schwarz. 2017. Durham: Duke University Press.

Halliwell, M. *Equity and Good Conscience*. 2nd Edition. 2004. London: Old Bailey Press.

Han, B.C. *Psycho-Politics: Neoliberalism and New Technologies of Power*. Translated by Erik Butler. 2017. London: Verso.

Harcourt, B.E. Fantasies and Illusions: On Liberty, Order, and Free Markets. *Cardoza Law Review*, Vol. 33, No. 6 (August 2012), pp. 2413–2428.

Harpham, G.G. *Language Alone: The Critical Fetish of Modernity*. 2002. London: Routledge.

Harpum, C., Bridge, S., Dixon, M. *The Law of Real Property*. 8th Edition. 2012. London: Sweet & Maxwell.

Harrington, B. *Capital Without Borders: Wealth Managers and the One Percent*. 2016. Cambridge: Harvard University Press.

Harris, J.W. *Property & Justice*. 1996. Oxford: Oxford University Press.

Harvey, D. *A Brief History of Neoliberalism*. 2005. Oxford: Oxford University Press.

Hay, D. *Albion's Fatal Tree: Crime and Society in Eighteenth-Century England*. 1975. London: Pantheon.

Hayek, F.A. *The Road to Serfdom*. 2001. London: Routledge Classics.

Hayek, F.A. *Law, Legislation and Liberty*. 2013. London: Routledge Classics.

Hedley, S. Is Private Law Meaningless? *Current Legal Problems*, Vol. 64 (2011), pp. 89–116.

Hedlund, R. The Theological Foundations of Equity's Conscience. *Oxford Journal of Law and Religion*, Vol. 4, No. 1 (2015), pp. 119–140.

Heilbroner, R. *The Worldly Philosophers*. 2000. London: Penguin Books.

Heller, M.A. The Tragedy of the Anticommons: Property in the Transition from Marx to Markets. *Harvard Law Review*, Vol. 111, No. 3 (January 1998), pp. 622–688.

Herian, R. The Castrated Trustee: Jouissance and Breach of Trust. *Pólemos*, Vol. 10, No. 2 (September 2016), pp. 97–115.

Herian, R. The Conscience of Thomas More: An Introduction to Equity in Modernity. *The Heythrop Journal* (early access), 2020, pp. 1–12.

Hobsbawm, E. *The Age of Revolution 1789–1848*. 1992. London: Abacus.

Hobsbawm, E. *The Age of Capital 1848–1875*. 1997. London: Abacus.

Hodgson, G. M. *Conceptualizing Capitalism: Institutions, Evolution, Future*. 2015. Chicago: University of Chicago Press.

Holdsworth, W.S. *Sources and Literature of English Law*. 1925. Oxford: Clarendon Press.

Holdsworth, W.S. Blackstone's Treatment of Equity. *Harvard Law Review*, Vol. 43, No. 1 (November 1929), pp. 1–32.

Honoré, A.M. Ownership. *Readings in the Philosophy of Law*. Edited by Jules L. Coleman. 2013. New York: Routledge, pp. 563–574.

Hopkins, N. How Should We Respond to Unconscionability? Unpacking the Relationship between Conscience and the Constructive Trust. *Contemporary Perspectives on Property, Equity and Trusts Law*. Edited by Martin Dixon and Gerwyn LL H Griffiths. 2007. Oxford: Oxford University Press, pp.3–18.

Hudson, A. *The Law of Finance*. 2nd Edition. 2013. London: Sweet & Maxwell.

Hudson, A. *Great Debates in Equity and Trusts*. 2014. London: Palgrave.

Hudson, A. *Equity and Trusts*. 9th Edition. 2017. London: Routledge.

Hudson, A. Law as Capitalist Technique. *King's Law Journal*, Vol. 29, No. 1 (2018), pp. 58–87.

Ireland, P. From Lonrho to BHS; The Changing Character of Corporate Governance in Contemporary Capitalism. *King's Law Journal*, Vol. 29, No. 1 (2018), pp. 3–35.

Jackson, R. Civil Justices Reform and Alternative Dispute Resolution. *Judiciary of England and Wales*, 20 September 2016. https://www.judiciary.uk/wp-content/uploads/2013/03/lj-jackson-cjreform-adr.pdf.

Johnson Jr, J.F. Natural Law and the Fiduciary Duties of Business Managers. *Journal of Markets and Morality*, Vol. 8, No. 1 (Spring 2005), pp. 27–51.

Jolowicz, J.A. General Ideas and the Reform of Civil Procedure. *Legal Studies*, Vol. 3, No. 3 (November 1983), pp. 295–314.

Jones, J.W. *The Law and Legal Theory of the Greeks*. 1956. Oxford: Clarendon Press.

Kairys, D. (ed.). *The Politics of Law: A Progressive Critique*. 3rd Edition. 1998. New York: Basic Books.

Kant, I. *The Moral Law*. Translated by H. J. Paton. 2005. London: Routledge Classics.

Kelly, P. Bentham. *Political Thinkers from Socrates to the Present*. Edited by David Boucher and Paul Kelly. 2003. Oxford: Oxford University Press, pp. 307–323.

Kennedy, D. The Role of Law in Economic Thought: Essays on the Fetishism of Commodities. *The American University Law Review*, Vol. 34, No. 4 (Summer 1985), pp. 939–1001.

Kerly, D.M. *An Historical Sketch of the Equitable Jurisdiction of the Court of Chancery: Being the Yorke Prize Essay of the University of Cambridge for 1889*. 1889. Leopold Classic Library.

Kerruish, V. *Jurisprudence as Ideology*. 1991. London: Routledge.

Keynes, J.M. *The Essential Keynes*. Edited by Robert Skidelsky. 2015. London: Penguin Classics.

Klinck, D.R. Doing "Complete Justice": Equity in the Ontario Court of Chancery. *Queens Law Journal*, Vol. 32, No. 1 (Fall 2006), pp. 45–81.

Klinck, D.R. *Conscience, Equity and the Court of Chancery in Early Modern England*. 2010. Farnham: Ashgate.

Krips, H. *Fetish: An Erotics of Culture*. 1999. Ithaca: Cornell University Press.

Lacan, J. *Écrits: A Selection*. Translated by Alan Sheridan. 2001. London: Routledge Classics.

Laycock, D. The Triumph of Equity. *Law and Contemporary Problems*, Vol. 56, No. 3 (Summer 1993), pp. 53–82.

Le Guin, U.K. *Dancing at the Edge of the World: Thoughts on Words, Women, Places*. 1989. New York: Grove Press.

Lefebvre, H. *Critique of Everyday Life*. 2014. London: Verso.

Legendre, P. *Law and the Unconscious: A Legendre Reader*. Edited by Peter Goodrich. Translated by Peter Goodrich with Alain Pottage and Anton Schütz. 1997. Basingstoke: Palgrave Macmillan.

Letwin, S.R. *The Pursuit of Certainty: David Hume, Jeremy Bentham, John Stuart Mill, Beatrice Webb*. 1998. Indianapolis: Liberty Fund.

Lippit, Victor D. *Capitalism*. 2005. London: Routledge.

Lobban, M. Preparing for Fusion: Reforming the Nineteenth-Century Court of Chancery, Part I. *Law and History Review*, Vol. 22, No. 2 (Summer 2004a), pp. 389–427.

Lobban, M. Preparing for Fusion: Reforming the Nineteenth-Century Court of Chancery, Part II. *Law and History Review*, Vol. 22, No. 3 (Fall 2004b), pp. 565–599.

Lobban, M. Mapping the Common Law: Some Lessons from History. *New Zealand Law Review*, Vol. 2014 (2014), No. 1, pp. 21–67.

Loughlin, M. *The Idea of Public Law*. 2003. Oxford: Oxford University Press.

Lukács, G. *History and Class Consciousness: Studies in Marxist Dialectics*. Translated by Rodney Livingstone. 1971. London: Merlin Press.

Main, T.O. ADR: The New Equity. *University of Cincinnati Law Review*, Vol. 74 (2005), pp. 329–404.

Maine, H. *Ancient Law*. 1972. London: J.M. Dent & Sons Ltd.

Maitland, F.W. *Equity: A Course of Lectures*. 1969. Cambridge: Cambridge University Press.

Mannoni, O. *Freud: Theory of the Unconscious*. Translated by Renaud Bruce. 2015. London: Verso.

Marcuse, H. *One-Dimensional Man: Studies in the Ideology of Advanced Industrial Society*. 2002. London: Routledge.

Markovits, D. Sharing Ex Ante and Sharing Ex Post. *Philosophical Foundations of Fiduciary Law*. Edited by Andrew S. Gold and Paul B. Miller. 2014. Oxford: Oxford University Press, pp. 209–224.

Martin, J.E. *Modern Equity*. 19th Edition. 2012. London: Sweet & Maxwell.

Marx, K. *A Contribution to the Critique of Political Economy.* 1859. https://
www.marxists.org/archive/marx/works/1859/critique-pol-economy/pre
face.htm.

Marx, K. *Capital Volume 1.* 1930. London: J.M. Dent & Sons Ltd.

Marx, K., Engels, F. *The German Ideology.* Edited by C.J. Arthur. 1970. London:
Lawrence & Wishart.

Marx, K., Engels, F. *Collected Works, Volume 3 1843–1844.* 1975. London:
Lawrence & Wishart.

Marx, K., Engels, F. *The Communist Manifesto.* Edited by David McLellen. 1998.
Oxford: Oxford World Classics.

Mason, A. The Place of Equity and Equitable Remedies in the Contemporary
Common Law World. *Law Quarterly Review,* Vol. 110 (April 1994), pp. 238–
259.

McGowan, T. *Enjoying What We Don't Have: The Political Project of Psychoanalysis.* 2013. Lincoln: University of Nebraska Press.

McGowan, T. *Capitalism and Desire: The Psychic Cost of Free* Markets. 2016.
New York: Columbia University Press.

Meagher, R.P., Gummow, W.M.C., Lehane, J.R.F. *Equity Doctrines & Remedies.*
3rd edition. 1992. Sydney: Butterworths.

Mill, J.S. *Principles of Political Economy and Chapters on Socialism.* Edited by
Johnathan Riley. 2008. Oxford: Oxford University Press.

Millett, P.J. Equity's Place in the Law of Commerce. *Law Quarterly Review,* Vol.
114 (April 1998), pp. 214–227.

Mirowski, P. *Never Let a Serious Crisis Go to Waste.* 2013. London: Verso.

Mitchell, C., Mitchell, P. (eds.). *Landmark Cases in Equity.* 2012. London:
Bloomsbury.

Mitford, J. *A Treatise on the Pleadings in Suits in the Court of
Chancery by English Bill.* 1876. New York: Baker, Voorhis & Co.
Publishers. http://www.mindserpent.com/American_History/reference/equ
ity/1876_mitford_by_jeremy_equity_pleading.pdf.

Moberly, R.B., Kilpatrick, J. Introduction: The Arkansas Law Review Symposium
on Alternative Dispute Resolution. *Arkansas Law Review,* Vol. 54, No. 2
(2001), pp. 161–170.

Neuberger, L. The Stuffing of Minerva's Owl–Taxonomy and Taxidermy in
Equity. *Cambridge Law Journal,* Vol. 68, No. 3 (November 2009), pp. 537–
549.

Neuberger, L. *Equity, ADR, Arbitration and the Law: Different Dimension of
Justice.* The Fourth Keating Lecture. 19 May 2010. http://www.civilmedi
ation.org/downloads-get?id=98.

Neuberger, L. *Has Equity Had Its Day?* Hong Kong University Common Law
Lecture 2010. 12 October 2010. Hong Kong. http://webarchive.nationala

rchives.gov.uk/20131202164909/http://judiciary.gov.uk/Resources/JCO/
Documents/Speeches/mr-speech-hong-kong-lecture-12102010.pdf.

Neuberger, L. *Has Mediation Had Its Day?* The Gordon Slynn Memorial
Lecture. 11 November 2010. http://www.judiciary.gov.uk/Resources/JCO/
Documents/Speeches/moj-speech-mediation-lectureA.pdf.

Neuberger, L. *Developing Equity—A View from the Court of Appeal.* Chancery
Bar Association Conference, London. 20 January 2012. www.judiciary.uk/
wp-content/uploads/JCO/Documents/Speeches/mr-speech-chancery-bar-
assoc-lecture-jan12.pdf.

Neuberger, L. *Equity—The Soul and Spirit of All Law or a Roguish Thing?*
Lehane Lecture 2014, Supreme Court of New South Wales, Sydney. 4 August
2014. https://www.supremecourt.uk/docs/speech-140804.pdf.

Neuberger, L. *Keynote Address: A View from on High.* Civil Mediation Conference. 12 May 2015. www.supremecourt.uk/docs/speech-150512-civil-mediat
ion-conference-2015.pdf.

Newman, R.A. (ed.). *Equity in the World's Legal Systems: A Comparative Study
(dedicated to Rene Cassin).* 1973. Brussels: Établissements Émile Bruylant.

Nozick, R. *Anarchy, State and Utopia.* 1974. New York: Basic Books.

Oppermann, J.P. Tending the Garden: Equity and Exscription. *Pólemos,* Vol. 10,
No. 2 (September 2016), pp. 117–136.

Pashukanis, E.B. *Law & Marxism: A General Theory Towards a Critique of the
Fundamental Juridical Concepts.* Translated by Barbara Einhorn. Edited by
Chris Arthur. 1989. London: Pluto Press.

Pawlowski, M. Unconscionability as a Unifying Concept in Equity. *The Denning
Law Journal,* Vol. 16 (2001), pp. 79–96.

Pearce, R., Barr, W. *Pearce & Stevens' Trusts and Equitable Obligations.* 6th
Edition. 2015. Oxford: Oxford University Press.

Penner, J.E. *The Idea of Property in Law.* 1997. Oxford: Oxford University Press.

Perreau-Saussine, A. Bentham and the Boot-Strappers of Jurisprudence: The
Moral Commitments of a Rationalist Legal Positivist. *Cambridge Law
Journal,* Vol. 63, No. 2 (July 2004), pp. 346–383.

Pierson, C. *Just Property, Volume Two: Enlightenment, Revolution, and History.*
2016. Oxford: Oxford University Press.

Piketty, T. *Capital in the Twenty-First Century.* Translated by Arthur Goldhammer. 2014. Cambridge: The Belknap Press of Harvard University Press.

Polanyi, K. *Great Transformation: The Political and Economic Origins of Our
Time.* 2001. Boston: Beacon Press.

Polanyi, K. *Economy and Society: Selected Writings.* 2018. Cambridge: Polity
Press.

Posner, Richard A. *Economic Analysis of Law.* 3rd Edition. 1986. Boston: Little,
Brown and Company.

Postema, G.J. Law's System: The Necessity of System in Common Law. *New Zealand Law Review*, Vol. 2014, No. 1 (2014), pp. 69–105.

Potter, H. *An Introduction to the History of Equity and Its Courts.* 1931. London: Sweet & Maxwell.

Pound, R. The Decadence of Equity. *Columbia Law Review*, Vol. 5, No. 1 (January 1905), pp. 20–35.

Probert, R. Trusts and the Modern Woman—Establishing an Interest in the Family Home. *Child and Family Law Quarterly*, Vol. 13, No. 3 (2001), pp. 275–286.

Pugsley, D. Coleridge, John Duke, First Baron Coleridge (1820–1894). *Oxford Dictionary of National Biography.* 2004. Oxford: Oxford University Press. http://www.oxforddnb.com/view/article/5886.

Radin, M.J. *Reinterpreting Property.* 1996. Chicago: University of Chicago Press.

Rai, S., Chandra, S., Mullick, S. ADR Processes: A Jurisprudential Understanding. *The Icfai University Journal of Alternative Dispute Resolution*, Vol. 7, No. 4 (2008), pp. 74–91.

Rancière, J. *Disagreement: Politics and Philosophy.* Translated by Julie Rose. 1999. Minneapolis: University of Minnesota Press.

Robinson, J. *Economic Philosophy.* 1964. Harmondsworth: Penguin Books.

Roemer, J.E. *Theories of Distributive Justice.* 1996. Cambridge: Harvard University Press.

Rose, N. *Powers of Freedom: Reframing Political Thought.* 1999. Cambridge: Cambridge University Press.

Samet, I. *Equity: Conscience Goes to Market.* 2018. Oxford: Oxford University Press.

Samet, I. Equity. *Research Handbook on Private Law Theories, Hanoch Dagan & Benjamin Zipursky eds., Forthcoming.* 2020. https://papers.ssrn.com/sol3/papers.cfm?abstract_id=3600193.

Selden, J. *Table Talk of John Selden.* 1856. London: J.R. Smith. https://archive.org/details/tabletalkofjohns00seldiala.

Schumpeter, J.A. *Capitalism, Socialism and Democracy.* 2010. London: Routledge Classics.

Schroeder, J.L. *The Triumph of Venus: The Erotics of the Market.* 2004. Berkeley: University of California Press.

Scott, B.R. *Capitalism: Its Origins and Evolution as a System of Governance.* 2011. Berlin: Springer.

Shaxson, N. *Treasure Islands: Tax Havens and the Men Who Stole the World.* 2011. London: Vintage.

Singer, J. *Entitlement: The Paradoxes of Property.* 2000. New Haven: Yale University Press.

Sitkoff, R. The Economic Structure of Fiduciary Law. *Boston University Law Review*, Vol. 91 (2011), pp. 1039–1049.

Smith, H. Why Fiduciary Law is Equitable. *Philosophical Foundations of Fiduciary Law*. Edited by Andrew S. Gold and Paul B. Miller. 2014. Oxford: Oxford University Press, pp. 261–284.

Sorabji, J. *English Civil Justice After the Woolf and Jackson Reforms: A Critical Analysis*. 2014. Cambridge: Cambridge University Press.

Standing, G. *The Corruption of Capitalism: Why Rentiers Thrive ad Work Does Not Pay*. 2017. London: Biteback Publishing.

Stebbings, C. *The Private Trustee in Victorian England*. 2002. Cambridge: Cambridge University Press.

Stiegler, B. *For a New Critique of Political Economy*. 2010. Cambridge: Polity Press.

Stiglitz, J.E. *The Price of Inequality*. 2013. London: Penguin Books.

Stoller, R.J. *Observing the Erotic Imagination*. 1985. New Haven: Yale University Press.

Stychin, C.F., Mulcahy, L. *Legal Methods and Systems*. 3rd Edition. 2007. London: Sweet & Maxwell.

Tawney, R.H. *Religion and the Rise of Capitalism*. 1990. London: Penguin Books.

Thompson, E.P. *The Making of the English Working Class*. 2013. London: Penguin Modern Classics.

Tomšič, S. *The Capitalist Unconscious: Marx and Lacan*. 2015. London: Verso.

Towers, R. Man for the Millennium. *The Law Society Gazette*, 17 December 1999.

Virgo, G. *The Principles of Equity & Trusts*. 2012. Oxford: Oxford University Press.

Virgo, G. *The Principles of the Law of Restitution*. 3rd Edition. 2015. Oxford: Oxford University Press.

Von Mises, L. *Liberalism: The Classical Tradition*. Edited by Bettina Bien Greaves. 2005. Indianapolis: Liberty Fund.

Von Mises, L. *The Anti-Capitalist Mentality*. 2009. Mansfield Centre: Martino Publishing.

Watt, G. *Equity Stirring: The Story of Justice Beyond Law*. 2012. Oxford: Hart Publishing.

Watt, G. *Trusts & Equity*. 6th Edition. 2014. Oxford: Oxford University Press.

Watts, P. Taxonomy in Private Law—Furor in Text and Subtext. *New Zealand Law Review*, Vol. 2014, No. 1 (2014), pp. 107–144.

Weber, M. *The Protestant Ethic and the "Spirit" of Capitalism and Other Writings*. Edited and Translated by Peter Baehr. 2002 London: Penguin Books.

West, Edwin G. Property Rights in the History of Economic Thought: From Locke to J.S. Mill. *Property Rights: Cooperation, Conflict, and Law*. Edited by Terry L. Anderson and Fred S. McChesney. 2003. Princeton: Princeton University Press, pp. 20–42.

Whish, R., Bailey, D. *Competition Law*. 8th Edition. 2015. Oxford: Oxford University Press.

Williams, F. *Magnificent Journey: The Rise of the Trade Unions*. 1954. London: Odhams Press.

Williams, R. *Keywords: A Vocabulary of Culture and Society*. 1988. London: Fontana Press.

Wolff, J. *An Introduction to Political Philosophy*. 1996. Oxford: Oxford University Press.

Wolin, S.S. *Tocqueville Between Two Worlds: The Marking of a Political and Theoretical Life*. 2001. Princeton: Princeton University Press.

Wood, E.M. *The Origins of Capitalism: A Longer View*. 2017. London: Verso.

Woodward, L. *The Age of Reform 1815–1870*. 1962. Oxford: Clarendon Press.

Woolf, L. *Access to Justice: Final Report*. 1996. http://webarchive.nationalarch ives.gov.uk/20060213223540/http://www.dca.gov.uk/civil/final/contents. htm.

Worthington, S. *Equity*. 2nd Edition. 2006. Oxford: Oxford University Press.

Yip, M., Lee, J. The Commercialisation of Equity. *Legal Studies*, Vol. 37, No. 4 (2017), pp. 647–671.

Zinn, H. *A People's History of the United States from 1492 to the Present*. 2nd Edition. 1996. London: Longman.

Žižek, S. *The Sublime Object of Ideology*. 1989. London: Verso.

Žižek, S. *The Ticklish Subject: The Absent Centre of Political Ontology*. 1999. London: Verso.

Žižek, S. *How to Read Lacan*. 2007. New York: W.W. Norton & Company.

Žižek, S. *For They Know Not What They Do: Enjoyment as a Political Factor*. 2008. London: Verso.

MISCELLANEOUS ONLINE RESOURCES

http://hansard.millbanksystems.com/.

https://www.taxjustice.net/.

Art. XII—The Chancery Reform Association reporting on and quoting, H.W. Weston, Secretary to the Chancery Reform Association. *Chancery Infamy, or a Plea for an Anti-Chancery League; Dedicated to All Chancery Suitors and Reformers*. 2nd Edition. 1850. London: Effingham Wilson.

Art. XII—The Chancery Reform Association. *Law Review, and Quarterly Journal of British and Foreign Jurisprudence*, Vol. 13, No. 1 (November 1850), pp. 193–208.

Founding Statement of the Mont Pelerin Society, Switzerland, April 8, 1947. https://www.montpelerin.org/statement-of-aims/.

Ministry of Justice. *Civil Justice Statistics Quarterly, England and Wales (Incorporating The Royal Courts of Justice 2015).* 2016. https://www.gov.uk/gov ernment/uploads/system/uploads/attachment_data/file/527018/civil-jus tice-statistics-january-march-2016.pdf.
New York (State). Commissioners on Practice and Pleadings. *The Code of Civil Procedure of the State of New-York.* 1850. Albany: Weed, Parsons & co., public printers. https://archive.org/details/codecivilproced00fielgoog.
The Stanford Encyclopedia of Philosophy. Edited by Edward N. Zalta. 2018. https://plato.stanford.edu/archives/sum2018/entries/bentham/.

CASE-LAW AND LEGISLATION

Access to Justice Act 1999 (c.22).
Alec Lobb (Garages) Ltd v Total Oil (Great Britain) Ltd [1983] 1 WLR 87.
Bank of Credit and Commerce International S.A. v. Aboody and another [1990] 1 Q.B. 923.
Campbell v Griffin [2001] W & TLR 981 (CA).
Cheese v Thomas [1994] 1 WLR 129.
Chukorova Finance International Ltd v Alfa Telecom Turkey Ltd [2013] UKPC 20.
Cloutte v Storey [1911] 1 Ch 18.
Co-Operative Insurance Society Ltd. Respondents and Argyll Stores Ltd. Appellants [1997] 2 WLR 898.
Cobbe v Yeoman's Row Management Ltd and another [2008] 1 WLR 1752.
Consumer Credit Act 1974 (c.39).
Companies Act 2006 (c.46).
Cowcher v Cowcher [1972] 1 WLR 425.
Dunbar Bank plc v Nadeem [1998] 3 All ER 876.
Earl of Chesterfield v Janssen (1751) 2 Ves Sen 125.
Earl of Oxford's Case (1615) 1 Ch Rep 1.
Eves v Eves [1975] 1 WLR 1338.
Fry v Lane (1888) 40 Ch D 312.
Gissing v Gissing [1971] AC 886.
Greenwood v Greenwood [1937] P 157.
Hart v O'Connor [1985] AC 1000.
Human Rights Act 1998 (c.42).
In Re Colgate (A Bankrupt), Ex parte Trustee of the Property of the Bankrupt [1986] Ch 439.
In re Sussex Brick Company [1904] 1 Ch 598.
Ingram v Little [1961] 1 QB 31.
Jennings v Rice [2002] EWCA Civ 159 (CA).
Jones v Kernott [2011] UKSC 53.

Kingstreet Investments Ltd v New Brunswick (Finance) [2007] 1 SCR 3.

Law of Property Act 1925 (c.20).

Lloyd's Bank Ltd v Bundy [1975] QB 326.

Lonrho plc. v Fayed and Others (No. 2) [1992] 1 WLR 1.

Mahoney v Purnell and others (Baldwin and another, third parties) [1996] 3 All ER 61.

Meinhard v Salmon 249 N.Y. 458 (N.Y. 1928).

Multiservice Bookbinding Ltd v Marden [1979] 1 WLR 243.

Murphy v Burrows [2004] EWHC 1900.

Ottey v Grundy [2003] EWCA Civ 1176 (CA).

Pao On v Lau Yiu Long [1980] AC 614.

Prestney v Corporation of Colchester (No 2) (1883) 24 Ch D 376.

Re Coslett Contractors Ltd [1998] Ch 495.

Senior Courts Act 1981 (c.54).

Sheddon v Goodrich (1803) 8 Ves 481.

Supreme Court of Judicature Act 1873 (c.66).

Supreme Court of Judicature Act 1875 (c.77).

Supreme Court of Judicature (Consolidation) Act 1925 (c.49).

Supreme Court Act 1970 (NSW).

Taylor v Salmon (1838) 4 My & Cr 134.

Tracy v Atkins (1977) 83 DLR (3d) 47 (BCSC).

Uglow v Uglow [2004] Civ 987 (CA).

Westdeutsche Landesbank Girozentrale v Islington LBC [1996] AC 669.

Zurich Insurance plc UK v International Energy Group Ltd [2015] UKSC 33.

INDEX